Drawing on the Artist Within

Betty Edwards is Professor of Art at California State University. She was for some years a working artist, and when she began teaching drawing she found herself increasingly interested in the problem of helping people to learn *how* to draw.

The brain research carried out by Professors Jerome and Bruner and Roger Sperry, which brought a new understanding of the functions of the right and left hemispheres of the brain, led her to develop teaching techniques that encouraged students to use the right – or creative – side of the brain. The results were astounding, even with her most unpromising pupils, and she has now perfected her techniques into a system that enables anyone at all to acquire a real skill in drawing.

Betty Edwards' original contributions to the art of drawing and creativity have reached far beyond the classrooms where she has taught for many years. Her work has been praised by a wide range of distinguished psychologists and educationalists, and she has conducted creativity seminars and workshops for leading businesses, including IBM, and research organizations in many different parts of the United States and Europe.

"The mind in creation is
as a fading coal which
some invisible influence,
like an inconstant wind,
awakens to transitory
brightness; this arises
from within . . . and the
conscious portions of our
natures are unprophetic
either of its approach or
of its departure."
PERCY BYSSHE SHELLEY

*A Guide to
Innovation,
Invention,
Imagination
and
Creativity*

Drawing on
the Artist Within

Betty Edwards

Fontana/COLLINS

Also by Betty Edwards:
Drawing on the Right Side of the Brain

First published in Great Britain by William Collins 1987
First issued in Fontana Paperbacks 1988
Second impression May 1989

Copyright © 1986 by Betty Edwards

Designed by Joe Molloy
Typeset in Berthold Times Roman
by Mondo Typo
Instructional drawings by Betty Edwards

Printed and bound in Great Britain by
William Collins Sons & Co. Ltd, Glasgow

The publisher and author wish to thank the museums, galleries, and private collectors for granting permission to reproduce the works of the art in their collections. Photographs are included by permission of the owners or custodians of the works reproduced. The author gratefully acknowledges the generosity of students in allowing her to retain their drawings during preparation of the manuscript.

Permission to reproduce the *Portrait of the Artist* by Henri Fuseli appearing on the book cover is by courtesy of the Victoria and Albert Museum, London.

Permission to reproduce Pablo Picasso's portrait drawing of Léon Bakst is by courtesy of the Picasso Museum in Paris and S.P.A.D.E.M.

The poem by Marilyn Thompson is reproduced by permission of the author.

The passage of Eran Zaidel's article, "The Elusive Right Hemisphere of the Brain," is from *Engineering and Science* publication of the California Institute of Technology, Pasadena, California.

The photograph of Elizabeth Layton and her drawings are reproduced by permission of the artist.

The drawings and quotation by Rudolf Arnheim from his books *Visual Thinking* and *Entropy and Art* are reproduced by permission of the University of California Press.

The photograph by William Duke of Los Angeles is reproduced by permission of the photographer.

The advertisement in Chapter Seven is reproduced by permission of the R. J. Reynolds Tobacco Company, Salem, North Carolina.

The quotation from the biography of Robert Musil by David S. Luft is by courtesy of the University of California Press.

Permission to reproduce the Grid diagrams in Chapter Nine was granted by Foote, Cone & Belding, Chicago and New York.

The quotation and diagram from Victor Rauzino's article in Chapter Eleven are reproduced by permission of *Datamation* magazine, copyright by Technical Publishing Company, a Dun & Bradstreet Company, 1983—all rights reserved.

The engravings of Tweedledee and Tweedledum are reproduced by permission of the British Museum, London.

The photograph of the sea anemone from Kozloff, *Seashore Life of the Northern Pacific Coast* is reproduced by permission of the University of Washington Press.

The diagram titled "Star Trek, Management, and the Brain" is reproduced by courtesy of the Business Publishing Division of the Georgia State University Business Publishing Division.

The drawing of the *Angel's Head* by Leonardo da Vinci on the Part I page is reproduced by courtesy of the Museo Torino, Turin, Italy.

The double photographs in Chapter Eighteen are reproduced by permission of the photographer, Nancy Webber.

The *Self-Portrait* by Leonardo da Vinci on the Part II page is reproduced by courtesy of the Museo Torino, Royal Library, Turin, Italy.

The drawing by Rembrandt on the Part III page is reproduced by courtesy of Mr. and Mrs. Robert Engel, Pasadena, California.

The photograph of Governor Edmund G. Brown is reproduced by permission of the *Los Angeles Times*.

I am grateful to my family, friends, colleagues, and students for encouraging me throughout this project.
I dedicate this book to all of them.

ACKNOWLEDGMENTS

I wish to thank the many individuals who contributed to this endeavor. In particular, my thanks go to the teachers who have worked with me over the past several years, teaching the studio/lab sections of my drawing classes for university students. Students' drawings throughout the book reflect the fine teaching of these exceptional instructors: Marka Hitt-Burns, Arlene Cartozian, Lynda Greenberg, Linda Jo Russell, and Cynthia Schubert. In addition, my thanks go to J. William Bergquist, Anne Bomeisler Farrell, Brian Bomeisler, Don Dame, Frederic W. Hills, Burton Beals, Joe Molloy, Carol Wade, Diane McHenry, Jim Drobka, Harold Roth, Peter Hoffman, Stanley Rand, Stephen Horn, and Robert Ramsey for their generous giving of time, thought, and effort on my behalf. And last, I wish to acknowledge my indebtedness to Roger W. Sperry and to thank him for his kindness and generosity.

CONTENTS

Drawing in the Dark

Writing this book has been a process of discovery. I started with a glimmer of an idea that visual perception, drawing, and creativity might somehow be linked. The writing took the form of a search, a hunt for clues that might allow me to capture bits and pieces of this concept and fit them together finally into a comprehensible whole.

At the start of writing, I was far from clear in my mind what shape the final manuscript might take. And in fact, as the writing progressed, it seemed somehow to take on a life of its own, leading *me* in my search rather than vice versa. In a strange way, therefore, I found myself writing *about* creativity while at the same time engaged in the very same process—the search and the object of the search becoming one and the same.

My search began with an investigation of the written words of many creative individuals. And there, by their own assertion, I learned that words alone were often inadequate to describe the creative process as they had experienced it. Some individuals advised that to be truly creative we must somehow turn ourselves away from usual modes of thought in order to see things differently, to look at the world from a different point of view. Still others expressed serious concern that verbal language can be inappropriate for certain creative tasks and that words at times can even *hinder* thinking.

My friend mathematician J. William Bergquist invented the adjective "numerate" (as a parallel to "literate") to describe the ability to understand and use numbers. "Numerate" has gone into the language and is now frequently used. What new word would describe the ability to understand and use visual information?

Yet verbal language and analytic thought have dominated human life for so long a time now that it is hard to imagine that there might be other means of translating experience, valuable for thinking yet altogether different. We have grown used to the idea of other languages, to be sure: the languages of music, of dance, of mathematics and science, the relatively new computer languages, and of course the language of art itself—certainly not a new idea. But the notion that we might benefit from a visual, perceptual language as a parallel to verbal analytic thought processes is, perhaps, an idea of our own time. It is an idea derived from the pioneering research, first published in 1968, of psychobiologist and

Nobel Laureate Roger W. Sperry, whose discoveries about the dual nature of human brain function and human cognition have radically changed modern conceptions of thinking. In fact, the global, visual, perceptual mode of the human brain is gradually being accepted as a partner equal in value to the sequential, verbal, analytic mode in the thinking process.

Thus, everywhere I looked I seemed to find confirmation of my belief that *direct perception*, a different kind of "seeing," is an integral part of the thinking—and hence the creative—process. And if that was, indeed, true, I thought it would be helpful to have a means to access that vision, not in words but in a form appropriate to vision. Therefore, in searching for a key to creativity, I also began to explore ways in which to express the visual, perceptual thinking mode of human brain function. Not surprisingly, I found such a language already in use—the language of drawing, which can record what we see, either in reality or in our mind's eye, in a way not totally dissimilar to the way we record our thoughts and ideas in words. Drawings, like words, have *meaning*—often beyond the power of words to express, but nonetheless invaluable in making the chaos of our sensory impressions comprehensible.

Thinking in a Different Language

With that realization, I believed I had found the link I sought between visual perception, drawing, and creativity. But my search was not yet over, for now I faced the further question of what role the visual language plays in the creative process, and how, if possible, it could be put to *use*. That, in essence, is the purpose of this book. In it, you will learn how to draw—but that is only the means, not the end. For in learning how to draw, I believe you will learn how to *see differently*. And that, in turn, will enhance your powers of creative thought.

You will be surprised, I think, to discover how quickly and skillfully you will be able to learn to draw; equally surprised to learn how much of the language of visual, perceptual thought you already know, right at this minute, perhaps without realizing it. And it is my hope that you will also discover that this new language, when integrated with the language of verbal, analytic thought, may provide the ingredients essential not only for true creativity—that is, new or novel ideas, insights, inventions, or discoveries that have social value—but also for useful creative solutions to the problems of everyday life.

The exercises in this book look like exercises in art, but they are not really intended as such. Art is something different—just as poetry is something different from basic instruction in reading. Professor Don Dame, artist and teacher, suggested that perhaps a new word is needed:

"The word 'art' is muddied. What you need is a word for 'order,' 'health,' 'beauty,' 'balance,' and 'quality of relationship.' What you are talking about in your book is a much more natural process than art. That natural process is orderly, constant, available, dispassionate. Seeing is totally different from looking. Looking is for survival on a more mundane level.

"Drawing is the time-bound activity of seeing. It stills the brain's noise and gives us a window to a process as independent as the autonomic nervous system. It seems peculiar that the process should be so elusive.

"If you have found a door to the process (with the exercises in this book), I think your discovery has little to do with art. Art is a specialist's activity in this culture, and is just a *symptom* of the process of seeing."

In conversation, Santa Monica, California, September 15, 1984.

Part I

A New Look at the Art of Seeing

"There is something antic about creating, although the enterprise be serious. And there is a matching antic spirit that goes with writing about it, for if ever there was a silent process, it is the creative one. Antic and serious and silent."
JEROME BRUNER
On Knowing: Essays for the Left Hand, 1965.

1

Creativity: The Chameleon Concept

What on earth is creativity? How can a concept be so important in human thinking, so crucial to human history, so dearly valued by nearly everyone yet be so elusive?

Creativity has been studied, analyzed, dissected, documented. Educators discuss the concept as if it were a tangible thing, a goal to be attained like the ability to divide numbers or play the violin. Cognitive scientists, fascinated by creativity, have produced volumes of bits and pieces, offering tantalizing glimpses and hints, but have not put the parts together into an understandable whole. To date we still have no generally accepted definition of creativity—no general agreement on what it is, how to learn it, how to teach it, or if, indeed, it can be learned or taught. Even the dictionary finesses definition with a single cryptic phrase: "*creativity*: the ability to create," and my encyclopedia avoids the difficulty altogether with no entry, even though another admittedly elusive concept, "intelligence," is allotted a full-length column of fine print. Nevertheless, books abound on the subject as seekers after creativity pursue a concept that seems paradoxically to recede at the same pace at which the pursuers advance.

Drawing on Treasure-Hunt Notes

The trail, fortunately, is at least marked with pointers to guide the chase. Letters and personal records, journals, eyewitness accounts, descriptions, and biographies are in abundance, gathered from creative individuals and their biographers over past centuries. Like clues in a treasure hunt, these notations spur the quest, even though (as in any good treasure hunt) they often seem illogical and indeed frequently contradict each other to confuse the searcher.

Recurring themes and ideas in the notes, however, do reveal some hazy outlines of the creative process. The picture looks like this: the creative individual, whose mind is stored with impressions, is caught up with an idea or a problem that defies solution despite prolonged study.

As an example of the contradictory nature of accounts of creative processes, the wife of Robert Browning, the poet, reported that "Robert waits for an inclination, works by fits and starts: he can't do otherwise, he says." But later, W. M. Rosetti, speaking of Browning's writing procedures, said that Browning wrote "day by day on a regular, systematic plan—some three hours in the early part of the day."
F.G. KENYON
Life and Letters of Robert Browning,
1908.

A period of uneasiness or distress often ensues. Suddenly, without conscious volition, the mind is focused and a moment of insight occurs, often reported to be a profoundly moving experience. The individual is subsequently thrown into a period of concentrated thought (or work) during which the insight is *fixed* into some tangible form, unfolding, as it were, into the form it was intended to possess from the moment of conception.

This basic description of the nature of the creative process has been around since antiquity. The story of Archimedes' sudden insight, while he was sitting in the bathtub mulling over the problem of how to determine the relative quantities of gold and silver in the king's crown, has put his exclamation "Eureka!" (I have found it!) permanently into the language as the "Ah-Ha!" of creativity.

A Scaffolding of Stages

Successive steps in the creative process, however, were not categorized until late in the nineteenth century, when the German physiologist and physicist Herman Helmholtz described his own scientific discoveries in terms of three specific stages (Figure 1-1). Helmholtz named the first stage of research *saturation*; the second, mulling-over stage *incubation*; and the third stage, the sudden solution, *illumination*.

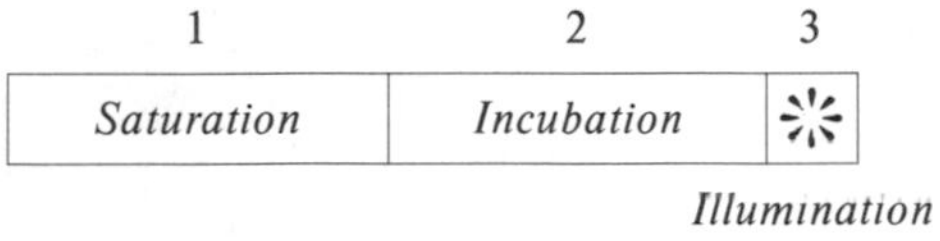

1	2	3
Saturation	Incubation	☀

Illumination

Fig. 1-1. Helmholtz' conception of creativity.

Helmholtz' three stages were supplemented in 1908 by a fourth stage, *verification*, suggested by the great French mathematician Henri Poincaré. Poincaré described the stage of verification as one of putting the solution into concrete form while checking it for error and usefulness (Figure 1-2).

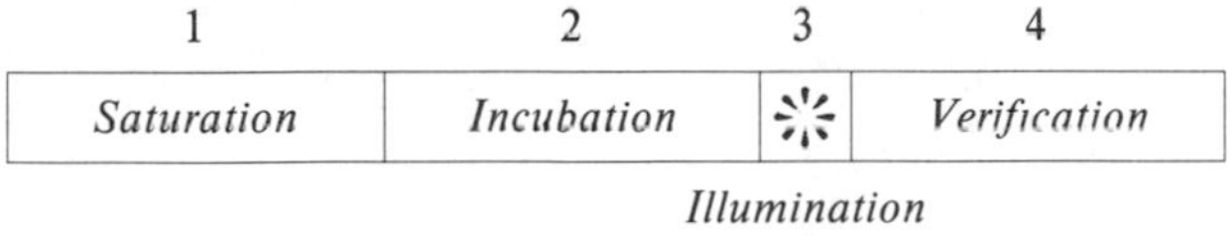

1	2	3	4
Saturation	Incubation	☀	Verification

Illumination

Fig. 1-2. Poincare's conception of creativity.

Then, in the early 1960s, the American psychologist Jacob Getzels contributed the important idea of a stage that *precedes* Helmholtz' saturation: a preliminary stage of problem *finding* or *formulating* (Figure 1-3, page 4). Getzels pointed out that creativity is not just solving problems of the kind that already exist or that continually arise in human life. Creative individuals often actively *search out* and discover problems to solve that no one else has perceived. As Albert Einstein and Max Wertheimer state in the margin quotations, to ask a productive ques-

"I can remember the very spot in the road, whilst in my carriage, when to my joy the solution occurred to me." From *The Life and Letters of Charles Darwin*, 1887.

"The formulation of a problem," said Albert Einstein, "is often more essential than its solution, which may be merely a matter of mathematical or experimental skill. To raise new questions, new possibilities, to regard old questions from a new angle, requires creative imagination and marks real advances in science."
A. EINSTEIN and L. INFELD
The Evolution of Physics, 1938.

Max Wertheimer echoed Einstein's point: "The function of thinking is not just solving an actual problem but discovering, envisaging, going into deeper questions. Often in great discoveries the most important thing is that a certain question is found. Envisaging, putting the productive question is often a more important, often a greater achievement than solution of a set question."
M. WERTHEIMER
Productive Thinking, 1945.

The five stages of creativity.

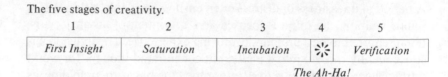

1	2	3	4	5
First Insight	*Saturation*	*Incubation*	☀	*Verification*

The Ah-Ha!

Fig. 1–3. Getzel's conception of creativity.

tion is a creative act in itself. Another American psychologist, George Kneller, named Getzel's preliminary stage *first insight*—a term that encompasses both problem solving (of existing problems) and problem finding (asking new and searching questions).

    Thus we have an approximate structure of five stages in the creative process: 1. First Insight 2. Saturation 3. Incubation 4. Illumination 5. Verification (Figure 1–3). These stages progress over time from one stage to the next. Each stage may occupy varying lengths of time, as indicated in the diagrams below (Figure 1–4), and the time lengths may possibly be infinitely variable. Only Illumination is in almost every case reported to be brief—a flash of light thrown on the subject. With the notable exception of the Gestalt* psychologists, for whom creativity is an unsegmented process, a single consistent line of thinking for the purpose of solving a *whole* problem, researchers have generally agreed on the basic concept that creativity involves progressive stages which occur over varying lengths of time.

*A school of psychology, active first in Germany in the 1930s and later in the United States, which interprets phenomena as organized wholes rather than aggregates of distinct parts and maintains that the whole is more than the sum of its parts.

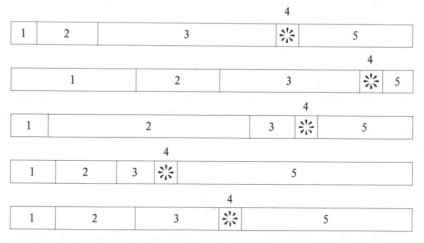

Fig. 1–4. Variations of the creativity process.

Except for the Illumination, which is usually brief, each stage may vary in the length of time required. Also, one project may require repeating the cycle of stages.

Building on this sketchy outline, however, twentieth-century researchers have continued to embellish the elusive concept of creativity and debate its various aspects. Like Alice in Wonderland, it has undergone one transformation after another, thus increasing one's sense that despite a general notion of its overall configuration, this chameleon concept will forever change before our eyes and escape understanding.

And now the concept is metamorphosing again. Changes in modern life, occurring at an increasingly rapid pace, require innovative responses, thus making it imperative that we gain greater understanding of creativity and control over the creative process. This necessity, coupled with the age-old yearning of individuals to express themselves creatively, has markedly enhanced interest in the concept of creativity, as is shown in the growing number of publications on the subject.

In these publications, one question explored by many writers is whether creativity is rare or widespread among the general population. And the question "Am I creative?" is one we all ask ourselves. The answer to both questions seems to depend on something we usually call "talent"—the idea that either you have a *talent* for creativity or you don't. But is it really as simple as that? And just what is talent?

Talent: The Slippery Concept

The drawing course I teach is usually described in the college catalog as follows: "Art 100: Studio Art for Non-Art Majors. This is a course designed for persons who cannot draw at all, who feel they have no talent for drawing, and who believe they probably can never learn to draw."

The response to this description has been overwhelming: my classes are always full to overflowing. But invariably one or more of the newly enrolled students approaches me at the start of the course to say, "I just want to let you know that even though you've taught a lot of people how to draw, *I am your Waterloo!* I'm the one who will *never* be able to learn!"

When I ask why, again almost invariably the answer is "Because I have no talent." "Well," I answer, "let's wait and see."

Sure enough, a few weeks later, students who claimed to have no talent are happily drawing away on the same high level of accomplishment as the rest of the class. But even then, they often discount their newly acquired skill by attributing it to something they call "*hidden* talent."

Turning the Tables on this Strange Situation

I believe the time has come to reexamine our traditional beliefs about creative talent—"hidden" or otherwise. Why do we assume that a rare and special "artistic" talent is required for drawing? We don't make that assumption about other kinds of abilities—reading, for example.

Before embarking on his life as an artist, Vincent van Gogh wrote of his yearning to be creative, which caused him to feel like "the man . . . whose heart is . . . imprisoned in something. Because he hasn't got what he needs to be creative. . . . Such a man often doesn't know himself what he might do, but he feels instinctively: yet am I good for something, yet am I aware of some reason for existing! . . . something is alive in me: what can it be!" Quoted in BREWSTER GHISELIN, ed. *The Creative Process*, 1952.

" 'Talent' is a slippery concept." GERHARD GOLLWITZER *The Joy of Drawing*, 1963.

What about so-called "naturally talented" persons? I believe that these are individuals who somehow "catch on" to ways of shifting to brain modes appropriate for particular skills. I mentioned my own experience in my 1979 book *Drawing on the Right Side of the Brain*:

"From an early age, perhaps the age of eight or nine, I was able to draw fairly well. I think I was one of those few children who accidentally stumble upon a way of seeing that enables one to draw well. I can still remember saying to myself, even as a young child, that if I wanted to draw something, I had to do 'that.' I never defined 'that,' but I was aware of having to *gaze* at whatever I wanted to draw for a time until 'that' occurred. Then I could draw with a fairly high degree of skill for a child."

What if we believed that only those fortunate enough to have an innate, God-given, genetic gift for reading will be able to learn to read? What if teachers believed that the best way to go about the teaching of reading is simply to supply lots of reading materials for children to handle and manipulate and then wait to see what happens? Such a teacher would, of course, never tamper with a child's spontaneous attempts to read for fear of spoiling "creativity" in reading. If a child asked, "How do you read this?" the teacher would respond, "Just be free! Do what comes into your head. Use your imagination and just enjoy it! Reading should be fun!" Then the teacher would watch to see which children showed "talent" for reading—the idea being that it's no use trying to teach the skill of reading because if a child isn't "talented," instruction won't help.

It's easy to see that if this were the situation in reading classes, probably only one or two or perhaps three children in a class of twenty-five might somehow manage to learn how to read. *They* would be designated as "talented" for reading, and no doubt someone would say, "Well, you know, Sally's grandmother was good at reading. Sally probably got it from her." Or "Oh, yes, Billy's good at reading. The family is quite literate, you know. It's in the genes, I guess." Meanwhile, the rest of the children would grow up saying of themselves, "*I can't read.* I haven't got any talent for it, and I'm sure I could *never* learn."

In an obscure 1916 book, two insightful teachers recommended intensive drawing instruction in the early grades as an aid to learning other subjects. The book offers evidence that good instruction *counts* at least as much as "talent."

The authors showed drawings before instruction by four children representing "*A*, the best; *B*, somewhat above the average; *C*, somewhat below the average; and *D*, the poorest in a class of thirty-five." (Figure 1–5). They then showed drawings done after instruction by the *same four children.* (Figure 1–6).

The authors reported that "the difference between the two drawings was often so great that the children were highly amused at their first drawings."
WALTER SARGENT and
ELIZABETH MILLER
How Children Learn to Draw, 1916.

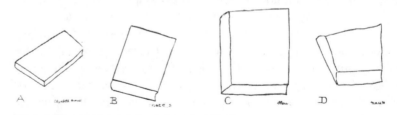

Fig. 1–5. First drawings of a book from the object.

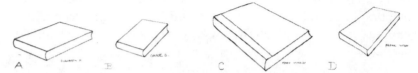

Fig. 1–6. Second drawings of a book from the object.

What I've described, of course, is more or less the way it is with drawing. Surely parents would object mightily if the concept of talent were used as a roadblock in learning to read the way it is used in learning to draw. But for some reason, most people, parents *and* students, accept the verdict "No talent for drawing" with quite surprising meekness and even crestfallen agreement.

This situation continues right up to college art classes. There, anxious students, already worried because their drawing skills are weak and fearful that they have no talent, are sometimes confronted on the first day by an instructor who might start the course with "Well, there's the still-life setup. Do a drawing of it." All too often the students fear an implied warning: ". . . and we'll see which of you should stay in this class."

A comparable situation might be to enroll in a beginning French conversation class and to be told at the start, "Go ahead and talk in French," with an implied warning that if you can't already speak French, you shouldn't bother to stay. Very few college students in art classes, I imagine, would stand for that. Yet students usually don't object to noninstruction, as they surely would in almost any other course, perhaps because they feel so bad—almost guilty—that they have no "talent" for drawing.

Talent is, indeed, a slippery concept, no matter what the form of creativity. But perhaps "artistic talent" has always *seemed* rare and out of the ordinary only because we *expect* it to be rare and out of the ordinary. We have become accustomed to thinking of artistic ability as basically unteachable, and teaching methods have remained unexamined. Moreover, many educators, parents, and students have shared an unspoken belief that artistic abilities are largely nonessential in our modern, technological society.

Yet we do value creativity. We constantly seek ways in which to be more creative ourselves, whatever our occupations or fields of interest. But must we have a mysterious God-given talent to be creative? Or is it possible that creativity *can* be taught?

The Basic Skills of Thinking

In my work with groups of artistically untrained people, I have discovered that any person of sound mind can learn to draw; the probability is the same as for learning to read. It is simply a matter of learning basic perceptual skills—the special ways of seeing required for drawing. I claim that anyone can learn enough *seeing* skills to draw a good likeness of something seen "out there" in the real world.

Once these basic perceptual skills are learned, their use can be as varied as subsequent uses of basic language and arithmetic skills. A few individuals may stay with art and eventually become artists, just as a

A paradox: Teachers fear that teaching drawing skills will harm or hinder a child's "creativity in art"—yet the criterion for selecting children who are "gifted in art" is usually *ability to draw realistically.*
A further paradox: Picasso, the most prolifically creative artist of our century, was systematically trained in classical drawing skills to the point that, as has been said, he "could draw like an angel."
And even a further paradox: all the major artists in the history of art had learned how to draw without, apparently, any damage to their creativity. Only in this century—specifically, post-Dewey and post-Gestalt psychology—have fears of "damage to creativity" prevented instruction in drawing.

few stay with language or mathematics and eventually become writers or mathematicians. But almost everyone can use perceptual skills—again, like language and math skills—to enhance *thinking* skills.

To go a step further, I propose that perceptual skills are deeply involved in the five stages of the creative process. I also propose that visual, perceptual skills are enhanced by training, just as the verbal, analytic skills benefit by education. And finally, I propose that learning to see and draw is a very efficient way to train the visual system, just as learning to read and write can efficiently train the verbal system. That is not to say that the visual system is better, morally or otherwise, than the verbal system. But the two systems *are* different. And when trained as equal partners, one mode of thinking enhances the other, and together the two modes can release human creativity.

Summing Up a Point of View

At present, our culture provides few opportunities for such training. We are used to thinking by means of the language system of the brain, and that mode has proved its effectiveness over the centuries. But we are only now beginning to understand the complex dual functions, verbal *and* visual, of the human brain, and new possibilities are opening up. As I see it, unlocking the doors to perception and releasing the potential for creativity is a twofold process: first, removal of the deterrent concept of talent as a requirement for learning basic perceptual skills; second, teaching and learning based on new knowledge of how the human brain works.

My claim is quite modest: if you can catch a baseball, thread a needle, or hold a pencil and write your name, you can learn to draw skillfully, artistically, and creatively. Through learning to draw perceived objects or persons, you can learn new ways of seeing that guide strategies in creative thinking and problem solving just as, through learning to read, you acquire verbal knowledge and learn the strategies of logical, analytical thought. Using the two modes together, you can learn to think more productively, whatever your creative goals may be. The products of your creative responses to the world will be uniquely your own, your mark on the world. And you will have taken a giant step toward attaining a *modern* brain. For in the years ahead, I believe that perceptual skills combined with verbal skills will be viewed as the basic necessities for creative human thought.

Through learning to draw perceived objects and persons, you can learn new ways of seeing. Drawing by student Kevin Bresnahan. "Street Scene," November 7, 1984.

2 Drawing on Gleams from Within

Following Emerson's advice, I am taking a chance on one of those gleams from within. Largely on the basis of a hunch, a persistent idea, plus evidence from the notes and journals of creative individuals; on my own experience in attempting to do some original work; and on what seemed to be an illumination—an "Ah-Ha!"—about the connection between seeing and creativity, I believe that learning to draw *can* enhance creativity.

The fairly recent but now familiar research on how the human brain halves differ in style and function indicates that drawing ability relies mainly on the visual, spatial functions of the right hemisphere. A brief review of that research will perhaps be helpful. I have found that for some of my students, the information seems somehow to slip out of their minds and lose its aura of interest and importance. My half-serious theory about why this happens is that perhaps the left (verbal) brain does not necessarily want to know about its silent partner and, having heard the message, perhaps proceeds to forget it as soon as possible.

The Right and Left of Thinking

The two major modes of human brain-hemisphere function (which I call simply L-mode and R-mode) were first described by psychobiologist Roger W. Sperry in his pioneering work during the late 1950s and early 1960s. Sperry's research, which was honored by a Nobel Prize for Medicine in 1981, has shown that the right and left hemispheres of the human brain use contrasting methods of information processing. Both thinking modes are involved in high-level cognitive functioning, but each brain half specializes in its own style of thinking and each has its own special capabilities. The two modes are able to work in a cooperative, complementary way while at the same time retaining their individual styles of thinking.

10

Nevertheless, these styles of thinking are *fundamentally* different and can cause each mode, in a sense, to view reality in its own way. Thus, in response to an event "out there," one brain half or the other may "jump in" first and dominate conscious awareness—or, in other instances, the two modes may have different and even conflicting responses to the same event. In some situations, one response or the other may be somehow suppressed and kept out of conscious awareness. A child, for example, whose angry mother says through clenched teeth, "I'm disciplining you because I love you," may, as a subconscious protective device, choose to believe the words and deny (at the conscious level) seeing the anger. On the other hand, conflicting responses to an event may both reach conscious awareness and both views may be expressed in words. For example, someone who has just viewed a televised political speech might say, "The words sound okay, but there's something about this person that I just don't like."

L-Mode: Linear, Logical, Language-Based Thinking

The left hemisphere (for the majority of human beings) specializes in verbal, logical, analytic thinking. Naming and categorizing are among its favorite things to do. It excels in symbolic abstraction, speech, reading, writing, arithmetic. In general, its system of thought is linear: first things first, second things second. It tends to rely on general rules to reduce experience to concepts that are compatible with its style of cognition. Its preference is for clear, sequential, logical thought, uncomplicated by paradox or ambiguity. Perhaps because of its bewildering complexity, our culture generally tends to emphasize L-mode thinking, thus funneling complexity down into manageable words, symbols, or abstractions and enabling us to cope, more or less, with many aspects of modern living.

A good example from everyday life of a task appropriate for L-mode's style of thinking is balancing your checkbook. Using words and numbers and following a prescribed procedure, checkbook balancing is a language-based, sequential, linear process.

At the start, the assumption is made that if you have kept all the records straight, you can expect to end with a balance of $0.00. If in fact you end up with a balance of, say, $1.06, R-mode (which is not interested in this process) may nudge you with the (unspoken) impulse "Let's just erase that and write in $0.00. It doesn't really matter." L-mode, however, would feel that it *does* matter and would respond indignantly, "No, no, *no*! I must go back to the beginning and go through the procedure step by step until I find the error." L-mode, of course, is the appropriate mode for balancing a checkbook, as its style of cognition is suited to the task. R-mode is simply not equipped for this L-mode job, and surely the last thing wanted is creative checkbook balancing.

"It is a common condemnation these days of our Western educational system that it discriminates against the right hemisphere. There is no doubt that our educational system is half-brained, but is it left-brained? To be sure, there are important differences in the learning styles of the two cerebral hemispheres: the left is constructive, algorithmic, stepwise, and logical. It benefits from narrow examples and from trial and error; it can learn by rule. The right hemisphere, on the other hand, does not seem to learn by exposure to specific rules and examples. Our studies show that it does not have an internal model of its own solution processes, which it can then interrogate and update. It needs exposure to rich and associative patterns, which it tends to grasp as wholes. Programmed instruction is certainly not for the right hemisphere, but I am not sure what is the proper method of instruction for our silent half. It is part of the elusiveness of the right hemisphere that we find it easier to say what it is not than what it is."
ERAN ZAIDEL
"The Elusive Right Hemisphere of the Brain," 1978.

L-Mode and R-Mode

At the close of a lecture, someone
thrust into my hand these little
drawings. I think they do a good job
of describing the situation:
L-mode sits upright, four-square and
unimpeachable, eyes closed against
the world. R-mode, always taking a
different slant on the world, playfully
views its surrounding upside-down,
with its eyes wide open.
(The artist's name, unfortunately,
is unknown to me.)

L-mode	R-mode
Verbal	Nonverbal
Syntactical	Perceptual
Linear	Global
Sequential	Simultaneous
Analytic	Synthetic
Logical	Intuitive
Symbolic	Concrete
Temporal	Nontemporal
Digital	Spatial

The above functions, while generally
attributed to the left and right hemispheres respectively for most individuals, may vary considerably in *location*
in the brain hemispheres of specific
individuals, particularly left-handed
and ambidextrous individuals.
Moreover, recent research indicates
a less-clear division of functions
between the hemispheres than was
thought to be the case in earlier investigations. I have coined the terms L-
mode and R-mode to designate *style
of thinking* rather than a more rigid
conception of *location* of functions
in one hemisphere or the other.

R-Mode: Visual, Spatial, Relational Thinking

In contrast to L-mode, the right half of the brain (for most individuals)
functions in a nonverbal manner, specializing in visual, spatial, perceptual information. Its style of processing is nonlinear and nonsequential,
relying instead on simultaneous processing of incoming information—
looking at the whole thing, all at once. It tends to seek relationships
between parts and searches for the ways parts fit together to form wholes.
Its preferences are for perceiving information, searching for patterns or
relationships that satisfy requirements for visual fit, and seeking spatial
order and coherence. It seems undaunted by ambiguity, complexity, or
paradox, perhaps because it lacks the "reducing glass" of L-mode, which
opts for general rules and resists acknowledging ambiguity and paradox.
Because of its quickness, complexity, and nonverbal nature, R-mode
thinking is, almost by definition, difficult to put into words.

A good example from ordinary life of R-mode functioning is freeway driving. Freeway driving requires rapid processing of constantly
changing simultaneous, visual, perceptual information. L-mode is ill
suited to this task. If *it* were in charge of driving on the freeway, it
would have to process the information linearly and verbally, like this:
"Now the Dodge is approaching from the right at approximately 55 miles
per hour and will overtake in 4.2 seconds; now the van is approaching
on the left at approximately 62 miles per hour and will overtake in . . ."
and so on. Clearly, this system is too slow for the requirements of freeway
driving. Thus, L-mode (which will rarely admit to incapability) says, in
effect, "I don't like to drive. It's boring. I'll let old you-know-who take
care of this job." And L-mode bows out of the task.

R-mode, on the other hand, is eminently well suited to this complex
visual, perceptual task and can handle the job with ease, even while
simultaneously engaged in other areas of thought. Many of my students
report that they do a lot of creative thinking while on the freeway. Some
report that, deep in thought about some problem, they occasionally go
right beyond their destination, meanwhile accomplishing all the enormously complex visual, perceptual processing required for driving
without conscious monitoring. A few students have even reported being
aware of starting out on a trip and aware of arriving at their destination,
but that the time between was lost in thought, the route taken unknown.

Working Together: Two Major Modes of Thinking

The two modes of cognition, L-mode and R-mode, share and communicate their separate views of reality principally by means of a large cable of
nerve fibers called the *corpus callosum* which connects the two hemispheres of the brain and transmits the separate processes of the two
modes to each other. In this way, the two views of reality are reconciled,
thus preserving our sense of being one person, an "I," a single identity.

12

Additionally, in many activities of daily living both major brain modes can work concurrently and cooperatively on the same information or task, each hemisphere playing its special role. To illustrate by analogy: in sewing, one hand holds the cloth while the other hand works the needle; or in tennis, the legs carry the player to the right spot and the hand/arm wields the racquet. Thus, in music, for example, L-mode reads the musical notation and keeps the beat while R-mode handles tone, melody, and expression. In most human activities, the sense of difference and separateness between the brain modes is muted and outside of conscious awareness.

Consciousness from Deep Within

Yet some inner acknowledgment of the duality of the brain seems to be harbored deep in human consciousness, surfacing, like an iceberg's tip, in language itself. For example, philosophers through the ages have proposed two ways of knowing the external world: through the intellect or through the emotions; through logical analysis or through metaphorical synthesis. Dichotomous terms abound: Yin and Yang, rational and poetic, abstract and concrete, scientific and imaginative. Individuals often speak of themselves as if two separate personalities existed in tandem: "Part of me wants to do such and such, but on the other hand I know I'm better off doing so and so." Or "Sometimes I'm really rational, on time, and dependable, but at other times I'm just off the wall."

The notable human characteristic of handedness is, of course, the most visually evident outward sign of brain duality, the right hand controlled by the (usually) dominant, verbal left hemisphere, the left hand by the subdominant visual right hemisphere. Marilyn Thompson's poem presents an artist's view of the characteristics often assigned to the right and left hands and, by implication, to the brain hemispheres themselves.

The So-Called "Minor" Hemisphere

By all accounts, R-mode, usually positioned as the second half of the dichotomy (although alternately positioned in Thompson's poem), is the more elusive and the less accessible of the two modes of cognition. Language seems to prevail over the nonverbal brain half to the extent that the age-old question "Can there be thought without words?" has been endlessly pondered and debated. Roger Sperry's work appears to have settled that argument at last with the answer "Yes," but perceptual cognition is a vastly different kind of thought. Because the verbal system is not well suited even to describing its silent partner, R-mode remains largely outside of everyday conscious, verbal awareness, even for ordinary activities that require the spatial, perceptual processing of R-mode, such as freeway driving.

"The specialization of the isolated hemispheres should not be overstated. . . . The right half of the brain does have some rudimentary linguistic ability. Moreover, there are doubtless many tasks where the two hemispheres ordinarily act in concert."
NORMAN GESHWIND
"Specializations in the Human Brain," 1979.

Poem for the Left and Right Hands
by Marilyn Thompson

The left hand trails in the water
The right is tying knots

The right stitches a seam
The left sleeps in the silk

The right eats
The left listens under the table

The right swears
The left wears the rings

The right wins, the right loses
The left holds the cards

The left strikes chords while the right
runs, runs   up and down, up and down

and when the right can't sleep
   and travels around the world
   against the clock
the left is buried

Oh left hand you're so quiet
Do you have children, a dog,
   mistresses, debts

It's the right that buys the groceries
shifts gears
runs for high office
feeds the baby little silver spoonfuls
It's the right that grabs the knife
to hack off the left hand

The left hand waits
a blind dog

holding in its mouth
the right's glove

The knife falls, clatters
The left hand

is the right's only chance

Atlantic Monthly, September, 1975, Vol. 236, No. 3, p. 38. Reprinted by permission of the author.

In a courageous book of self-explora-
tion, the British writer Marion Milner
(who wrote under the name Joanna
Field) discovered that most of her life
had been spent in "blind thinking,"
her term for the incessant chattering of
her mind. As she gradually learned to
escape the constriction of "blind"
thought and achieved access to what
she called "seeing" thought, she wrote:
"So it was that I came to the conclusion that the ordinary everyday perception of things which serves us
pretty well when going about daily
practical affairs is not the only kind of
perceiving that the mind can do. . . .
Only a tiny act of will was necessary in
order to pass from one to the other, yet
this act seemed sufficient to change
the face of the world, to make boredom and weariness blossom into
immeasurable contentment."
JOANNA FIELD
A Life of One's Own, 1936.

The creative process is decidedly no ordinary activity: what it is
and how it is done are still hidden behind a dark glass despite centuries
of speculation and investigation. But Sperry's contribution to knowledge about the brain suggests some new thoughts about creativity. For
example, creativity may seem to occur in stages, perhaps because the
requirements of each stage *cause* the brain to "shift gears"—that is, to
make cognitive shifts from one major brain mode to the other and back
again. Joanna Field describes this kind of mental shift in the margin
quotation.

Drawing, often considered a form of creativity, can provide actual
evidence of such mental shifts: a drawing can show whether one brain
mode or the other was "in charge" during the process of drawing, even
though the *person* might be unaware that the drawing is being influenced by a particular mental set. I believe that learning to draw mainly
requires learning to be aware of which brain mode is dominating and,
more important, learning to *control* mental shifts in brain mode. And
I believe that these skills are also prime requisites for increasing crea-
tive-thinking abilities.

Controlling Mental Shifts

Before we further explore these ideas, I suggest that you try an interesting experiment: follow the directions given below to obtain a record of
your present "state of mind" concerning visual information, as demonstrated through drawing. This record—three drawings—can be used for
comparison with later drawings, both in terms of acquired drawing skills
and in terms of new thinking skills. Even though you may have drawn
before, or perhaps have had some previous instruction, it is important
to do the preinstruction drawings. You will see progress, no matter what
the present level of your skills.

At the very first meeting of every class, before any instruction whatsoever, I suggest this experiment to my students. Besides showing the
students' progress, the preinstruction drawings are important for
another reason: a form of amnesia concerning previous abilities seems
to set in as students gain new ability to see and draw and to control
brain-mode shifts. You must remember that L-mode would perhaps
prefer that you not draw at all, thus retaining its usual dominance, and
will sometimes tend to find fault even with obviously skillful drawing.
The "Before" and "After" drawings provide powerful visual evidence of
progress that prevents "forgetting" and is very hard to deny.

Painful though it might be, therefore, I urge you to follow the brief
instructions and do the three preinstruction drawings. You need not
show them to anyone; just put them aside in a safe place for comparison
at a later time with drawings from later exercises. The preinstruction
drawings will be your "Before" drawings, similar to those in the sets of

14

"Before and After" student drawings I will show you next. Just as my students are always delighted to see the extent of their progress, so will you be happy, I believe, to have a visual record of where you started and how far you progressed.

Preinstruction Drawings

Use a pencil and inexpensive typing paper. Have an eraser handy. Take as long a time as you wish to do the three drawings; most students take ten, fifteen, or twenty minutes for each drawing. Be sure to title (*Preinstruction Drawing #1*, etc.), date, and sign each drawing.

Preinstruction Drawing #1: Draw a picture of a person—either the whole figure, a half-figure, or the head only. Persuade someone to pose for you, or draw someone watching TV—or you may draw yourself by looking in a mirror.

Preinstruction Drawing #2: Draw a picture of your own hand. If you are right-handed, draw your left hand, and vice versa if you are left-handed. Your hand may be in any position you choose.

Preinstruction Drawing #3: Draw a picture of an object, such as a chair or table, or of a group of objects—say, a drawing of your breakfast table *after* breakfast, or a potted plant, a pair of shoes, a stack of books on a table: any "still-life" of your choosing.

When you have finished, you might write on the back of each drawing what you think about the drawing. This last suggestion is not obligatory, but your comments might be interesting to review after you have learned to see and draw.

Drawing Out the Students

Let me show you a group of student drawings. (Figures 2–1 to 2–18 on the following pages.) The "Before" drawings were done at the beginning of the semester, prior to any instruction, and the "After" drawings following approximately twelve weeks of instruction.

The students who made these drawings never considered themselves to be artistically talented. They all expressed great surprise at their progress and great pleasure at discovering abilities within themselves that had not been evident before. Additionally, they stated that learning to *see* by learning to draw had caused other changes in their perceptions of the life around them. When asked to describe these changes, the replies varied from student to student: "I'm seeing more now"; "There's so much out there that I never noticed before"; "I just seem to be looking at things differently—in some way, *thinking* differently."

I am always curious about these statements and have asked a number of students, "Tell me, if your perceptions seem so different now, after learning to see and draw, what were they like before?" The most

Fig. 2-1. A. Francis Ampudia, September 6, 1984.

Fig. 2-2. Self-Portrait by A. Francis Ampudia, December 13, 1984.

Fig. 2-3. Scott Elderkin, September 8, 1984.

Fig. 2-4. Self-Portrait by Scott Elderkin, December 9, 1984.

Fig. 2-5. Farida Jalali, September 6, 1984

Fig. 2-6. Self-Portrait by Farida Jalali, December 13, 1984.

Fig. 2-7. Theresa Trucker, September 9, 1984.

Fig. 2-8. Portrait of a fellow student by Theresa Trucker, November 3, 1984.

Fig. 2–9. Steve Goldstone, September 8, 1984.

Fig. 2–10. Self Portrait by Steve Goldstone, December 9, 1984.

Fig. 2–11. Lauri Henderson, September 6, 1984.

Fig. 2–12. Portrait of a fellow student by Lauri Henderson, December 13, 1984.

Fig. 2–13. Debbie Grage, January 31, 1984.

Fig. 2–14. Portrait of a fellow student by Debbie Grage, April 26, 1984.

Fig. 2–15. Ray Ju, February 2, 1984.

Fig. 2–16. Self-Portrait by Ray Ju, May 17, 1984.

Fig. 2–17. Sheila Schumacher, January 31, 1984.

Fig. 2–18. Portrait of a fellow student by Sheila Schumacher, March 30, 1984.

usual response has been "It's really hard for me to say, but I think I was mostly just naming things—looking at things but not really seeing them." These comments, I think, demonstrate the influence of L-mode, which dominates—even intimidates—and forces one into seeing things *its* way.

Taking a Fresh Point of View

To reverse this influence, in the next exercise I will ask you to do one further drawing, this time not painful, but fun. The exercise presents a way to control your mind-set by tricking L-mode into staying out of the job. The procedure is designed to demonstrate several points. First, that when special conditions enable you to "set aside" L-mode, you are able to see and draw *right now*. Second, that when what is "out there" is placed in an unfamiliar orientation, the usual processes of recognizing and naming are slowed down and impeded, to the extent that L-mode gives up on trying to name and categorize. Third, that the (unnamed) parts of what is "out there" become interesting in themselves, as do the relationships between the parts. And last, that the mind can be surprised, even shocked, when the special conditions are changed back to "normal" and (verbal) recognition can occur.

The special condition that I propose is drawing upside down.

An Inspiration Born of Frustration

My first experience with upside-down drawing was illuminating. I was teaching in a high school in 1965, my first year of public-school teaching, and I was dismayed that I wasn't able to teach all of my students how to draw. A few seemed to be catching on, but I wanted *everyone* to learn. I couldn't understand what the problem might be. It had always seemed to me that drawing, compared with other kinds of learning, was easy: after all, everything you need to know in order to draw is *right there in front of the eyes*. Just look at it, see it, and draw it. "Why can't they see what is right in front of their eyes?" I wondered. "What is the problem?"

To a student who was having trouble with a still-life drawing, I would say, "Can you see that the apple is in front of the bowl?" "Yes, I see that," the student would answer. "Well, in your drawing, you have the apple sitting in the same space as the bowl." "I know," said the student, sounding puzzled. "I didn't know how to draw that." "Well," I said, pointing toward the still-life setup, "just look at the apple and the bowl, and draw what you see." "I don't know what to see," said the student. "Well," I said, "everything you need is right there, right in front of you. Just look at it." "I *am* looking at it," said the student, "but I can't draw it."

These conversations left me tongue-tied and baffled. Then one day, out of sheer frustration, I announced to my class, "Right. Today we are going to draw upside down." I placed some copies of master drawings upside down on the students' desks: I told them *not* to turn the drawings right-side up, and to make a copy of the original, doing their own drawing also upside down. The students, I believe, thought that I had gone "round the bend." But the room became suddenly quiet, and the students settled into the task with obvious enjoyment and concentration. When they had finished and we turned the drawings right-side up, to my surprise and to the students' surprise, every person in the class, not just a few, had made a *good* copy, a good drawing.

I hardly knew what to make of my impulsive experiment. It went against common sense, after all, to think that it might be easier to see and draw something upside down rather than right-side up. "What is going on?" I wondered.

I quizzed my students, hoping for enlightment. "Well," they said, "we didn't know what we were drawing, so we could do it." "Do what?" I asked. "See it," they said. "Well," I asked, "why can't you see it right-side up? It's the same thing, after all—I mean, the *lines* don't change." "It's too hard the right way up," they said. "Too confusing." I pondered their answers. I knew they were right, but I didn't know what it meant.

Drawing on a One-Track Mind

Another puzzlement arose during my years of high school teaching. Doing demonstration drawings, perhaps a portrait of a student, my wish was to explain what I was doing—what angle or curve I saw and how it fitted into the portrait. But strangely, I would hear myself stop talking, often right in the middle of a sentence. I felt I *should* continue talking, but could not. If I did struggle back into speech, I found that I would lose track of the drawing. Again I couldn't understand what the problem might be—why couldn't I talk and draw at the same time? I have since then somehow trained myself to "double-track," so to speak—to continue talking while doing demonstration drawings in the classroom—but students tell me that I sound very odd, as if I were talking "from a long way off," as they put it.

Other puzzlements arose during those years. For example, the progress of my students often resembled a flip-flop more than a steady and gradual acquisition of skills. A student who one day couldn't draw suddenly, the next day, had "caught on."

A Sudden Insight and a Lucky Break

It was some years later, about 1968, when by chance I happened to read accounts in various journals and newsmagazines of Roger Sperry's work on brain-hemisphere research, that I experienced something akin to the "Ah-Ha!" of Illumination. "That must be it!" I said to myself. "Drawing requires a certain brain mode, maybe a shift to another way of seeing things."

An early jazz pianist who worked with singer Billie Holiday said: "Billie would sometimes come at a note from a long way off." KUSC Radio, Los Angeles, August, 1982.

22

Fig. 2-19.
EUGENE DELACROIX (1798–1863)
An Arab on Horseback Attacked by a Lion, 1839. Pencil on tracing paper. Fogg Art Museum, Harvard University, Cambridge, Mass. (Meta and Paul J. Sachs Collection.)

It is very difficult to identify and understand upside-down images. In contrast, notice how quickly you grasp the whole picture when you turn this image right-side up.

Each of my puzzlements could be fitted into the hemisphere-function theories. Upside-down drawing forced a shift away from the naming, categorizing L-mode of the brain to the visual, perceptual R-mode—which is the appropriate mode for drawing. I couldn't talk and draw at the same time because, for me, the verbal L-mode conflicted with the visual R-mode. And the flip-flop of student skills could be viewed as a cognitive shift in brain mode—seeing by means of the mode inappropriate for drawing (L-mode) one day, the appropriate mode (R-mode) the next.

Turning the Tables on L-Mode

Let's try upside-down drawing now. Remember, the purpose of this drawing is to trick L-mode into bowing out of the job, which occurs possibly because L-mode finds it too difficult to name and categorize visual information presented upside down. To demonstrate that to yourself first, try to read the handwritten sentence in the margin, and try to decipher the upside-down reproduction (Figure 2–19). Then turn the book around to have a look right-side up.

Drawing on Gleams from Within

While looking at the upside-down writing and the upside-down Delacroix drawing, did you notice a slight sense of irritation? And were you surprised at how differently you perceived the Delacroix reproduction when you looked at it right-side up? It's almost as if L-mode, when forced to regard something in an upside-down orientation, says, in effect, "Listen, I don't do upside-down things. I like things to be the way they *always* are, so that I know what I'm looking at. If you're going to look at things upside down, count me out." Perfect! For drawing, just what we want!

Fig. 2–20
PABLO PICASSO (1881–1973)
Portrait of Léon Bakst, 1922. Pencil.
S.P.A.D.E.M., Paris, France.

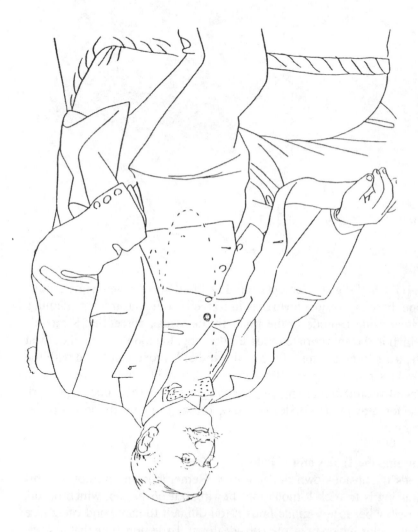

24

Drawing Upside Down

Figure 2–20 is a portrait drawing by Pablo Picasso. The image is upside down. You will be copying the image just as you see it, and therefore your drawing will also be upside down. Resist—no, refuse!—the impulse to turn the book around in order to see what it is.

Remember, you want *not to know* what it is you are drawing, and you do not *need* to know, in the usual sense of being able to put it into words. Remember, too, that if you come to a part of the drawing you can't help recognizing and naming, don't say it! Try not to talk to yourself in words. Ask your L-mode to "Kindly be quiet, please."

Please read all of the instructions before you begin your drawing:

1. Use a pencil to draw with—any ordinary pencil will do. Keep an eraser handy.

2. Use a piece of typing paper or plain bond paper.

3. You may copy the drawing the same size as shown in Figure 2–20, or larger, or smaller—whatever size you wish. Your copy, of course, will be upside down, just as the drawing in the book is upside down.

4. You may start the drawing at whatever point you wish. Since the parts all fit together, there is no special sequence— no "first things first, second things second." R-mode can start anywhere, skip around if it wishes, and end up back where it started. You may, however, decide to start at the top of the upside-down image and work down from there; but in any case, I recommend working from line to adjacent line and from line to adjacent space, as shown in Figure 2–21.

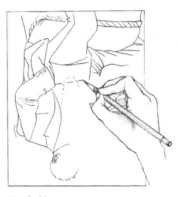

Fig. 2-21

5. If you talk to yourself at all, speak only of *relationships* and of how things fit together. For example, what is the angle of this line relative to the edge of the paper? Relative to the first line, what is the angle of that next line? Relative to the whole width of (say) the top edge of the paper, how far over is this curve? What is the shape of this open space? Don't make it hard for yourself by saying anything negative (for example, "This will be hard," or "I was never good at ____"). Just go right on drawing, checking angles and curves relative to the edges of the paper, and placing shapes and spaces relative to each other.

6. You might compare different points on the drawing: by dropping an imaginary line (parallel to an edge of the paper) from one point to another, as shown in Figure 2-22. This will help locate various parts relative to each other.

The parts will fit together like a jigsaw puzzle, and you may find yourself becoming *interested* in seeing how it all goes together so (visually) logically.

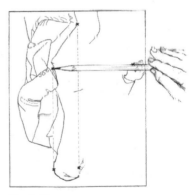

Fig. 2-22
While drawing, check where points lie in relation to each other by using imaginary vertical and horizontal lines (or you may want to actually draw in the lines, or to lay your pencil down on the drawing as a means of checking points).

7. If possible, try to take note of what goes on in your brain during the upside-down drawing. Try to notice your state (or states) of mind. And most important, be observant of your reaction at the moment when you've finished and turn the drawing right-side up.

8. Find a quiet place to draw where no one will interrupt you. You will need twenty minutes or so to complete this drawing. Some individuals draw more rapidly, some more slowly. Both are valued, one not more than the other.

Start your drawing now.

When you turned your finished drawing right-side up, you were probably very surprised—and pleased—to see how good it was. You *can* draw! And someone looking at your drawing would no doubt say, "I didn't know that you're so talented!" And did you also notice that while you were doing the drawing, you seemed to be seeing the lines and spaces in front of you in a different way? But then, when you turned it right-side up, you suddenly saw the shapes and spaces the way you usually would. That, I think, is the cognitive shift we were after. Try to think back now and recapture the difference between the two ways of seeing.

Look at some other reactions you may have had. Were you surprised, for example, to find that you drew the left knee coming toward you, in foreshortened view, without knowing it? Were you surprised at how strongly three-dimensional the figure in the drawing appears? The way the left hand fits into the pocket so convincingly? Were you surprised at the expression on the face? Surprised that the features "look right"?

Some of my students are puzzled and even a bit disturbed to find that they drew things they didn't know they were drawing. That is one of the paradoxes of drawing—a difficult proposition to swallow for the more logical L-mode. But—to satisfy L-mode's need to name and recognize—the portrait drawing is of Picasso's friend the Russian painter and designer Léon Bakst.

What can we learn from these surprises? Mainly, I think, that looking at things upside down forces one to "see differently." Things are seen *apart* from their usual connections. A line that is just a line, interesting in itself when viewed upside down, seems to disappear into a *familiar form* when viewed in the usual orientation.

I believe that this phenomenon of things sinking into a familiar context is one of the true blocks to creativity. Upside down, one sees things—parts and wholes—with a separate clarity that becomes lost in normal orientation. In drawing as in creative thinking—again, paradoxically—it is sometimes extremely valuable *not* to know what you are seeing, or what you are looking for. Preconceptions, whether they are visual or verbal, can blind one to innovative discoveries.

"An act that produces *effective surprise*—this I shall take as the hallmark of creative enterprise.... Effective surprises ... have the quality of obviousness about them when they occur, producing a shock of recognition following which there is no longer astonishment."
JEROME BRUNER
"The Conditions of Creativity," 1979.

26

Drawing and Thinking from the Down Side Up

You now have in hand your preinstruction drawings and your upside-down drawing. Both are valuable as a record of your present abilities—contradictory as the drawings may be. The preinstruction drawings show how you *think* you can draw, and the upside-down drawing demonstrates your actual capabilities for drawing. Possibly the same contradiction may exist for your conception of your creative abilities as well. The message of upside-down drawing, I believe, is that you can already draw—that is, the capability is there in your brain, ready to be used, *if the conditions of the task engender an appropriate perceptual response to the job.*

I hope you will do more upside-down drawing, to reinforce that cognitive shift which I believe is essential for drawing—and for creative thinking. Figure 2-23, the *Study of a Nude* by the great Flemish artist Peter Paul Rubens, and Figure 2-24, *Odalisque with a Moorish Chair* by Henri Matisse, are shown upside down on pages 28 and 29, ready for you to try your hand (and eye). Right-side up, either of these drawings might *seem* difficult and complicated, but with upside-down orientation you will find that you can accomplish even "difficult" drawings such as these.

And finally, there is an episode from the history of creative invention which demonstrates an elegant solution that resulted from turning the problem upside down.

In 1838, the American inventor Elias Howe turned his attention to devising a sewing machine. After perfecting various features, he remained with one major problem: the needle. Needles had always had a point at one end and an eye at the other to hold the thread. Howe's problem: how could such a needle pass all the way through a piece of cloth and come back up again in a continuous action when it had to be fastened at its eye end to the mechanism itself? The machine couldn't "let go" of the needle to pull it through to the other side of the fabric, as happens when a person is sewing with a needle.

Howe could not "see" a needle in any other way until one night he dreamed of being attacked by savages carrying spears that had eye-shaped holes near their tips. Ah-Ha! Howe awakened from his dream and immediately whittled a sewing machine needle with the hole at the pointed end. The problem was solved, essentially by being turned upside down—by Howe's "seeing" the needle, its point, and its eye for the thread in a different orientation.

Fig. 2–23
PETER PAUL RUBENS (1577–1640)
Study of a Nude, Charcoal, white gouache. Courtesy of the Ashmolean Museum.

These two drawings provide additional opportunities to practice upside-down drawing.

Fig. 2-24
HENRI MATISSE (1869–1954)
Odalisque with a Moorish Chair. Pen and ink.
Collection, The Museum of Modern Art, New York.
Acquired through the Lillie P. Bliss Bequest.

3

Taking a Long Look at Creativity

"The problem of creativity is beset with mysticism, confused definitions, value judgments, psychoanalytic admonitions, and the crushing weight of philosophical speculation dating from ancient times."
ALBERT ROTHENBERG
quoted in James H. Austin, *Chase, Chance, and Creativity*, 1978.

Over the past eight or nine years, I have been reading everything I could about creativity. I have found in my research that many writers agree about certain aspects of the creative process—for example, naming and categorizing, in L-mode fashion, the five stages of the creative process: 1. First Insight 2. Saturation 3. Incubation 4. Illumination 5. Verification. Many writers also agree that for creativity to occur, thinking needs "freeing up."

But again and again, just as I thought I was making progress in understanding the process, questions would come rushing back. I saw that in pursuit of creativity, the pursuer must still ask, "How do I get started when I don't even know what to create?" "Once I've found an area of interest and have acquired information, how do I know when enough information is enough? (In my own investigation of creativity, for example, how many *more* books and papers on creativity should I go on reading?) Then, "How do I get into the incubation stage?" And "How do I know that illumination (or inspiration or insight—the "Ah-Ha!") will be there when I need it?" "How am I supposed to know when an insight is the *right* insight? In fact, how do I know an insight when I see one?" "How do I know that I am in touch with reality and not simply daydreaming—that my insight will result in something new and useful?" "How do I know when to just stand there and when to do something?" In short, "How do I know if I am—or if I can become—truly creative?"

Puzzles That Left Me Puzzled

A. F. Osborn states that creativity is activated by such "stabs" as "What if . . .? What about . . .? What else . . .? And again, What else . . .?"
Applied Imagination: Principles and Procedures of Creative Problem-Solving, 1957.

Hopeful that taking some action myself would answer these questions, I took a "stab" at the so-called "creativity" exercises and tests sprinkled through most books on the subject. I counted the "fs" in the farmhand paragraph; I figured the area of the square; I took the Alternate-Uses tests (for example, the brick-uses test); I divided the area of a circle into ten parts using only three lines; and I did the Nine Dots experiment. (I

Fig. 3–1. How good an inspector are you? Count the f's.

The necessity of training farmhands for first class farms in the fatherly handling of farm livestock is foremost in the minds of farm owners. Since the forefathers of the farm owners trained the farmhands for first class farms in the fatherly handling of farm livestock, the farm owners feel they should carry on with the family tradition of training farmhands of first class farms in the fatherly handling of farm livestock because they believe it is the basis of good fundamental farm management.

Total number of f's _____

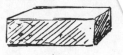

Fig. 3–2
The Alternative Uses Test.
As rapidly as you can, list the uses for an ordinary brick.

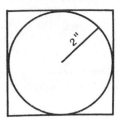

Fig. 3–3
What is the area of the square?

invite you to try these puzzlements out. Answers appear at the end of the chapter.)

You will probably find, as I did, that these and similar exercises require that you "look" at a problem in some new and different way. And once you have figured out the solution (or have read the answer), your response was probably "Of course—it was there all along. Why didn't I see it in the first place?" Those who do see it, it might be assumed, are more "creative" than those who do not.

Most creativity exercises have specific goals: to increase fluidity or fluency in idea production (Have you ever tried "brainstorming"?); to enhance visualization and fantasy (Try these: 1. Visualize your front door. 2. Put your mother on the ceiling. 3. Walk up the wall like a fly); to remove cultural, environmental, verbal, or emotional blocks; to increase self-confidence and reduce self-criticism; and to increase the number of specific thinking strategies. The supposition is that creativity can be practiced, like golf or tennis.

I discovered through further reading, however, that this approach has shortcomings. Though the tests and exercises are often interesting and fun to do, and though the validity of some measures of creativity has been established, evidence is somewhat sparse that becoming adept at creativity exercises actually increases creative output—that is, original work or ideas. In fact, truly creative individuals—people who have been *producing* creative work—may *or may not* do well at tests or exercises in "creative" problem solving.

The reason seems to be that most of these tests are "knowledge-poor," to use writer Morton Hunt's phrase. They are not *about* anything; they have little content. I found that they did indeed test my powers of perception and stimulate thinking, but I also had the feeling that they were awfully intricate and time-consuming for what seemed to be very little payoff for all that mental effort.

Furthermore, one category of exercises—those known as the

The Nine Dots Experiment.
Draw four continuous *connected* straight lines through the nine dots.

From GERARD I. NIERENBERG
The Art of Creative Thinking, 1982.

"There is no convincing evidence that courses in problem solving can increase one's ability to make the imaginative leaps that are often crucial in problem solving."
MORTON HUNT
The Universe Within, 1982.

picture-meaning tests—left me truly baffled. Although these exercises are not actually intended to measure creativity, they too test your perceptions. You are asked to look at pictures and establish a relationship between them. My problem, I discovered, was that I didn't always see what I was *supposed* to see. As it turned out, my bafflement was fortunate; it led me to a new thought about the connection between seeing and creativity.

Allow me to baffle you too with a few of these exercises. The first (Figure 3–5) is relatively straightforward:

Fig. 3–5
From GERALD I. NIERENBERG
The Art of Creative Thinking, 1982.

The intended analogy, apparently, is that the "*blossoming fruit-tree branch*" is to "*honey*" as the "*sea, sand, shore, and shellfish*" are to "_____(?)" The "suggested answer" is "*b*," the sea gull, which I can in (more or less) accept, though there is also an argument for "a": *honey* eventually ends up in a glass jar, just as moisture from the ocean can eventually end up in a water glass. But the next test (Figure 3–6) set my mind going in circles:

Fig. 3–6
From GERALD I. NIERENBERG
The Art of Creative Thinking, 1982.

The analogy, as I read it, is: "*sea gull*" is to "*ocean, shore, and shellfish*," as "*woman cooking*" is to "_____(?)" The "suggested answer" is "a or b," the supermarket or the man. What does that mean? That the sea gull gets its food from the sea as the woman gets food from the supermarket? Or, alternatively, the sea gull forages for food for its mate as the woman cooks up food for *her* mate? Against my will, alternative interpretations come to mind: the sea gull ignores the ocean and finds its food elsewhere, while the woman ignores the supermarket and cooks from scratch. Or, the sea gull *depends* on the ocean for its food, as the woman *depends* on the man for her keep (an old-fashioned notion, I admit). But why ignore the possibility of "c" as the correct answer? The sea gull is linked conceptually to the sea as cooking with gas is linked to gas in the gas pump. My mind, and the reader's too, perhaps, goes on generating more and more possible solutions, and annoyance builds when I am told that only this or that answer can be the *correct* answer.

Finally, it occurred to me that the source of the difficulty lies in the nature of drawings: unlike diagrams, word and number problems, and many puzzles, which are often "knowledge-poor," drawings are "information-rich"—even simple little sketches like the picture-meaning drawings. The test maker must necessarily ignore that information richness in order to provide a single "answer." (Note that in the second example, Figure 3–6, the test maker provided *two* possible answers—an unusual concession, but still inadequate to match the visual complexity of the drawings.)

Another example from a well-known and widely used picture-meaning test illustrates the problem more clearly (Figure 3–7):

Fig. 3–7
Visual Reception subtest.
Reproduced from the Illinois Test of Psycholinguistic Abilities by S. A Kirk, J. J. McCarthy, and W. D. Kirk, 1968, with the permission of the University of Illinois Press.

The special instructions clearly ask for the *functional* similarity rather than the perceptual similarity between the drawings. The "correct" answer prescribed by the test makers is to match the hourglass with the watch rather than with the coffee maker that *looks* like the hourglass.

Using this and similar exercises, a research scientist tested three adult patients, all of whom had previously suffered damage to their left (language-based) brain hemispheres. The object of the experiment was to determine the ability of each patient's right hemisphere (the hemisphere specialized for visual-perceptual information processing) to perform the verbal-conceptual analysis normally ascribed to the left hemisphere. Following testing, the researcher reported that the scores of the three patients' responses to picture tests were very low, on the level of a 5-to-6-year old child. The patients had missed the "correct" answers.

Drawing Away from a Single Answer

But is there a single correct answer to a test like the one shown in Figure 3–7? Even closely following directions, I can make a case for several other equally correct answers for that particular picture analogy. I agree that keeping time is one functional similarity between the hourglass and the watch, but an equally valid functional similarity is that the hourglass allows some matter (sand) to shift from its top container to the bottom container, and the coffee maker functions in the same way, moving liquid from top to bottom. Additionally, the shovel moves sand from one place to another (into the bucket) while the hourglass performs a similar function. Furthermore, the Bunsen burner will eventually force the liquid in the test tube to move out into the atmosphere by means of heat, while the force of gravity causes the sand to move from one part of the hourglass to the other. And so on.

Another picture-meaning test was presented to the same three patients. This one illustrates the difficulty more precisely (Fig. 3–8):

Fig. 3–8
Reproduced from the Illinois Test of Psycholinguistic Abilities by S. A. Kirk, J. J. McCarthy, and W. D. Kirk, 1968, with the permission of the University of Illinois Press.

The test maker asks the question "Which of the four items on the right is related to the middle item on the right in the same way that the top item on the left is to the bottom one?"

The researcher himself recognized at this point that something was going wrong, for he wryly states in his paper, "Whenever I try this test [on colleagues and students], I get many more answers than I care to hear." Nevertheless, he continues: "The semantic relationship I want

34

you to recognize here is that of equal temperature. Both the iron and the burning wood are hot, whereas the ice cream and ice water are cold." That, apparently, is the "correct" answer, and again, the patients' scores on the test were very low.

But wait a minute! As I see it, this time the so-called "correct" answer isn't correct at all! The iron is clearly cold: the cord is unplugged and neatly wound, and the iron is resting flat on a surface. No one ever puts a *hot* iron down flat; therefore, it *must* be cold. The analogy, then, must be as follows: *hot* to *cold*. The fire, which is clearly hot and burning (smoke is rising), is to the cold iron as the *hot* tea (clearly shown as hot—the steam is rising) is to the cold water in the glass with ice cubes. The test maker's answer, at least to my way of thinking, definitely does not *fit* the visual information presented to me.

It seems to me that whoever made up this test has ignored that complex visual information and has said in effect, "I don't care what the picture happens to show; I insist that you ignore the wound-up cord on the iron and the fact that the iron is flat down on a surface; pay no attention to the steam rising from the tea. You must get *my* idea in your mind: a semantic relationship, a category. All of that pictorial detail is immaterial. Don't see what you see. Fires are *hot*, and irons are *hot*, and that's all there is to that."

Such rigidity is maddening, and I believe its eventual effect on student test takers with undamaged brains is to make them try *not* to see what is in front of their eyes, but instead to arrive at abstract verbal concepts which may in fact contradict their visual perceptions. Furthermore, the test takers, whose damaged left (verbal) hemispheres had perhaps produced a condition in which they were *unable* to see in the accepted way, were judged mistaken for having seen. And with that realization, it occurred to me that much of modern education trains for exactly this kind of thinking, thus by default downgrading direct perception.

To See or Not to See

Why? I asked myself. How can there be an advantage in not seeing? How much not-seeing is going on? How much not-seeing do I do myself, having come up through an educational system that rewards not-seeing? If, as I believed, seeing is somehow tied in with creativity, what is the effect of not-seeing on creativity?

Certainly a case can be made for screening out visual data. Two plus two is categorically four, no matter how the appearance of the numbers changes, and close attention paid to variations in the look of alphabet letters would be counterproductive. The spelling of words, the value of various coins and paper currency, recognition of objects, persons, and places are all more efficiently processed by means of rigid linguistic categories.

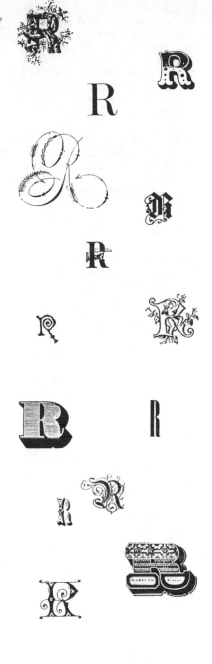

"There are times, after all, when one word is worth a thousand pictures."
PROFESSOR DON DAME
Art Department, California State
University, Long Beach

But what happens if an individual's lifetime educational experience consists almost entirely of screening out visual data and opting for linguistic concepts? Would one finally lose the ability to see, figuratively speaking? Or is it a partial loss, operating only selectively? What is different in my own training that causes me, like the patients in the test, to *have to see* visual information, at least at times, and even, at times, against my will? And what about those individuals who don't easily learn the trick of suppressing visual data in favor of verbal categories? What decisions are made about them as individuals, about their potential capabilities, their life opportunities, their futures?

Trying to Focus on Connections

Questions were piling on top of questions at this point, and in an effort to sort it all out, I tried to focus more specifically on the connections, if any, among seeing, drawing, and creativity, connections I had tentatively explored in my first book. In that book, I stated my hope that learning to draw would enhance creativity and increase artistic confidence. Concerning the latter goal, I felt on fairly certain ground: almost without exception, my students have gained confidence in their artistic ability.

On the promise to enhance creativity, however, the case was not so clear. Many students told me that they *felt* more creative as a result of learning to draw, and certain individuals provided instances of creative accomplishments. I knew, too, that drawing somehow releases creativity—but precisely how I could not say, nor was I able to express that idea clearly.

I felt quite sure, however, that the connections between drawing and creativity were somehow tied to *seeing*. And then it occurred to me that the process of drawing was, in many ways, a replication of the creative process itself. First, in drawing, one works for long periods, deeply immersed in seeing, without a sense of time passing. This quality of timelessness is a striking characteristic of drawing, one that seemed to me to be in some way similar to the outside-of-consciousness incubation stage of creativity. In drawing, one is aware that cognition is occurring, but in a different, even remote part of the mind.

Second, while drawing, one has a sense that the object being perceived is somehow at once itself yet simultaneously very like something else—hair that seems like an ocean wave, a hand that is poised like a flower on a stem. This metaphoric, analogic thinking is embedded in the drawing process and is also deeply involved in the creative process as reported by researchers and creative individuals.

Third, the characteristic need of creative persons to work in isolation is analogous to the need for isolation while drawing, particularly the need for freedom from verbal interruption. Most artists work best in silence and alone.

Finally, and most important, since ability to draw requires above all perceptual skill—the ability to see—it occurred to me that perhaps the three most elusive of the five stages of creativity (First Insight, Incubation, and the "Ah-Ha!" of Illumination) might in some way be closely connected with visual perception, not in the usual sense of the word *seeing* but rather in the special sense in which visual perception is used by an artist.

This special way of seeing includes the ability to see a whole field while at the same time perceiving parts within the field in relationship to each other as well as to the whole (the process you were engaged in while doing upside-down drawing); the ability to see with undistracted attention what is actually "out there," quite apart from language considerations; the ability to perceive both the thing as it is and its possible metaphorical overtones.

The inner gleam was hazy and indistinct as I pondered these tentative connections between visual perception and creativity without making much progress. Meanwhile, with some uneasiness and uncertainty, I continued my search until, paradoxically, I found a key clue hidden in language.

"Drawing turns the creative mind to expose its workings. Drawing discloses the heart of visual thought, coalesces spirit and perception, conjures imagination; drawing is an act of meditation."
EDWARD HILL
The Language of Drawing, 1966.

Fig. 3–9. Some answers to the puzzles on page 31.

The "F" Test
Answer: We tend to overlook the "f" in the word "of." There are thirty-six "f's."

The Alternative Uses Test
Responses are judged to be more creative if a variety of categories are included—for example: to build a wall; to grind up and make red paint; to throw at your worst critic; to make a plumb bob . . .
Additionally, the ability to generate a large number of responses in a given time is judged to indicate a higher level of flexibility in thinking—one aspect of creativity.

The Area of a Square
Changing the relationship of the radius of the circle to a closer connection with the square changes the problem and simplifies it.

The Nine Dots Experiment
Most people tend to be frozen into the boxlike pattern. When they stop thinking of boxes and think of the problem, connecting nine separate dots, the solution opens up. Three or two lines or even one line can connect all the dots.

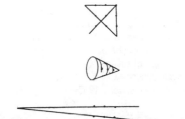

4

Drawing on Definitions

Still searching for clues about the precise role of seeing in creative thought, I went back to the statements, letters, and journals of creative individuals. After an unfruitful period of browsing, I suddenly for some reason *focused* on the words I was reading and *saw* them in a new light: in nearly every case, I realized, creative individuals have described Illumination, the fourth stage of creativity, in terms of vision.

Statement after statement used the verb *to see*: "All at once I saw the answer!" "It came to me in a dream in which I saw the solution to the problem." The French poet Paul Valéry described inspiration this way: "Sometimes I have observed this moment when a sensation arrives at the mind; it is as a gleam of light, not so much illuminating as dazzling. ... You say 'I see, and then tomorrow I shall see more.' There is an activity, a special sensitization; soon you will go into the dark-room and the picture will be seen to emerge."

This discovery was intensely exciting. My eyes were open at last to the link between seeing and creativity—a link that had been staring me in the face all along. And once my eyes were open to the idea, I found again, again, and yet again that words of vision, mainly from the verb *to see*, were used to describe the moments of invention, of discovery and investigation, and of the sudden, exhilarating resolution of a problem.

How could I *not* have seen it? A pointer toward the prize, but deeply hidden in language, masked by language forms that had become so familiar I could no longer see them or be aware of what they signified. Even creativity itself, I found, is most often defined in terms of vision: "Creativity is the ability to see problems in new ways." "Creativity is the ability to see things in a new light (or from a different perspective)." "Creativity is the knack of looking for answers in unexpected places." I had the feeling that I too had gone "into the dark-room," and that the picture would soon begin to emerge.

Unmasking Clues Rooted in Language

I found, first of all, that the term Illumination itself, Helmholtz' name for the moment of inspiration, the fourth stage of the creative process, is defined in the dictionary as "throwing light on a subject in order to see it better." Spurred on by that discovery, I investigated two terms often used interchangeably with Illumination: *intuition* and *insight*. Both words revealed more clues hidden within their origins. The root of *intuition* is *intuitus*, the past participle of the Latin verb *intueri*, to look at, and the word is defined as "the power or faculty of attaining direct knowledge or cognition without rational thought and inference"— seeing something directly, or, in other words, "getting the picture," without having to figure it out.

Investigation of the word *insight* led me down other interesting pathways. A partner to intuition, *insight* paradoxically refers directly to seeing and vision but means seeing something not necessarily visible, such as "seeing into" something, or "apprehending" something. To apprehend, "to grasp with understanding," and *discernment*, a synonym of insight, "to detect with the eyes (or with other senses)," or "to come to know or recognize mentally," pointed toward the connection of seeing and understanding—in short, grasp of meaning, a key element in creativity.

The terms *foresight*, *hindsight*, and *clear-sightedness* are variations of the same idea. Other phrases subtly shift the emphasis to differentiate specifically the kind of "seeing" or grasp of meaning that is taking place: to see in perspective, to see in proportion, to see things differently, to see through someone (or some deception), to see the light, to get things in focus. In fact, when a person has struggled to understand something, and "daylight breaks," or "the light dawns," the most commonly heard expression is "I *see* it now!"

Language Clues Linked to Drawing

It struck me at this point that the exhilarated exclamations of creative individuals—the Eurekas and the "Ah-Ha!"s of discovery—were echoed by my drawing students when, finally, they had *seen* something with the special perception induced by drawing. It also dawned on me that to the students this was a form of *insight*. Moreover, the experience was a conscious one. (Recall the moment when you finished your upside-down drawing, turned it right-side up, and suddenly *saw*, all at once, the "whole picture.")

To me, the picture was not yet completely whole, but the thought occurred to me that the experience of seeing through drawing could be used to clarify the concept of insight—to demonstrate what it is, how to know and recognize it, and how to set up conditions conducive to attaining it. After all, logical reasoning and analysis depend on prelim-

"George Washington gave instructions to his orderly not to be disturbed during the darkest period of the revolutionary war. Washington wanted to turn his deep problems over to the creative, intuitive part of his mind. . . . By his own testimony, George Washington used that kind of insight to guide his decisions throughout his presidency. So did Abraham Lincoln, among others. The founding fathers thought this was so important that they tried to remind us of it on the back of the dollar bill. There you will find an unfinished pyramid with an eye over the top of it. The meaning of this symbol is thousands of years old. The structure is not complete, whether it is the individual's life or the nation, until the all seeing eye is in the capstone position, until this creative, intuitive part of our mind is playing a major role in guiding our decisions."
WILLIS W. HARMAN
"This 20 Year Present," *Public Management*, 1980.

"I understand this picture exactly, I could model it in clay. I understand this description exactly, I could make a drawing of it. In many cases we might set it up as a criterion of understanding, that I'm able to represent the sense of a sentence in a drawing (I am thinking of an officially instituted test of understanding)."
LUDWIG WITTGENSTEIN
quoted in Andrew Harrison, *Making and Thinking*, 1979.

inary training not in logic and analysis but in verbal and numerical skills. If insight, intuition, and illumination *are* what the roots of the words indicate—grasp of meaning through special perception—prelimi- nary training in perceptual skills might be an appropriate means of attain- ing a greater understanding of the whole creative process.

"But wait a minute," you may object, "I'm not blind. I can see perfectly well."

And of course that's true; every sighted person is capable of ordinary seeing. But I am talking about a different kind of seeing, the kind of seeing developed through drawing that is quantitatively and qualitatively differ- ent from ordinary seeing.

Drawing a Parallel in Language

A parallel in language may illustrate the difference: a person who has never learned to read and write can nevertheless use language—can talk. In talking, that person may show humor, flexibility, intelligence, and understanding. But important uses of literacy will be blocked off: access to written work of the present or past centuries, the ability to fix ideas into writing for others to use, and the ability to increase knowl- edge through reading. Almost everyone will agree that learning to read and write makes a qualitative difference in terms of *thinking*.

So it is with seeing. A person untrained in perceptual skills may nevertheless see well, perhaps may even have very sharp perception in the sense of noticing, for example, minute changes of facial expression, small errors in computations, or subtle movement patterns in sports. But my students generally agree that learning to see by means of draw- ing makes a qualitative difference. They had never before realized how much more there was to see, how very different things could appear, and how radically this kind of seeing could affect their thinking.

The Value of Perceptual Skills

Thus, to restate my thesis, the *use* of learning to see and draw is not limited to making works of art, just as the use of learning to read and write is not limited to writing works of literary art. Nor is the purpose of learning the artist's way of seeing simply to see more or to see better; and it certainly is not (for most people, at least) for the purpose of becoming a professional artist, though that may happen in a few cases. Perceptual skills, like verbal skills, are valuable because they improve thinking.

Thus, I gradually assembled the pieces of the puzzle. But how to put them all together? Where in the process of creative thinking do verbal and perceptual skills seem to fit?

The Accessible Two

To answer that question, I thought that as a logical first step I might separate out the two stages that seemed the least mysterious of the five: Saturation and Verification, the second and fifth stages of creativity. Saturation, simply put, is information gathering. Volumes have been written on how to do research. Libraries are organized to help researchers gather information—facts, figures, data, procedures. Especially in the Western world, a person becomes educated largely by gathering and memorizing information: What year did Columbus discover America? Who wrote *Hamlet*? What is the product of 7 times 7? At higher levels of education, students usually specialize in a subject area in order better to saturate their minds with finer and finer details of facts and procedures. The process of gathering information, therefore, is at least familiar.

Verification, the last stage of creativity, is also fairly well understood. A new idea needs to be verified and put into a form that makes it available for use by others. Though creative thinkers report many instances of rapid Verification—simply a matter of writing down what appeared in a dream or in a flash of inspiration—the process can also be difficult and time-consuming, sometimes requiring years of labor to produce a convincing, unassailable proof. But the process itself is accessible to human understanding, involving as it does procedures that have been studied, analyzed, codified, and specified. Again, a major aim of Western education is to teach students how to verify ideas. The challenge "Prove it!" rings through countless schoolrooms.

The Mysterious Three

The sticking point comes with the first and middle stages of creativity: First Insight, Incubation, and Illumination. These three, by all accounts, are mysterious and seem to elude human understanding. What is going on in the brain that produces First Insight—the question? During Incubation, what is the brain doing with the information gathered during the previous stage of Saturation? The great French mathematician Jacques Hadamard, quoted in the margin, described his creative mode of thought. But what was going on in Hadamard's brain when he was "really thinking"? He quoted the French philosopher Etienne Souriau, who spoke of the need for "thinking aside." But *where* or *what* is that "aside"? And what went on in Einstein's brain when he stepped away from his friend in order to "a little think"? These are the elusive aspects of creativity. And Illumination, the moment of inspiration, is perhaps the most mysterious of all.

In the creative process as a whole, it seems to me that Saturation and Verification fit best with our usual conception of *conscious* thought, while First Insight, Incubation, and Illumination seem to fit with our conception of unconscious or subconscious thought. Saturation and

"The saturation phase [of creativity] is a thorough investigation of the possibilities of the germinal idea. Before attempting *The Ancient Mariner* and *Kubla Khan* Coleridge read widely in the literature of travel. To prepare for *Moby Dick* Melville immersed himself in accounts of whaling from classical time to his own."
GEORGE KNELLER
The Art and Science of Creativity, 1965.

"A classic example of the arduousness of [verification] is the search of the Curies for the undiscovered element in pitchblende. The excitement they felt at discovering a new source of energy was buried under years of exhausting toil."
GEORGE KNELLER, 1965.

"Pour inventer, il faut penser à côté."
("In order to invent, one must think aside.")
ETIENNE SOURIAU
Théorie de l'Invention, 1881.

"I insist that words are totally absent from my mind when I really think and I shall completely align my case with Galton's in the sense that even after reading or hearing a question, every word disappears at the very moment I am beginning to think it over. . . . I fully agree with Schopenhauer when he writes, 'Thoughts die the moment they are embodied by words.'"
JACQUES HADAMARD, 1945.

A favorite story told by physicist Albert Einstein's friends:
When discussing a scientific problem with a colleague, Einstein would sometimes step away from his friend, saying in his charming, German-influenced English, "I will a little think."
From *Einstein: A Centenary Volume*, A. P. French, ed., 1979.

Verification fit with logical analytic thinking, while First Insight, Incubation, and Illumination fit better with our general conception of imagination and intuition. Turning to the field of drawing, Saturation and Verification seem more like looking and naming; First Insight, Incubation, and Illumination seem more like seeing and visualizing in the artist's way.

I have long believed that drawing requires a cognitive shift in brain mode from the dominant verbal, conceptual L-mode to the subdominant visual, perceptual R-mode. Whether or not that is the case, artists attest to the fact that drawing produces a slight change in consciousness, a perceptible shift in mental state, often described as "seeing differently." If artists are asked, "Are you in a different state of mind when you're working?" most will answer "Yes," not even asking what you mean. They know what you mean by the question, because to do art at all generally requires such mental shifts. Note, however, that an artist is aware only *after the fact* of having been in the state of "seeing differently," and is often reluctant to probe too deeply into the nature of that different mental state. As the French artist Georges Braque said, the mystery "must be respected."

Certain aspects of "seeing differently," however, can be examined. For example, one is unable to carry on a conversation (as in my difficulty in talking while demonstrating drawing), and interruption is seriously resented. Also, the mental state produces a sense of alert concentration, quite the opposite of "daydreaming." And there is a loss of the sense of time passing, a lack of any sense of boredom, a sense at times of near-revelation or near-mystical insight. As Frederick Franck put it in the margin quotation, the ego is liberated as the mind takes "a dive into reality."

A Hypothetical Structure

Continuing my efforts to put all the pieces of the puzzle together, I sketched a hypothetical structure of mental shifts during the stages of creativity. I conjectured that if cognitive shifts similar to those which seem to occur in drawing also occur during the process of creativity, the picture might look something like this:

1. Suppose that an area of investigation is located—a problem surfaces. This stage, First Insight, requires an intuitive leap best accomplished by "seeing" large amounts of information—the "whole picture"—and searching for the parts that are missing, that don't fit, or that "stand out" in some way. Something is noticed, and a key question flashes into the mind often concerning something that *isn't there* or something seen in a new, imaginary orientation. Because L-mode is not suited to such vast and vague exploration, I believe that First Insight is largely an R-mode function.

French artist Georges Braque was reluctant to probe too deeply into his art:
"There are certain mysteries, certain secrets in my own work which even I don't understand, nor do I try to do so. ... The more one probes the more one deepens the mystery: it's always out of reach. Mysteries have to be respected if they are to retain their power. Art disturbs: science reassures."
Quoted in GEORGE KNELLER, *The Art and Science of Creativity*, 1965.

"Looking and seeing both start with sense perception, but there the similarity ends. When I 'look' at the world and label its phenomena, I make immediate choices, instant appraisal—I like or dislike, I accept or reject what I look at, according to its usefulness to 'Me.'
"The purpose of 'looking' is to survive, to cope, to manipulate . . . this we are trained to do from our first day. When, on the other hand, I *SEE*, suddenly I am all eyes, I forget this Me, am liberated from it and dive into the reality that confronts me."
FREDERICK FRANCK
The Zen of Seeing, 1973.

2. Suppose, then, that L-mode comes forward in the Saturation stage, as it gathers, sorts out, and categorizes information on the area of interest. This second stage is mainly one of conscious awareness, the "normal" verbal, analytic, linear mode. During this stage, the mind does indeed become saturated with information, ideally up to the limit of its ability to obtain that information.

3. At this point, perhaps, L-mode falters. Recall from the journal notes of creative thinkers that when lines of investigation peter out, when logical questions defy answers, when the puzzle resists solution and dead ends block further progress, a sense of unease, anxiety, and frustration sets in. Thinking loses structure. The gathered bits of information, like pieces of a jigsaw puzzle spread out on a table (a few fitted together perhaps—an edge here, a corner there), refuse to yield to logical analysis. The pattern, the organizing principle, the key that would reveal the whole picture is missing. Since further L-mode progress seems blocked and frustrated, the problem is often "set aside."

Suppose that the problem at this point is "handed over," so to speak, to the other, more obscure mode of the brain, the visual, perceptual, global, intuitive, pattern-seeking R-mode, which proceeds to deal *on its own*—that is, outside of conscious awareness—with information gathered during the L-mode–dominated Saturation stage. This is the Incubation stage. And in its timeless, wordless, synthesizing fashion, R-mode perhaps manipulates the gathered information in imagined visual space, shifting positions of particles and chunks, trying for the "best fit," attempting to form coherent patterns even though parts of the puzzle may be missing, trying to see the whole picture, trying to "fill in" the blank spaces, trying to form a visually logical structure with all the parts in the "right relationship" to each other and to the whole. Note that this structure is not formed by rules of logical analysis—the syntactical rules of linear language—but instead by the heuristics or rules of visual logic.

An Aside: A Different Kind of Logic
On this point, studies are said to have shown that the right hemisphere of the brain does not have an internal model of its own solution processes and does not seem to learn by exposure to specific rules and examples. But although this statement may be true for certain R-mode processes, it doesn't fit with my own and others' experiences in drawing. The game of drawing has rules and heuristics that guide the process of seeing and drawing. The rules are not syntactical—that is, they are not like the orderly, grammatical rules of language that govern the way words are put together to form phrases, clauses, and sentences. The rules and heuristics of drawing are broad enough to allow for infinite variation—a necessary characteristic because the visual information "out there" is infinitely variable and complex. It may only *seem* as if R-mode has no

Evolution of a word:

heuristic: hyu-ris'-tic, adjective or noun.

Derived from the Indo-European *wer* (I have found); in Greek *heuriskein* (to discover), from which was derived Archimedes' cry "*Eureka!*" (I have found it!)
From LEWIS THOMAS, *The Lives of a Cell*, 1975.

Today's definition (Webster's):

heuristic:
general meaning: serving to guide, discover, or reveal;

specific meaning: a rule valuable for research but unproved or incapable of proof.

Fig. 4–1. One style of seeing . . .

Fig. 4–2. . . . . And another way to look at a chrysanthemum.

internal model of solution processes because the model is so different it cannot be seen when L-mode is used to look for it.

To illustrate, the petals of a chrysanthemum are all more or less the same shape. In (realistic) drawing, one *knows* that, but wants *not* to know it, because the requirement—the rule or heuristic—of drawing is to see *each* petal as a unique instance, yet at the same time to see it in relationship to all the other petals, as well as to the stem, to the leaves, to the space around the whole form (and the space around each petal, leaf, and stem), and simultaneously to see all of that in relation to the shape of the drawing paper, the lightness or darkness of each line, the crispness or fuzziness of each mark, and so on.

44

In a sense, this is the opposite of the thinking style of L-mode, which sees the myriad petals and asks, "What is the general shape of the *typical* petal?" and then proceeds to abstract a symbolic shape that can be used over and over, *without further thinking*, to "stand for" the general category "chrysanthemum petals." From there, L-mode moves to the next category, asking, "What is the general shape of chrysanthemum stems?" and from there, proceeds to determine the general shape of chrysanthemum leaves. "There. It's done," says L-mode. "The title is 'Chrysanthemum.' "

Figures 4–1 and 4–2 show the end results of the two different styles of thinking. The second drawing can be repeated over and over, fitting with the idea of an L-mode internal model which can be used for *any* chrysanthemum or, in fact, for the general category "Flower."

The first drawing, by Dutch artist Piet Mondrian, however, illustrates a completely different strategy, one based *not* on generalized forms but on exact, unique, exceedingly complex forms. Mondrian's drawing could be repeated only with great effort and difficulty because of this complexity. Furthermore, given another chrysanthemum, the artist would have to start again from the beginning. The same would be true even with the same chrysanthemum *if the position of the flower were changed even slightly.*

This willingness to accept enormous complexity and to deal with specific instances, I believe, is what L-mode cannot *stand* about R-mode. What sticks in the craw, perhaps, is that R-mode is so different—an idea that reminds me of a song from the musical *My Fair Lady*: "Why Can't a Woman Be More like a Man?" Why, says L-mode, can't R-mode be more like me? Why can't it go straight to the point the way I do and select out only what is important? Find the general rule and *stick to it*! Why bother with all that complicated stuff? What difference does it make if each petal is a little different? They're all more or less the same anyway. The differences aren't important. R-mode disagrees (just as L-mode disagrees that checkbook balancing is tedious and unimportant!), and, as did the Swiss artist Paul Klee, refuses to make hypotheses about what is seen, about what in reality exists "out there." Despite overwhelming complexity, R-mode opts for the unique instance.

This profound difference in styles of thinking is accompanied by a difference in the level of conscious awareness of the two processes. The R-mode process may be largely outside of conscious (L-mode) awareness; L-mode is—or, perhaps, *prefers* to be—unaware that R-mode is "thinking aside."

I suggest that this may be what is going on during the Incubation stage which ultimately produces the Illumination of creativity. The sheer amount of information and the simultaneous spatial perceptions are at levels of complexity beyond the capability and *unsuited to the style*

Drawing in Two Modes

The following brief exercise will help clarify the difference between these two methods of drawing:

1. On a piece of scratch paper, copy a bit of the Mondrian *Chrysanthemum*. Try a single leaf, perhaps, or a small section of petals. Try to copy the lines *exactly* as you see them.

2. Then, on the same sheet of paper, copy a single leaf of the second drawing, Figure 4–2, and perhaps a part of the petals. As you do the second drawing, note the difference in mind-set, speed of line, difficulty, and complexity.

3. As a last step, use a flower as model and draw it using both methods.

"I must begin not with hypothesis, but with specific instances."
PAUL KLEE
Altes Fräulein, 1931.

In 1922, the great atomic physicist Niels Bohr was mulling over the problems of atom dynamics, which seemed at the time to be at an impasse. In a 1980 address, Harvard physics professor Gerald Holton described Bohr's "well-nigh hopeless" state of mind:

"Bohr knew already that the problem was one involving not only physics but also epistemology. Human language is simply inadequate to describe processes within the atom, to which our experience is connected in only very indirect ways. But since understanding and discussion depend on the available language, this deficiency made any solution difficult for the time being.

"Bohr confessed that originally he had not worked out his complex atomic models by classical mechanics; they had come to him 'intuitively . . . as pictures,' representing events within the atom."
GERALD HOLTON
"On Tracing the Nascent Moment," 1980.

"Faraday, Galton, Einstein, and certain other noted scientists have reported that they solved scientific problems in visual images and only afterwards translated their thoughts into words.

"In a famous instance of this, Einstein, unable to reconcile his special theory of relativity with Newtonian physics, pictured a box falling freely down a very long shaft; inside it, an occupant took coins and keys out of his pocket and let them go. The objects, Einstein saw, remained in midair, alongside him, because they were falling at the same rate as he—a situation temporarily identical with being in space, beyond any gravitational field.

"From this visual construct, Einstein was able to sense some of those seemingly contradictory relationships about movement and rest, acceleration and gravity, that he later put into mathematical and verbal form in his general theory of relativity."
MORTON HUNT
The Universe Within, 1982.

of the linear, sequential, language-based mode of thought. L-mode, perhaps unaware of what is going on, may occupy itself with more "normal" conscious activities and with cognition more suited to its thinking style, while its partner meantime is . . . thinking aside.

Again, the letters and journals of creative individuals often describe this period as one of uneasiness and anxiety. Perhaps L-mode, the thought mode by which we consciously talk to ourselves and explain to ourselves what we are thinking about, as in Joanna Field's "blind thought," is aware in some sense that it is on hold, waiting for . . . it knows not what.

A Hypothetical Structure Continued . . .

Returning now to my conjectured structure of the creative process, the next stage may emerge as follows:

4. Suppose that the subconscious process of Incubation goes on for days or weeks or months. Perhaps L-mode continues to be in a state of uneasiness regarding the inquiry under investigation. Then suppose that one day the problem solver, while driving on the freeway or stepping on the bus, or, like Archimedes, sitting in the bathtub, finally "sees the light." Up to this moment, R-mode, still outside of conscious awareness, still in the midst of its continuing manipulation of the information in imagined visual space, following its unique rules and heuristics, has been searching for the pattern, the key to the puzzle. Suddenly the parts fall into place, everything fits, the configuration looks right, the spaces and the shapes mesh together and satisfy all the constraints of the problem. All is in focus. Illumination at last. "Ah-Ha!" "That's it! I see it now!" "Eureka. I have found it!"

In a flash of recognition, the Illumination is seen as *right*. The discoverer embraces the solution with elation, since it alleviates the uneasiness and anxiety experienced during Incubation. The notes and journals of creative individuals inform us that often accompanying Illumination is a deep sense of pleasure similar to the esthetic response to beauty. Solutions are often spoken of as being "beautiful," or "elegant." But more important, the Illumination feels right, "looks" right, and is somehow *known* to be right. A sense of certainty prevails, and the discoverer is exhilarated.

5. In a sense, R-mode has somehow presented the solution to the problem in a form compatible with L-mode. And as things quiet down, L-mode perhaps asks itself, "Where did that come from, that solution which just seemed to pop into my brain? I wasn't even thinking about the problem and here the answer shows up. Very strange! Just luck, I guess. I must have stumbled on the answer somehow, since it seems to have just come out of the blue. Oh, well, never mind. It doesn't matter. Somehow I know it's the right solution, and now that I've seen the

light, I can get on with the job—really get started. I can test it out, find out if it *really* works, and if it does, write up the proof." Thus L-mode takes over again in the final stage of the creative process, Verification.

Since both the Incubation stage and the resulting Illumination were outside of conscious awareness and arrived out of the blue as a surprise, an enigma, an inexplicable event, is it any wonder that the solution to a problem is often attributed to luck, to the Muses, or to something called "God-given talent"? The conscious, verbal left hemisphere of the brain often explains away (there's an interesting phrase!) the whole process by saying that the answer came as a "gift from heaven," or from "out of nowhere," or from "out of left field"—the last perhaps a subconscious acknowledgment of its silent partner, the right hemisphere, which does in fact—for most people—control the left hand and the left visual field.

But these musings about the source of the Illumination are usually brief, as L-mode proceeds with the final stage, doing what it does best. And with a new sense of confidence in the outcome, the creator writes the book, composes the sonata, draws the building plans, tests the mathematical formula, reorganizes the company personnel, or builds the machine part by part—in short, performs a step-by-step Verification of the "inspired" solution.

So far, so good, I said to myself—the five stages of creativity conceptualized to fit alternate combinations of modes of thought. First Insight, mainly R-mode, but triggered by consciously asked questions: "What if . . .?" or "I wonder why . . .?" or "How come . . .?"; Saturation, mainly L-mode; Incubation and Illumination, mainly R-mode, manipulating L-mode information in imagined visual space; and finally, Verification, mainly L-mode.

1	2	3	4	5
First Insight	*Saturation*	*Incubation*	☀	*Verification*

The Ah-Ha!

An "elegant" formulation indeed. Or so I thought. I had taken a step, at least, in the right direction. But I was still far from reaching the goal I had set for myself: first, how to gain access, in particular, to the obscure and elusive stages of First Insight, Incubation, and Illumination in the creative process; and second, how to teach that process. How could I find a way to draw out the artist from within?

In 1907, Albert Einstein recorded the creative moment when he grasped that the effect of gravity was equivalent to a nonuniform motion as "the happiest moment of my life."
Quoted in HANS PAGELS, *The Cosmic Code*, 1982.

Plato explained away the divine spark that inspires poets:
"And for this reason God takes away the minds of these men and uses them as his ministers, just as he does soothsayers and godly seers in order that we who hear them may know that it is not they who utter these words of great price when they are out of their wits, but that it is God himself who speaks and addresses us through them."
Quoted in JAMES L. ADAMS, *Conceptual Blockbusting*, 1974.

Not all creators find mental shifts from imagery back to language (for verification) an easy matter. The great nineteenth century geneticist Francis Galton wrote: ✺
"It is a serious drawback to me in writing, and still more in explaining myself, that I do not so easily think in words as otherwise. It often happens that after being hard at work, and having arrived at results that are perfectly clear and satisfactory to myself, when I try to express them in language I feel that I must begin by putting myself upon quite another intellectual plane. I have to translate my thoughts into a language that does not run very evenly with them. I therefore waste a vast deal of time in seeking for appropriate words and phrases, and am conscious, when required to speak on a sudden, of being often very obscure through mere verbal maladroitness, and not through want of clearness of perception. That is one of the small annoyances of my life."
Quoted in JACQUES HADAMARD, *The Psychology of Invention in the Mathematical Field*, 1945

Part II

Making Thought Visible

"The question is, who is interested in creativity? And my answer is that practically everybody is. This interest is no longer confined to psychologists and psychiatrists. Now it has become a question of national and international policy as well."

ABRAHAM MASLOW
The Farther Reaches of Human Nature, 1976.

5 Drawing on a Parallel Language

As a teacher, I must, of course, rely on words to instruct my students. But as a teacher of drawing, I also have available another language—the visual language of drawing itself. Thus, it was within the context of both forms of language that I approached the problem of how to teach the creative process.

But it was quite by chance that I came across a little-known essay by George Orwell titled "New Words," written probably in 1940 (apparently the exact date is uncertain). Though the essay is about verbal language, it linked together my research into the journals of creative individuals, my conception of the roles of L-mode and R-mode in the stages of creativity, and an idea I had been picking up and putting down again for nearly twenty years: that drawings—marks on paper with *or without* recognizable images—can be read like a language and that they reveal to the person making the marks (as well as to the viewer) what had been going on in the mind of the mark maker.

This was not a new or original idea, but I had become increasingly intrigued with the notion (introduced in Chapter Four with Mondrian's chrysanthemum drawing) that drawings also seem to reveal which brain mode, L-mode or R-mode, had dominated during the process of drawing. Moreover, I had been working with my students on the idea that pure drawing—that is, marks on the paper that represent pure expression, devoid of any realistic or symbolic images—can reveal thoughts of which even the thinker is unaware.

Dredging Up Visual Thought

In "New Words," Orwell used the phrase "making thought visible," and this seemed to me to be an idea I was looking for, a clue pointing toward an R-mode language, a language parallel to the verbal language of L-mode, yet entirely different, which might provide access to the obscure stages of the creative process in which R-mode appears to function.

"... drawing, within the visual arts, seems to me to hold the position of being closest to pure thought."
JOHN ELDERFIELD
Director of Drawings, Museum of Modern Art, New York, quoted in an interview by Michael Kimmelman.

The Orwell passages are from "New Words," 1940(?) in *The Collected Essays, Journalism, and Letters of George Orwell*, Vol. 2: *My Country, Right or Left*, 1968.

In his essay, Orwell speculated on the limited and limiting ability of words to describe thought—an echo of Galton's "small annoyance" (the margin quotation on page 47). Orwell said, "Everyone who thinks at all has noticed that our language is practically useless for describing anything that goes on inside the brain." As a way out of this problem, Orwell first suggested inventing new words, but he quickly acknowledged that chaos would result if everybody constantly invented new words to describe individual mental events. He then came around to the idea that the first step in producing words that could describe mental states and events would be to "make thought visible."

"In effect," Orwell wrote, "it must come down to giving words a physical (probably visible) existence. Merely talking about definitions is futile; one can see this whenever it is attempted to define one of the words used by literary critics (e.g. 'sentimental,' 'vulgar,' 'morbid,' etc.). All meaningless—or rather, having a different meaning for everyone who uses them. What is needed is to *show* a meaning in some unmistakable form, and then, when various people have identified it in their own minds and recognized it as worth naming, to give it a name. The question is simply of finding a way in which one can give thought an objective existence."

Orwell speculated further that film might be the medium that could communicate mental processes: "If one thinks of it, there is very little in the mind that could not *somehow* be represented by the strange powers of the film. A millionaire with a private cinematograph, all the necessary props and a troupe of intelligent actors could, if he wished, make practically all of his inner life known. He could explain the real reasons of his actions instead of telling rationalised lies, point out the things that seemed to him beautiful, pathetic, funny, etc.—things that an ordinary man has to keep locked up because there are no words to express them. In general, he could make other people understand him ...though putting thoughts into visible shape would not always be easy."

Poet Howard Nemerov was interested in the thought that, just by chance, we might have had another language, altogether different from verbal language. Nemerov noted that the French writer Marcel Proust "touches the thought, but almost at once lets it go."
Proust wrote: "And just as certain creatures are the last surviving testimony to a form of life which nature has discarded, I ask myself ... what might have been if there had not come the invention of language, the formation of words, the analysis of ideas.... It is like a possibility which has ended in nothing."
H. NEMEROV
"On Poetry, Painting, and Music," 1980.

"We are unknown, we knowers, ourselves to ourselves: this has its own good reason. We have never searched for ourselves—how should it then come to pass, that we should ever *find* ourselves?
FRIEDRICH NIETZSCHE
On the Genealogy of Morals, 1887.

Orwell noted that he had written these thoughts down hastily, but he concluded that the ideas had value: "It is curious that when our knowledge, the complication of our lives and therefore (I think it must follow) our minds develop so fast, language, the chief means of communication, should scarcely stir."

Drawing on Orwell's Idea

Orwell's idea seemed to me to fit with drawing. Drawing can objectify thought—can get it out in front, where it can be seen. Drawing is truly *different* from verbal language, particularly in its ability to deal, in Orwell's words, with the "complication of our lives." For example, drawing is not locked into linear time (in an L-mode sense) and is therefore able to clarify complicated relationships that may include past, present, and future. Also, in drawing one can express ideas or feelings that are too complicated or imprecise to fit into the "reducing lens" of words. Furthermore, drawings can show relationships that are grasped immediately as a single image, where words are necessarily locked into a sequential order.

Additionally, drawing is information-rich and can delineate differences as well as point up similarities. In drawing, R-mode presumably does not select information by categories, but sees whatever is "out there" (or inside the mind), at the same time looking for unifying patterns and connections that might link seemingly different parts. Put another way, drawing can help one get the whole picture, see how the land lies, bring things into focus, zero in on the problem, simultaneously see the forest *and* the trees, move the pieces around in visual space, see the light as plain as day. Could it also, I wondered, help one gain First Insight, locate a problem, ask the beautiful question?

Drawing on Possibilities

What would a visual language, useful for accessing R-mode of the brain, be like? What would be its rules? Would they be similar to the so-called "principles of art"—the rules of composition? If more complex, could they be translated into language, or would they always remain different and aside from language? Would there be a requirement for visual order and arrangement? Could a visual language make statements accessible to L-mode, or would the "reading" (I don't intend a pun) be too complicated for words? Could there exist a vocabulary and a grammar for visual and spatial relationships? What would be the role of chance or accident? With the gates wide open to experience, how would the user of such a language cope with overwhelming complexity?

These are the questions I have asked myself, and by no means do I have answers that are anywhere near complete. But I believe that capability for such a language does actually exist in the human brain. The

"always the beautiful answer who asks a more beautiful question."
E. E. CUMMINGS
quoted in Nathan Goldstein, *The Art of Responsive Drawing*, 1973.

form, however, the rules, the vocabulary, the possibility of translation for the moment all remain just out of reach.

Tentatively, one can at least say that the statements and propositions of such a language are probably visual, the grammar a set (perhaps unlimited) of perceptual strategies or heuristics, the vocabulary an open-ended set of unfixed, ever-evolving visual forms with recognizable *general meaning* yet almost infinite variability (to fit Orwell's requirements for making thought visible). The order or arrangement must necessarily be visual, spatial, relational, and simultaneous rather than linguistic, analytic, and sequential. If attainable, an R-mode language with the above characteristics would provide a language of depth, complexity, and flexibility possibly comparable to verbal language itself and possibly capable of actually making thought visible.

A parallel R-mode language would obviously depend on visual perception for "reading" the image, but capturing or translating the image back into words would be very useful—would make the visual ideas accessible for L-mode processing. There is no doubt, however, that translation would be difficult, as is shown by the picture-meaning tests in Chapter Three and, again, by Galton's "small annoyance" (in the margin quotation on page 47).

As I see it, the main problem is the difference in complexity between the two modes of expression: images are nearly always very complicated; words most often distill, simplify, and abstract complexity. To say that another way, the relationship of words to images is similar to that of *titles* of drawings to the actual drawings. Words (or titles) cannot fully substitute for images, but if well chosen for *fitting* the image, they can "tag" images so that the images can later be called up in the "mind's eye," thus retaining their complexity.

The Duality of Words and Images

Complexity aside, I am going to forge ahead and assume that a nonverbal, visual language of drawing exists as a possible parallel to verbal language, even though I cannot at this point spell it out in L-mode terms. A language of drawing, of course, is not the only possible parallel language. There exist, obviously, many nonverbal languages: the language of sound (music), the language of movement (dance or sports), of abstract symbolic thought (mathematics and science), of color (painting), of film (as Orwell suggested), and the language of Nature itself—the genetic code, for example. Each of these could perhaps serve equally well for encoding R-mode thought—for making thought visible.

But drawing is very simple. Other nonverbal languages, perhaps equally effective, are complicated by requiring equipment, space, materials, or physical agility. Music, for example (other than singing), requires instruments and is complicated by its dual brain-mode characteristics.

"As to words, they remain absolutely absent from my mind until I come to the moment of communicating the results in written or oral form. . . ."
JACQUES HADAMARD
The Psychology of Invention in the Mathematical Field, 1945.

Fig. 5-1
A drawing of Churchill painting.

"Painting is complete as a distraction. I know of nothing which, without exhausting the body, more entirely absorbs the mind. Whatever the worries of the hour or the threats of the future, once the picture has begun to flow along, there is no room for them in the mental screen. They pass out into shadow and darkness. All one's mental light, such as it is, becomes concentrated on the task. Time stands respectfully aside."
WINSTON CHURCHILL
Painting as a Pastime, 1950.

Painting requires materials that are often bulky and expensive—brushes, paints, stretcher bars, and canvas (though British Prime Minister Winston Churchill, sketched in Figure 5-1, among countless others, found those problems no impediment). Dance and sports require certain levels of physical fitness as well as space for performance. Mathematics and science require at least minimal levels of training. Nature, if her secrets are to be penetrated, requires advanced techniques of science, meditation, or philosophy. And, as Orwell pointed out, filming one's thoughts would require a millionaire's bankroll.

Thinking Simply by Means of Drawing

Drawing, on the other hand, requires the simplest of materials. The cave drawings by prehistoric human beings demonstrate clearly how uncomplicated the requisite materials are: a surface to mark on and something to make marks with. Using the crudest of drawing tools—a bit of charred wood or a pointed stick dipped in powdered clay—primitive tribespeople over the centuries have produced exquisite drawings, often based on natural forms, that made visible their ideas and beliefs.

Drawing has few physical requirements. Ordinary motor skills and eye-hand coordination—ordinary ability, as I have mentioned, to thread a needle or to catch a ball—are sufficient. Many handicapped individuals have demonstrated how little drawing skill depends on ordinary motor skills. Even deprived of use of the hands, a person can learn to draw, as is shown in beautiful drawings by paralyzed individuals, using their teeth to hold the pencil, or by amputee patients drawing with the pencil gripped by their toes or strapped to an arm. It is knowing how to

Fig. 5-2
Sorcerer, Trois-Frères, c. 15,000–10,000 B.C. 2 ft. high. Ariège, France.

54

Fig. 5–3
ELIZABETH LAYTON
Mothers Day, 1982.

Elizabeth Layton first began drawing at age 68 with the hope of finding relief from severe depression following a stroke. Drawing proved to be therapeutic, and Layton continued to draw. Since then, her drawings have been exhibited nationwide and are greatly admired. I think she should be acclaimed a national treasure.

see that counts.

In its simplicity, drawing is the silent twin to reading. Both reading and drawing can be done at any age from early childhood to the final day of a lifetime, if the eyes last that long. Both can be done in almost any environment, at any time of the day or night, by any person of any age who has minimal physical and mental health. Like reading, drawing can be taught in an ordinary room or classroom or out of doors, requiring none of the elaborate equipment of present-day art classrooms.

In considering drawing as a possible parallel to verbal language, a first step is to demonstrate to you, the reader, that a language of drawing exists, and that you are already able to read it—in part, at least. In light of the fact that prehistoric human drawings predate written language by about ten thousand years, it seems possible that a language of drawing may derive from innate brain structures, just as verbal language apparently derives from innate structure. (Psycholinguist Noam Chomsky has postulated for language a "deep structure" in the brain, composed of preexisting expectations of the ways in which the components of human languages go together.) The fact that you *know* (part of) the parallel visual language already—though you perhaps don't know that you know it, along the lines of Polanyi's statement—indicates at least a possible innate brain structure for visual language.

How, then, to tap into your natural ability to use—and understand—the expressive power of this visual language? Clearly, by drawing—and by learning how to draw—just as we tap into the power of verbal language by learning how to read and write.

A dark saying by philosopher Michael Polanyi.
"We know more than we know we know."

6　Making Telling Marks

Handwriting of the famous.

If you are a person who says of yourself, "I don't draw at all," that is not exactly a true statement. Nearly every day you do a drawing using line, one of the basic components of art: you "draw" your name. Embedded in that "drawing"—in the line of your signature, quite aside from the names the line spells out—is a great quantity of visual information. The information is there for all to see and "read."

Some individuals consider themselves expert at reading handwriting, and although handwriting analysis, called graphology, has never been taken very seriously by most people as a predicator of personality traits, no one denies that handwriting is unique to each individual. Your signature expresses you and only you. Your signature is, in fact, a legal possession, *owned* by you, as much a part of you as your fingerprints.

Since the alphabet letters do not vary—an *a* is an *a*, no matter what it looks like—the line with which you *draw* the letters of your name is the source of the uniqueness of your signature. The exact characteristics of the line come from within your psyche, your physiology, and your history. Therefore, no one else can precisely duplicate your signature, because the line you generate carries rich, complex information incapable of being produced by anyone but you.

Drawing Your Name

Take a plain piece of paper and try this:

First, simply write (draw!) your signature as you always write/ draw it.

Now, put the paper aside for a moment and look at the following set of signatures. The name is the same in each case in order not to confuse the issue. (I made up the name by simply pointing twice, eyes covered, at the phone directory—once for the first name and once for the last.)

What is David Jacoby like? Introverted or extraverted? What colors does he like? What kind of car does he drive? Would you lend him money? Would he be a good friend? Would you trust him? Is he careful about time—for example, keeping appointments? Do you think he has read a book lately? What kind of book?

Now, keeping that person in the back of your mind, think what this next David Jacoby is like:

This person is different from the first David Jacoby, isn't he? Is he introverted or extraverted? What colors does he like? What kind of car does he drive? Would you lend him money? Would he pay you back? What about time: does he keep his appointments? What is his favorite TV program?

Now, a third David Jacoby:

Again, is he introverted or extraverted? What kind of job does he hold? What are his favorite colors? What kind of car? (With this handwriting style, my students sometimes respond, "He rides the bus.") Favorite TV program? On time or not? Would you lend him money? Would he be a trustworthy friend?

Now, a fourth:

And a fifth:

David Jacoby

Now my question to you is "How did you know so much about these imaginary characters? The answer, I think (echoing Polanyi's statement), is that you know more than you know you know. The signatures *as drawings* are information-rich, and the language in which the information is embedded is read intuitively by you. Your grasp is immediate and does not require special training. And your intuition about the person behind each signature may be correct, at least to some extent, because personality characteristics influence handwriting.

Reading Your Own Line

Next, take out again the paper on which you wrote your own signature. Hold it at arm's length. Take a good look at it, *as a drawing* (which it is). Try intuitively to read the expressive quality of the line. Try for a moment to set aside the more or less automatic verbal judgments that come to mind: "My handwriting has never been very good." "That's pretty messy. If I try I can sometimes do better." "My handwriting gets worse all the time," and so on. Instead, try to see the shapes the lines make, the speed or slowness of the marks, the expressive quality of the whole "picture." You might try turning the paper upside down, better to see the expression inherent in the line.

The painter Wassily Kandinsky, who abandoned an academic career in Russia to become a painter in Germany in 1896, attempted to plot the grammar of a visual language. He wrote in 1947:
"Point—rest.
Line—inwardly animated tension created by movement.
The two elements—their intermingling and their combinations—develop their own 'language' which cannot be attained with words."
Point and Line to Plane.

You are looking at a picture of you. Present in that signature is information about you, your personality, your attitudes, your characteristics, all locked into a rich and complex language that is read visually, perceptually, and intuitively. This language, processed differently from verbal language, parallels verbal language and exists for everyone at some level of consciousness within the mind.

To test that, try the next step, shown in Figure 6–1. Using the hand not generally used to write with—that is, if you are right-handed, use the left, and vice versa—write your signature again underneath the first.

Now, look at *that* drawing. New and unfamiliar qualities will have emerged in the line—and you would be perceived differently by someone trying to read that drawing of you.

Next, shift the pencil back to the hand you usually use, but this time write your name backward—that is, rather than starting at the left and writing toward the right side of the paper, reverse the direction, writing the last letter of your name first.

Again, look at the drawing. You will see that the line is slower, more unsure, perhaps wobbly and awkward. What do you think about that "person" (thinking only of the line quality and pretending for a moment that you don't know that the signature was reversed)?

And last, use the nonusual hand to write your name again, but this time do not watch the hand as it writes; turn your head away and look in the opposite direction, or close your eyes. Then regard this last signature. It will show the greatest degree of distress, anxiety, and extreme unsureness. Again, since the names are the same in each of your signatures, it is the line quality that changes the effect on the viewer.

The Line Turns Inward to Outward
Return your gaze now to your first signature, written in your normal handwriting. This drawing gives the truest picture of you, undistorted by constraints imposed from outside—that is, my suggestions to write with the nonusual hand, backward, and so on. But it is important to note that the other signatures *also* give true pictures and accurate information: your responses to constraints imposed from the outside. Your handwriting made evident your mental and physiological state in each instance, including complex and intricate information about assurance or uncertainty, enjoyment or distress, ease or difficulty, clarity or confusion, pleasure or annoyance, speed or slowness of writing: all are objectified and made visible. The line can record *exactly* not only the "best case" (your normal signature) but all states of mind, in all their possible variability. Yet the line still uniquely and specifically reflects you and no one else.

The visual language of line—whether it is the line of a signature or of any other kind of drawing—can be translated into words, but only with great difficulty because the visual information is so densely packed and complex. Long strings of descriptive words could only begin to unravel the complexity of the set of signatures you have drawn. Yet the mind can grasp the whole signature in a split second, comprehending the "message" of the line by a "leap of insight." This insight, of course, can be increased and deepened by further study and thought, but the initial, instantaneous grasp of meaning is often essential for further understanding.

Reading the Language of Line
Apparently, the ability to "read" the language of line, as you have just demonstrated, is a widespread and common ability, but is little used at

For this exercise, follow the sequence demonstrated below by writer Geoffrey Harris:

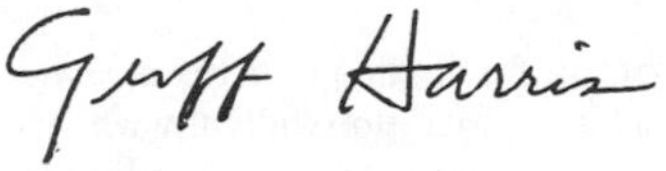

Signature as usually written.

Signature written with the other hand.

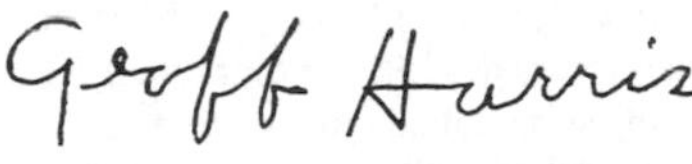

Usual hand, but written backward.

Other hand, without looking while writing.
Fig. 6-1

Hungarian artist and designer Laszlo Moholy-Nagy spoke of nonverbal grasp of meaning in *The New Vision*, 1947:
"The intuitive is most accurately understood as a speeded-up, subconscious logic, parallel to conscious thought, in all save its greater delicacy and fluidity. Usually the deeper meanings so often ascribed to the intuitive more properly belong to sensory apprehension. Here resides the ineffable. This kind of experience is fundamentally non-verbal but it is not inarticulate to the visual and other senses. Intuitive in the verbal universe is always potentially explicable. Intuitive in the plastic sense, in all the arts, including poetry, is a matter never, probably, capable of conscious verbalization."

"Especially fascinating to many investigators is a recognition difficulty which seems restricted to faces—a condition known as *prosopagnosia* (from the Greek *prosopon = face*, + agnosia). A prosopagnosic can generally identify objects with little difficulty. His language functions are good and he is most likely intellectually intact. He retains a clear memory of individuals he has known, and he can recognize them from hearing their voices, contemplating a verbal description of them, or noting some telltale mark, such as a mustache, pair of glasses, or favorite hat . . .
"Where the prosopagnosic fails is in identification of an unadorned face . . . in general there is no feeling of familiarity, even if the face belongs to a close acquaintance, a relative, or the patient himself! Told the identity of the face, the patient will . . . express his disbelief, perhaps adding that the individual (even himself!) has changed markedly since he last saw him."
HOWARD GARDNER
The Shattered Mind, 1975.

the *conscious level* in everyday life, especially in our predominantly verbal, numerical, technological, L-mode–oriented culture. Because of this cultural bias toward L-mode thinking, the visual language may at first seem unreliable, imprecise, ineffable, inconsequential, and ephemeral.

On the contrary, visual language is none of these: the language of line is precise, subtle, and powerful, accessible for rapid perusal, and esthetically, intellectually satisfying. To read the language of line requires a mode of thinking similar to the one we use for facial recognition, a complex and difficult task. In recognizing faces, we rely quite subconsciously on R-mode visual thought to process complicated and subtle information—not only to know *who* the person is but to know what kind of mood that person is in as well.

At the beginning of one of my courses, students are often surprised when I "read" their drawings during our weekly discussions of their work. I might say, "You needed to spend more time than the fifteen minutes you spent on this drawing." Or "I see you spent nearly three-quarters of an hour on this drawing." "I see you really liked drawing the shirt collar, but you didn't much like drawing this model's hair." Or "What was going on in the room at the time? Your drawing shows repeated distraction." Or "I can see you felt great joy in doing most of this drawing. But here is an area of distress. What happened at that point?" And so on.

Some revealing episodes have occurred during our discussions. For example, an assignment I often give requires students to draw their own feet. Following this assignment, I observed a student's drawing that showed anxiety and distress in every mark of the pencil. Although the drawing was beautifully and thoughtfully executed with apparently precise perception of details and relationships, parts of it were erased almost through the paper. (This was not detrimental to the drawing; the vigorous erasing and redrawing of lines gave the drawing a soft, expressive quality.) "Tell me about this drawing," I asked the student. "What do you mean?" she replied. "Well, it's an unusual and beautiful drawing. But it looks to me as if something was going on in your mind—that you were bothered by something perhaps. Can you tell me about that?"

The student looked surprised for a moment, then laughed in the most charming way, clutching her forehead in one hand for a moment. Then she said, "I'll tell you something. I really *hate* my feet."

Everyone laughed. Then another student said, "I think your feet are beautiful." This idea was echoed around the room, and gradually attention focused again on the student. She looked thoughtfully at her drawing and finally said with a note of surprise in her voice, "Maybe they aren't so terrible after all. I think I'll try drawing them again."

Drawing a Line, Seeing a Line

To demonstrate the language of line, let's start with the ABCs. On a sheet of paper, draw three lines: draw the first *very* rapidly—an instantaneous stroke of the pencil on the paper; draw the second line more slowly, at medium speed; and draw the third line as slowly as possible.

Fig. 6-2

In Figure 6-2, I've also drawn three lines at different speeds. I've mixed the order of the lines. Which one was drawn the fastest? How do you know?

The answer is, of course, that you know because you know. You can *see* the fastness or slowness: the qualities of *fastness* and *slowness* are inseparable from the mark. If you look at your three lines and mine side by side, you may be able to detect *six* different speeds, since our drawings will not be duplicates. Speed shows in the texture of the mark, its weight, its roughness or smoothness. Thus time itself is recorded in drawings—not in the linear, measured way of L-mode time, but in the way time is recorded in a human face, for example. Time becomes an embedded quality, which can be seen and comprehended.

Now, on the same paper, draw a new set of very fast lines. This time, try to duplicate the fast lines exactly, but draw the new set of lines very slowly. You will observe, as in the drawing below (Figure 6-3), that no matter how carefully the slow lines are drawn, they can never duplicate exactly the fast lines because—in the language of line—the exact speed at which a line is drawn is communicated by the line.

Fig. 6-3

Try this idea one more time: draw a curved line, very fast, and try to duplicate it very slowly, as shown in Figure 6-4. Next, reverse the procedure: draw a slow curve and try to duplicate it with a fast line.

Figures 6-5 through 6-9 are examples of drawings in which speed or slowness of the lines is one of the prime means of expression. Imagine the speed at which your hand would have to move to duplicate the Matisse drawing or the Kokoschka. Observe the Delacroix, though still still very rapidly drawn, has a slightly more deliberate quality to the line. Compare, now, the line Rembrandt used to draw the portrait of the preacher. The line is slowed down, is thoughtful and deliberate. And finally, regard the Shahn portrait of the physicist Robert Oppenheimer. Here the line is painfully slow, tight, even peevish and crabbed.

Try out these lines now. Enter the mental states of Matisse, Kokoschka, Delacroix, Rembrandt, and Shahn. Without attempting to copy the images contained in the drawings, simply duplicate the speed and gesture of the line—in other words, jump into the skins, for a brief moment, of these great artists, as shown in Figures 6-10 through 6-14. The mark, of course, can never be the same, for reasons mentioned previously: you are a different person, and your mark will always be *your* mark. Nevertheless, to experience within one's own mind even one element of the work of great artists—in this instance, simply the speed or slowness of the line—is instructive and illuminating.

Fig. 6-4

Making "French marks."

The contemporary British artist David Hockney, in a witty play on words, said that he used "French marks" to establish a French feeling in his stage design for the Metropolitan Opera House production of *L'Enfant et les Sortilèges* in 1981. Hockney felt that "French marks" are found, for example, in watercolor paintings by the French artist Raoul Dufy.

RAOUL DUFY
Detail, *Racetrack at Deauville*, 1929.
Fogg Art Museum, Cambridge, Mass.

62

Fig. 6-5
HENRI MATISSE (1869–1954)
Figure Study. Pen and ink
The Museum of Modern Art, New York.
Gift of Edward Steichen.

Fig. 6-6
OSKAR KOKOSCHKA (1886–1980)
Portrait of Mrs. Lanyi. Crayon.
The Metropolitan Museum of Art,
New York.

Fig. 6-7
EUGÈNE DELACROIX (1798–1863)
Detail, *Studies of Arms and Legs*, after
The Crucifixion by Rubens. Pen and
sepia ink. Courtesy of the Art Institute
of Chicago.

Fig. 6-8
REMBRANDT VAN RIJN (1606–1669)
Jan Cornelius Slyvius, Preacher:
Posthumous Portrait. Reed and quill
pens and ink. National Gallery of Art,
Washington, D.C.

Fig. 6-9
BEN SHAHN (1898–1969)
Dr. J. Robert Oppenheimer, 1954.
Brush and Ink. Museum of Modern
Art, New York.

Fig. 6–10
Matisse marks.

Fig. 6–11
Kokoschka marks.

Fig. 6–12
Delacroix marks.

Fig. 6–13
Rembrandt marks.

Fig. 6–14
Ben Shahn marks.

Getting a Line on the First Stage of Creativity

Thus, every line is a statement, a form of communication between the individual who made the line and the individual who views it. A drawing is a far more complex mode of expression, revealing of a wide range of thoughts and emotions, many of which originate in a realm beyond conscious awareness. We can "read" a line. Can we "read" a drawing? If so, perhaps we can take a step in the direction of gaining access to that part of the mind which knows . . . more than it knows it knows— the same part of the brain that asks the beautiful question, ponders the unsolved problem, takes the initial step in the creative process: First Insight.

7 Drawing Out Insight

Artist-theorist Max Bill believed that art was the medium that would make thought visible:

"Thought itself does not as yet seem to be directly expressible to the senses except through the medium of art. I therefore maintain that art can convey thought in such a way as to make it directly perceptible."

MAX BILL
"The Mathematical Approach in Art," 1955.

In his essay "New Words," George Orwell suggested that each of us has an outer and an inner mental life: the former expressed in the ordinary language we use in everyday life and the latter in another form of thought (or perhaps a better term is "thought about feelings") that rarely surfaces because ordinary words cannot express its complexity. Our goal is to dredge up that inner life of the mind by using an alternative, visual language (drawings, in this case) to give it tangible form—in short, to make inner thought visible.

Drawing Analogs from Deep Within

The first exercise will take us beyond the ABCs of slow and fast lines to drawings that reveal more of the complexity and subtlety of this visual language.

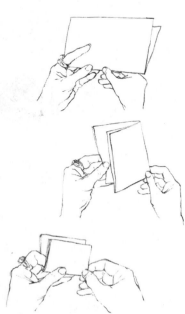

Please read through all of the instructions before you begin.

1. Divide a sheet of typing paper into eight sections by folding it in half, then in half again, then in half a third time, as shown at the left.

2. Number each section, 1 through 8, across the page as shown in Figure 7–1, placing the number at the bottom of each section.

3. Label each section, as shown in Figure 7–1, with the following words that "stand for" (in the L-mode sense) human characteristics or emotional states: 1. Anger 2. Joy 3. Peacefulness (or tranquillity) 4. Depression 5. Human Energy (or Power) 6. Femininity 7. Illness 8. _____ (This one is to be your choice—any human trait, quality, condition, or emotion. A few that come to mind: masculinity, loneliness, jealousy, anxiety, hysteria, hopefulness, guilt, ecstacy, love, hatred, adoration, fear.)

4. I have included examples of student analogs following the instructions, but do not look at them now. Most important, try to do this exercise without any idea whatever that the drawings "should" look a certain way. There is no "right" or "wrong," "good" or "bad" about

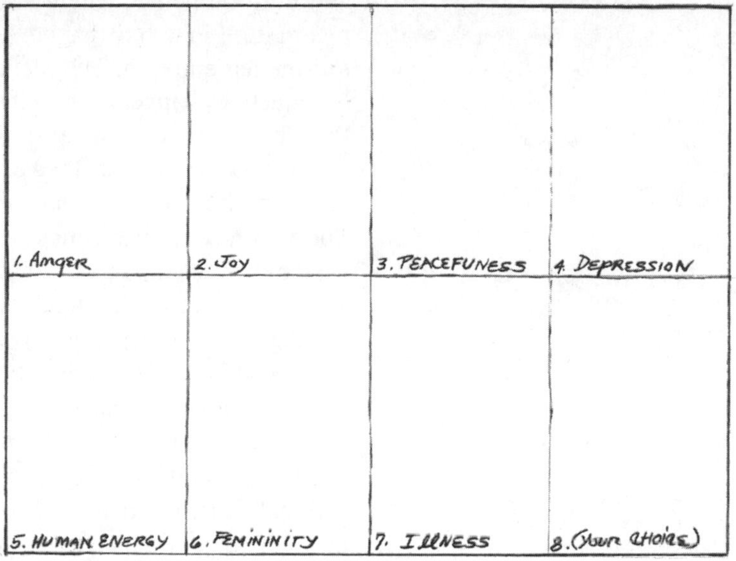

| 1. Anger | 2. Joy | 3. Peacefuness | 4. Depression |
| 5. Human Energy | 6. Femininity | 7. Illness | 8. (your choice) |

Fig. 7-1

these drawings. Each drawing will be the *right* drawing because it is right for you.

5. For the drawings, use a pencil rather than a pen. Each drawing will be made of marks—lines—in each section. You may want to use one line, many lines, or you may fill a whole section with lines if that seems right. You may use the point of the pencil, the side of the lead to make wide marks, heavy pressure or light, short marks or long. Use the eraser if you wish—anything goes in terms of *how* you use the pencil.

6. In each section, one at a time, make a drawing that *to you* represents what the word at the bottom stands for. Your drawings will be *analogs* of your thought on each concept, in the sense that the drawings will make subjective thought objective by giving it a visible form.

But there is one *definite* restriction (and only one): *you must not draw any pictures whatsoever or use any symbols at all.* No raindrops, no shooting stars, no hearts and flowers, no question marks, no lightning bolts, no rainbows, no clenched fists. Use only the language of line: fast lines, slow lines, light, dark, smooth, rough, broken, or flowing—whatever feels *right* for what you are trying to express. That expression will emerge from the marks on the paper, the parallel visual language of line.

7. The best way to do this exercise, I have found with my students, is as follows:

Read the word labeling the first rectangle: Anger. Think back to the last time you were really angry. Without using words at all, even to label the event or the reason for your anger, feel within yourself what that anger was like. Imagine you are feeling the emotion again, that it flows first from deep inside, then into your arm, down into your hand,

"The kind of mental image needed for thought is unlikely to be a complete, colorful, and faithful replica of some visible scene."
RUDOLF ARNHEIM
Visual Thinking, 1969.

and into the pencil, where it emerges from the point of the pencil to record itself in marks that are *equivalent* to the feeling—marks that *look like* the felt emotion. The marks need not be done all at once, but can be adjusted, changed, erased if necessary in order to achieve an image of the emotion that seems to fit the emotion *as it feels to you*.

8. You may take as long as you wish to do these drawings. Try not to censor the marks; they are private and need not be shown to anyone. You are simply trying to make marks that manifest—make evident—your personal, inner thoughts. Your aim will be to make visual images that are analogous to—can stand for—those thoughts.

Again, there is no right or wrong about these analog drawings. Each image you make will be right because it is right for you. Each image will be unique to you, since no one else in the world can exactly reproduce this visual manifestation of your mind, thoughts and emotions.

Understand that you need *not* know what the marks will be before you make them. Indeed, in a sense, you *cannot* know beforehand what they will look like. The marks will reveal to you what they look like as you make them. After they are made, *then* you will be aware of what they look like. *Therefore, do not try to visualize beforehand what the completed drawing will be like.* Allow the image to emerge in its own way— in short, to state itself what it means to say.

Try to complete the full set of analog drawings in one sitting. Fifteen to twenty minutes is the length of time my students usually need, though some like to have more time, and some finish in less time. I will show you a group of analog drawings by my students when you have finished. But don't look at them yet! Your mind must be clear of the analogs of others, in order for *your unique* images to emerge. Remember, there is no right or wrong, good or bad in these drawings. They simply are what they are for each person, just as your signature is what it is.

Begin the drawings now.

When you have finished, lay your page of analog drawings beside the student drawings shown in Figures 7–2 through 7–7, pages 70 to 72. We'll be looking for the differences that make your drawings and each set of drawings unique, but just as important, we will also be looking for similarities, in the broadest sense, both of which are a part of the "vocabulary" of a visual language.

The Vocabulary: Infinite Variability Within Broad Similarity

First, the broad similarities. You will notice that drawings in each of the separate categories have general characteristics that are similar—something like "family" resemblances. For example, in the rectangles marked "Anger" the lines are often dark, heavy, jagged. In the rectangles marked

"Joy," on the other hand, the line is frequently light, curved, and rising. In the rectangles marked "Tranquillity" or "Peacefulness," the line is frequently horizontal or softly curved and falling. "Depression" often elicits an image that is *low* within its allocated space.

You may find these resemblances in your drawings as well, though not necessarily. Your analogs may be entirely different from any that I have included. There is apparently no limit to the variability. Despite broad similarities within categories, I have never found two drawings that are alike, just as no two individuals are exactly alike.

I want to return later to the broad similarities, but for the moment, let's look at the seemingly infinite variability within a single category. Please look at the collected drawings of "Anger" on page 73 (Figure 7–8). Each of these drawings is by a different student.

In your mind, add your drawing of anger to this collection. As you can see, while your drawing labeled "Anger" may perhaps be broadly similar to the others, it is specifically unique—different from all the others in the same way a snowflake pattern is broadly similar to yet specifically different from all other snowflake patterns.

Looking at your own drawing in this context, then, realize that you have made a picture of your own anger (just as each of the students has portrayed his or her own anger). Each image is different because each individual is different and experiences anger in a way that is broadly similar to but specifically different in quality, intensity, duration, focus, and so on.

Your drawing makes your anger visible. That is what it looks like. Another person looking at your drawing would be able to "read" the visible manifestation of your anger and would intuitively know what it is like, just as you, looking at each of the students' drawings, know somehow in each instance what that anger is like. The knowing, of course, could probably be put into words, but because drawings pack tremendous complexity into even a small image, one would be hard put to express it all in words. (As an experiment, try at this point to find appropriate words or, perhaps, a statement that, to you, verbally expresses what your drawing visually "tells" you.)

Using Words to "Tag" the Image

A personal experience clarified for me this difficulty with words and analog drawings. A student brought me a page of drawings like the one you have just completed. Her drawing labeled "Anger" caught my eye and without thinking, I said, "Oh, I hope you never get angry at me!" Her drawing was something like this (Figure 7–9 on page 73). (I cannot, of course, exactly reproduce the original, since we are different individuals.)

The student asked why, and I was simply stumped for words. I *knew*

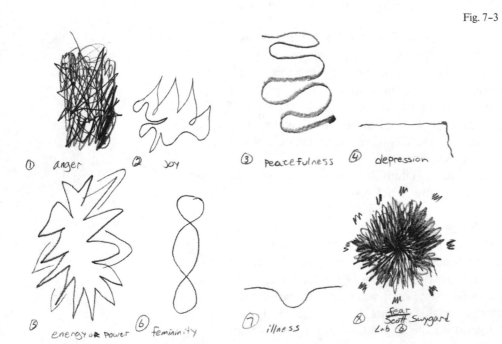

Fig. 7-2

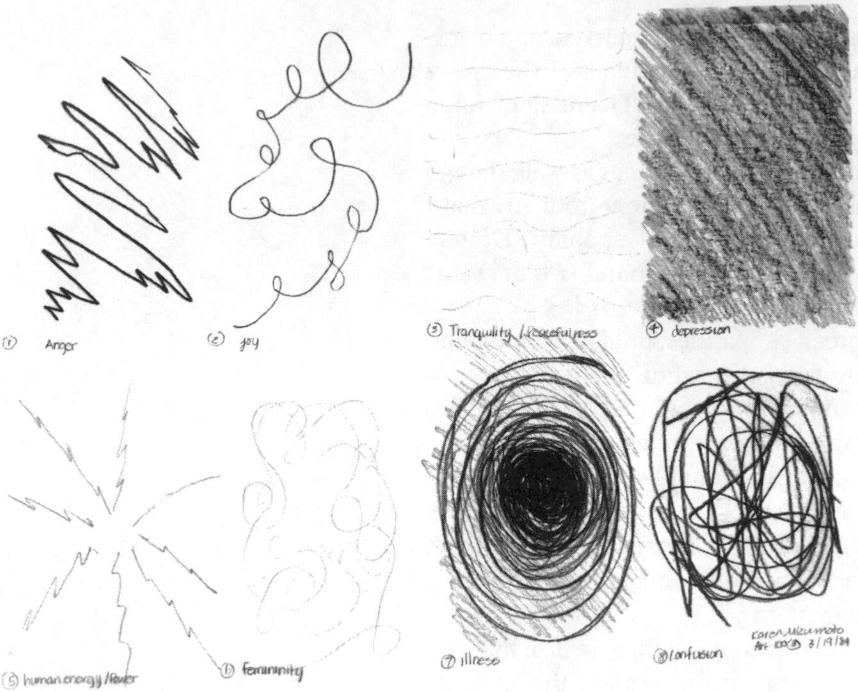

① Anger
② joy
③ Tranquility / Peacefulness
④ depression
⑤ human energy / Power
⑥ femininity
⑦ illness
⑧ Confusion

Karen Mizumoto
Art 100 ③ 3/19/04

Fig. 7-3

① anger
② joy
③ peacefulness
④ depression
⑤ energy or Power
⑥ femininity
⑦ illness
⑧ fear

Scott Suygard
Lab ⑥

Fig. 7-4

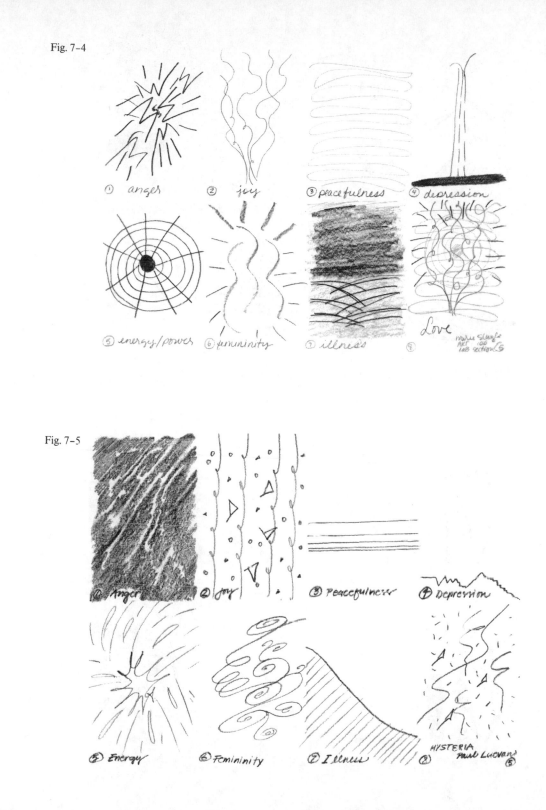

① anger ② joy ③ peacefulness ④ depression
⑤ energy/power ⑥ femininity ⑦ illness ⑧ Love

Fig. 7-5

① Anger ② Joy ③ Peacefulness ④ Depression
⑤ Energy ⑥ Femininity ⑦ Illness ⑧ HYSTERIA

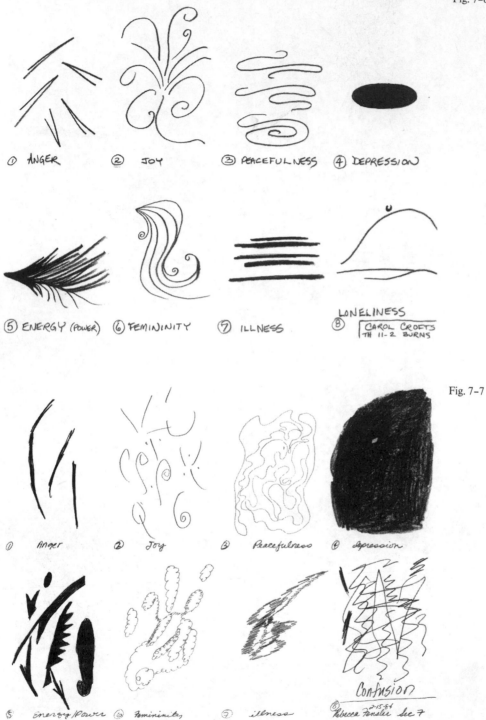

Fig. 7-6

① ANGER ② JOY ③ PEACEFULNESS ④ DEPRESSION

⑤ ENERGY (POWER) ⑥ FEMININITY ⑦ ILLNESS ⑧ LONELINESS

CAROL CROFTS
TH 11-2 BURNS

Fig. 7-7

① Anger ② Joy ③ Peacefulness ④ depression

⑤ Energy/Power ⑥ Femininity ⑦ illness ⑧ Confusion

Rebecca Fonsler Sec 7 2-15-84

72

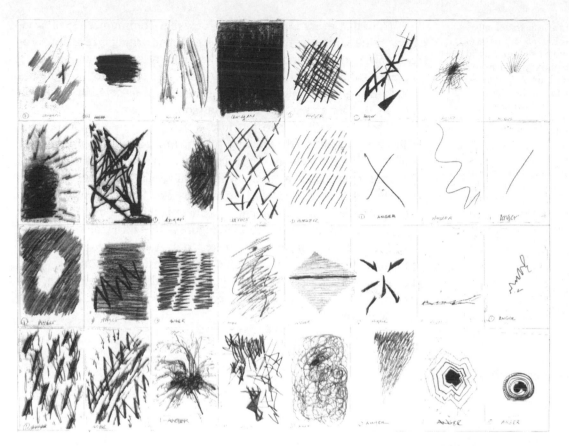

Fig. 7–8
Student analog drawings of the concept "Anger."

why, and I expect that you know why, and I feel sure that the student within herself knew why, yet none of us could find words precise enough to explain, beyond, perhaps, some rudimentary statement (which I did attempt) that the anger would go on for a long time. But there was so much more in her drawing that eluded my ability to express in words.

The same is true as I try to "tag" the thoughts and feelings made visible in the drawings reproduced here. To me, the first drawing in the upper left of Figure 7–8 seems to be anger that flares up, perhaps shifts from subject to subject. At this point, however, verbal language fails me and I am unable to say in words what meaning is conveyed by the heavy marks that cross in the center. I know, somehow, but I cannot say.

The next drawing in the top row of Figure 7–8: Yes, that is serious anger; I can see it. Can't you, too? The third in the top row: Yes, I recognize that anger. To me, it is sharp and stabbing anger. (The student who did this drawing told me that to his surprise, he found himself jabbing the pencil right through the paper—the short, sharp marks between the lines.) And the fourth: Yes, I believe I understand that brooding kind of anger . . . and so on.

ⓐ ANGER

Fig. 7–9
One student's concept of "Anger."

Note that every aspect of these drawings communicates information, in the same way that every aspect of handwriting is revealing. For example, in the drawing third from the left in the second row, (shown in Figure 7–10 below), the fact that the marks are shifted to the right and touch the right edge of the rectangle is important, as noted in the quotation by teacher and author Philip Rawson.

Again, it is difficult to put into words just how that positioning affects the meaning of the drawing, but you may be able to sense with me the effect of the placement. The image that comes to mind is of someone shouting away in anger—all the while, analogically speaking, backed up (or clinging?) to a wall, and forming, as Rawson suggests, a strong obstacle. Analogically speaking, this anger is different from anger that stands in the middle of a space, as in Figure 7–11. And it is also significant that the off-center "anger" form makes contact with the *right* side of the rectangle. If the form touched the left side instead, the analog would change—seem more aggressive, perhaps, and, for some reason, less defensive. This change can be seen when you look at the drawing upside down.

Fig. 7–10   Fig. 7–11

In his 1969 book *Visual Thinking*, Rudolf Arnheim described a brief experiment with thinking-by-drawing, carried out under his direction by two of his students. The small group of subjects, mostly fellow students of the experimentors, were asked to depict their notions of "Past, Present, and Future," "Democracy," "Good and Bad Marriage," and "Youth." Arnheim termed the resulting drawings "nonmimetic"—that is, without likenesses of objects or events. Verbal explanations were obtained from the subjects of the experiment during or after the drawing.

Past, Present and Future

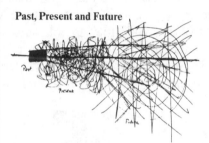

"The *past* is solid and complete, but still influences the present and the future. The *present* is complex and not only a result of the past and leading to future, thus overlapping both, but is an entity in itself (black dot). The *future* is least limited but influenced by both, past and present. One line runs through for all have one common element—time."

Democracy

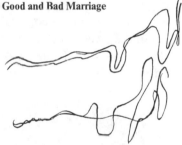

"All types can fit into system (outer circle) in harmony and without losing their identities, both persons and concepts. All contribute to the whole."

"Equality among individuals."

Good and Bad Marriage

"A good marriage (top) is two people together but as individuals. They both recognize each other as separate from each other but also involved with each other. A bad marriage (bottom) is one where two people support each other and are absorbed into each other. When a conflict occurs, they cannot help each other."

Left, good marriage; right, bad marriage.

The procedure seems to have been used as a means more to *illustrate* verbal thought (instructions included "Think aloud as you draw and explain what you are doing as you do it!") than to try to gain access to thought that is outside of awareness and inaccessible to the verbal mode of the brain. Arnheim said, "The drawings were intended to give an accurate visual account of a concept. As such they were purely cognitive, not different in principle from what scientists show in their schematic designs. However, they were apt to go beyond the visual enumeration of the forces constituting the patterns. The draftsmen tried to evoke, more or less successfully, a vivid resonance of these forces and thereby resorted to devices of artistic expression."

Nevertheless, the drawings apparently tapped into the same rich visual vocabulary that appears in the analog drawings. One set of drawings, in which students were encouraged to use as many sheets of paper as needed, apparently showed observable changes from drawing to drawing, which Arnheim considered to be a gradual refinement of concepts—an idea closer to his stated objective to use drawings for thinking.

Arnheim reported that his student subjects, who were apparently familiar with the arts, made no protest about the drawings required of them and entered into the drawing task with little hesitation. He wondered, however, whether persons of "a different educational level and less familiar with the arts might respond less well." On the contrary, my work with large groups of students unfamiliar with the arts indicates that these students are equally unhesitant and unquestioning. They question neither their ability to portray complex concepts nor whether the concepts are portrayable. Once the necessity to picture objects is removed, they simply proceed with competence and apparent enjoyment.

Meaning in Language and in Drawing

Why is this so? Or is it so? Does this parallel language "read" similarly for everyone, at least for people from similar cultures? How can a drawing have *meaning*? Turning to the other language—verbal language—one can agree with George Orwell that words, though limiting and limited, do generally mean what they mean, and that people usually concur on those meanings. As writer Gertrude Stein pointed out, the word "rose," after all, signifies a rose, and not something else. Can there also be general agreement on the meaning of drawings? If so, it would seem to provide additional evidence that there might be a "deep structure" of visual form underlying human art that is wired into the human brain in a manner similar, perhaps, to the way in which Noam Chomsky has postulated such a structure for human verbal expression. The analog drawings seem to indicate the possible existence of such a structure.

Symbolic language is intrinsically human, and the making of art—drawings, paintings, sculptures, and other objects that "stand for" or symbolize things or ideas—is also intrinsically human. The analog drawings before us, however, are not representational. By intention, they do not "stand for" any recognizable object. Thus, they do not communicate on the level of visual symbols that may be shared by many people. (Yes, that is the figure of a man, a tree, a bowl of fruit.) If, then, they do communicate, it must be on another level of shared awareness.

Richard Gregory, Director of the Brain and Perception Laboratory at the University of Bristol in Great Britain, proposed in 1971 the idea of a "deep structure" for perception.

"What is so special about human language is its grammatical structure, which, if Noam Chomsky is correct, is in all natural languages closely related to what he calls the Deep Structure of language, which is inherited, not learned, and which, we may suppose, is derived from and indeed may in large part be perceptual classification. A biological problem for Chomsky's theory is the rapidity, on a biological time-scale, of the development of grammatical language; possibly this has been so rapid because there has been a take-over of a perceptual Deep Structure having biologically ancient—indeed pre-human—origins."
R. GREGORY
Mind in Science, 1981, quoting his article "The Grammar of Vision."

Fig. 7–12
A precedent for analog drawings from modern art.
WASSILY KANDINSKY (1866–1944)
Black Lines. Oil on canvas.
The Solomon R. Guggenheim Museum, New York.
Kandinsky wrote extensively on the "language" of line.

Structure as Meaning

One would expect enormous variation among the analog drawings—and in fact, no two drawings are alike. What is surprising, however, is the *structural* similarity of the drawings that express a single concept such as "Anger" (Figure 7-8), "Joy" (Figure 7-13), "Peacefulness" (Figure 7-16), and so on. And this structural similarity occurs often enough to suggest that it is a *shared* intuition which contributes visually to our understanding of the concept the drawing means to express. These structural similarities are most easily seen if one views a large number of drawings at once. We have looked at a collection of "Anger" drawings. Let's look at drawings of the second concept, "Joy."

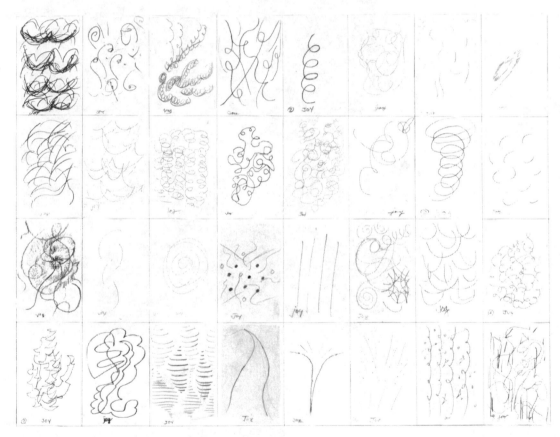

Fig. 7-13. Student analog drawings of the concept "Joy."

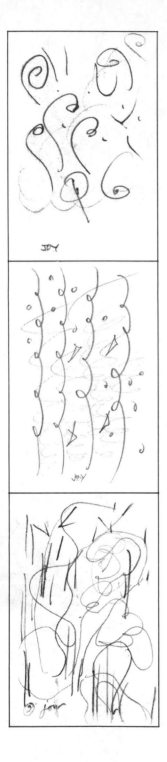

Fig. 7-14
VINCENT VAN GOGH (1853–1890)
Grove of Cypresses. Pencil and ink with reed pen.
Courtesy of the Art Institute of Chicago.

Student analog drawings of "Joy."

78

Fig. 7–15
SIMONE CANTARINI (1612–48)
Studies of an Infant in Various Poses.
Red chalk.
The Pierpont Morgan Library.

Analogs of Joy

Again, as with the "Anger" drawings, you can see that each drawing is unique. Yet the drawings share a basically similar structure. The concept "Joy" appears to generate not jagged, dark, pointed forms that almost overwhelm the format as does the concept "Anger," but instead light, curving, circular forms that tend to *rise* within the format (Figure 7–13). Figures 7–14 and 7–15 show how master artists use the language of line to express joy. The Van Gogh drawing in particular is profoundly expressive of the emotion, while at the same time the artist portrays the cypress trees and adds layer on layer of metaphoric meaning.

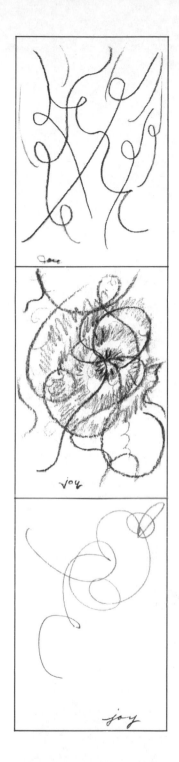

Student analog drawings of "Joy."

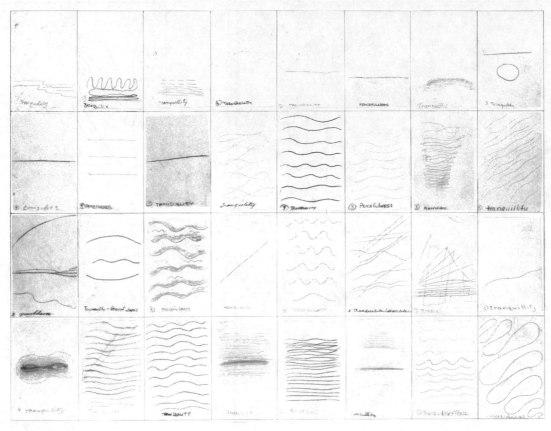

Fig. 7–16
Student analog drawings of
"Peacefulness."

Peacefulness Along Horizontal Lines
Another, even more striking instance of the structural similarity is
found in the analog drawings of "Peacefulness" or "Tranquillity." My
students mainly drew horizontal lines—although there were other interpretations of the concept. The collected drawings are shown in Figure
7–16. Your own drawing of this concept may also be horizontal. In turn,
this same horizontality appears in master drawings with the underlying
theme of peacefulness, as shown in Figures 7–17 and 7–18.

Fig. 7-17
JOHANN MARTIN VON ROHDEN (1778–1868)
Landscape. Pencil.
Staatliche Graphische, Munich.

Student analog drawings of "Peacefulness."

Fig. 7–18
MARTIN JOHNSON HEADE (1819–1904)
Twilight, Salt Marshes.
Charcoal, white and colored chalks.
Boston, Museum of Fine Arts.

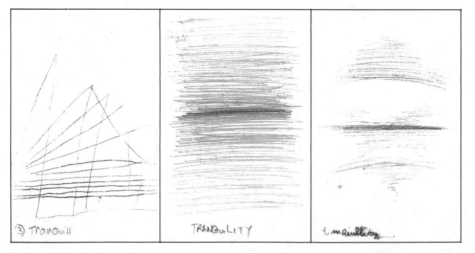

Student analog drawings of
"Tranquillity."

Fig. 7–19
Student analog drawings of
"Depression."

The Lowness of Depression

Student analogs for the concept "Depression" (Figure 7–19) are particularly interesting in their structural similarity. Many of my students placed lines and forms *low* in the rectangle, which was obviously deliberate, not accidental, as it occurs over and over again. I shouldn't have been surprised perhaps. The link of "depression" and "lowness" is in the language—in such expressions as "I'm feeling low today." This brings again to mind the interesting question: among early human cultures, was language developed to "tag" preexisting visual structures, or did language come first, with visual structures later fitted to verbal structures? Whatever the case, students intuitively expressed this concept by using the visual language in which the placement of forms within the four edges of the format is as significant as the forms themselves.

Student analog drawings of
Depression."

Fig. 7–20
FRANCISCO GOYA (1746–1828)
Sad Presentiments of What Must Come to Pass, from *The Disasters of War*.
Etching. Print Department, Boston Public Library, Boston, Mass.

In their analogs, students expressed "Depression" in three main
ways: descending lines, horizontal forms placed low in the format, and
hatched lines filling the format. The etching by Spanish artist Francisco
Goya *Sad Presentiments of What Must Come to Pass* (Figure 7–20)
combines these three aspects.

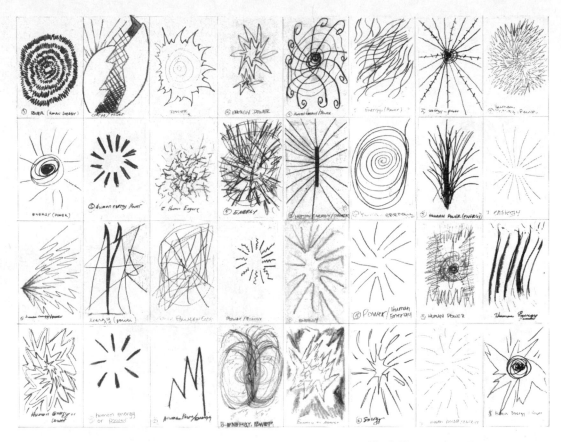

Fig. 7–21
Student analog drawings of "Human
Energy."

Drawing Lines on Human Power

One of the most intriguing groups of drawings was of the concept
"Human Energy" or "Power" (Figure 7–21). To my great surprise, drawing after drawing presented similar basic structural forms, with two main
variations: either an exploding image or rising triangular forms. Your
own analog of this concept may also present some version of these basic
visual structures—though, of course, it may be entirely different.

In an analysis of the drawings on "Human Energy" or "Power," the
numbers are interesting: in the first group of 83 students who did the
drawings, 47 drew individual versions of the exploding structure, 22
drew rising structures of triangular forms or lines, and 14 drew other
images. In the second group of 80 students, 41 drew individual versions
of the exploding structure, 23 drew rising triangular forms, and 16 drew
other structures—almost the same proportional percentages as the first
group. Yet, again, despite the similarity of basic structures, each of the
students' analog drawings is unique, expressing a visual message subtly
different from each of the other drawings.

ENERGY (POWER)

⑤ Human energy, Power

⑤ Power / Human Energy

Fig. 7–22
REMBRANDT VAN RIJN (1606–69)
The Mummers. Pen and ink with wash.
The Pierpont Morgan Library, New York.

Drawings by master artists, of course, laminate image and meaning on top of the deep structure, and therefore resonate in the mind of the viewer. Figures 7–22 and 7–23 show drawings by master artists based on the theme of human energy or power that reveal the underlying exploding structure. The drawing by Roy Lichtenstein is almost an analog itself. The underlying structure of the Rembrandt drawing *The Mummers* (Figure 7–22) may be hard to see at first. Nathan Goldstein,

Fig. 7-23
ROY LICHTENSTEIN (1923–)
Explosion Sketch. Pencil, color pencil and ink. 5½ x 6½".
Collection of Mr. and Mrs. Horace H. Solomon, New York.

author of well-known books on drawing, describes the configuration:

"Near the drawing's exact center, the hand holding the reins marks the center of an expanding burst of lines, shapes, and tones of such power that we sense its radiating directional force in the hat, collar, elbow, leg, and reins of the figure on the left. This force is continued in the neck and chest of the horse, and in the lines near the man on the right. The release of such explosive force warrants the thick, surrounding buffer of space. . . . The rhythm resulting from the many 'spokes' of direction that radiate from the drawing's center adds force to that action. . . . The empty area absorbs the 'shock waves' and sends them back again." (*The Art of Responsive Drawing*, 1973.)

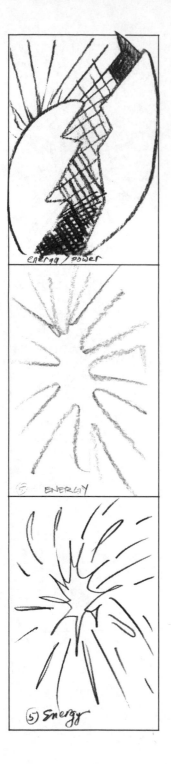

Fig. 7–24
WILLIAM DUKE
Photograph, 1984.

A similar structure can be seen in a photograph by William Duke (Figure 7–24). Duke said of his photograph, "I think of this as the story of a guy practicing his art, reaching a plateau, then finally breaking through." The theme: human energy and power; the underlying structure: the exploding image.

Fig. 7–25
PABLO PICASSO (1881–1973)
Detail, *Bathers*. Pencil drawing.
Fogg Art Museum, Harvard University (Bequest of Paul J. Sachs).

Fig. 7–26
AMEDEO MODIGLIANI (1884–1920)
Portrait of a Woman. Pencil.
The Museum of Modern Art,
New York.

Feminine Lines and Crossed Forms

For the concept "Femininity," my students drew mainly curving lines, lines similar to those used by Picasso (Figure 7–25), Modigliani (Figure 7–26), and Hokusai (Figure 7–27) in drawings of female figures. The curving lines were not unexpected, but a certain percentage of the

Fig. 7-27
KATSUSHIKA HOKUSAI (1760–1849)
A Maid Preparing to Dust.
Brush and ink.
Freer Gallery of Art, Smithsonian
Institution, Washington, D.C.

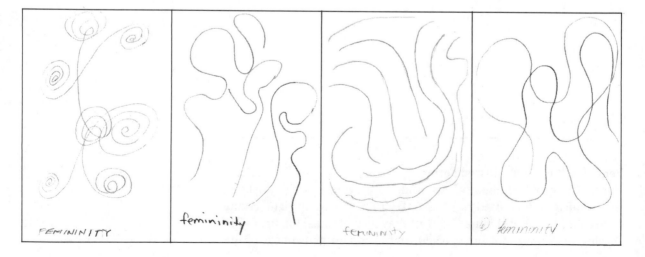

FEMININITY   femininity   femininity   femininity

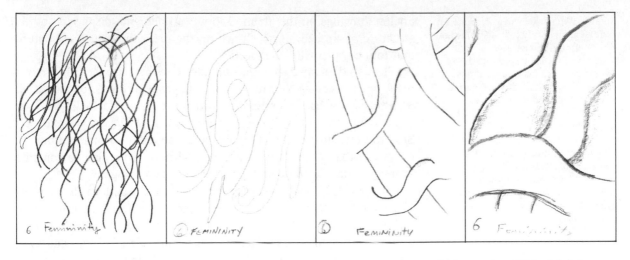

Student analogs of "Femininity"
showing "crossed forms."

Fig. 7–28
A drawing by Matisse showing
"crossed forms."
HENRI MATISSE (1869–1954)
Model Resting on Her Arms, 1936.
Pencil on paper.
The Baltimore Museum of Art.
The Cone Collection, formed by
Dr. Claribel Cone and Miss Etta Cone
of Baltimore, Maryland.

Ludwig Wittgenstein, in a celebrated letter written in 1919 to British philosopher Bertrand Russell, said:
"I don't know *what* the constituents of thought are, but I know *that* it must have such constituents which correspond to the words of language."
Russell then asked, "Does a thought consist of words?"
"No," Wittgenstein replied, "but of physical constituents that have the same sort of relation to reality as words. What those constituents are I don't know."
Quoted in R. L. Gregory, *Mind in Science*, 1981.

analog drawings on this theme—about ten percent—displayed an odd structure of crossed forms, shown on the preceding page, a structure that to me was totally unexpected.

The students had again presented me with a surprise. I had never really noticed a crossed-form structure at conscious level, nor connected it with the concept of femininity. And yet it was perfectly logical—the kind of thing that makes one say, "Yes, of course! What did you expect?" Still, this structure is not at all obvious. The really surprising thing, of course, is that students unacquainted with art were able to generate intuitively such a subtle and expressive visual analog.

Intrigued, I began watching for this unusual pattern in drawings and paintings of female figures, and I found a number of examples, such as Figure 7–28. I also came across an advertisement of which a detail is shown in Figure 7–29. There it was again! The chair legs and even the model's sweater echo almost exactly the students' intuitive analogs for the concept of femininity. Did the designer of the advertisement deliberately use crossed forms, or was it subconscious? Does the advertisement "work" because the viewer of the design subconsciously reads the meaning of this visual language?

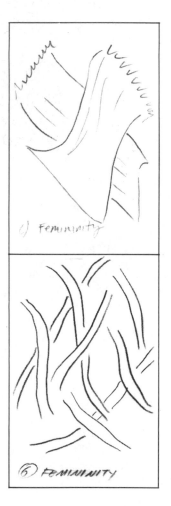

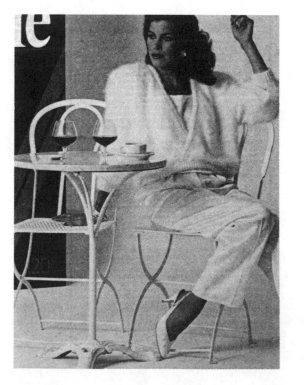

Fig. 7–29

92

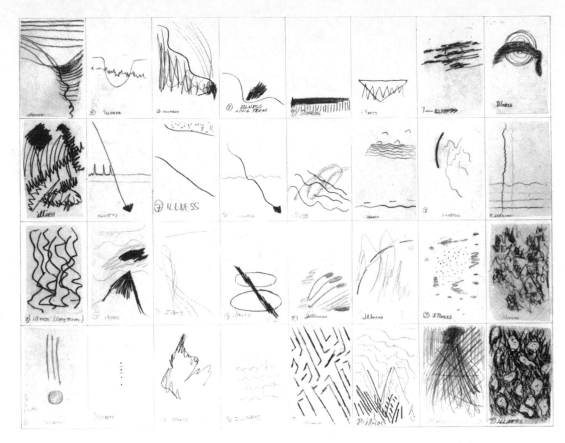

Fig. 7-30

Form on Top of Form

Student drawings of the concept "Illness" were another surprise for me. The drawings generally show a form of one type superimposed on a form of another character (Figure 7–30). Again, this makes sense—one says, "Yes, of course"—but again, the underlying structure is nonobvious and subtle.

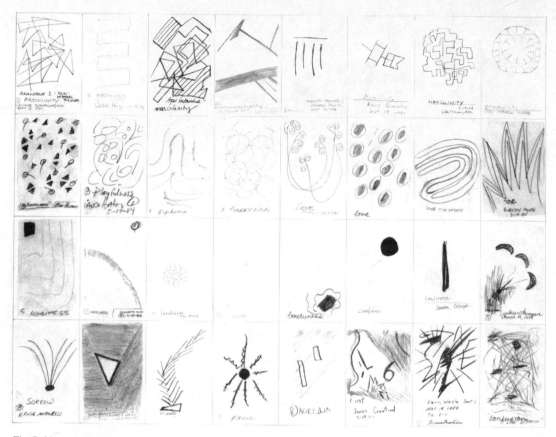

Fig. 7-31
Student analogs of a variety of
concepts.

As for the drawing of concepts of my students' own choosing (Figure 7–31), the range was wide, including such large ideas as "Death," as well as more specific concepts such as "Curiosity," "Playfulness," and "Indecision." But even though there are a limited number of analogs of one concept, even here similarities of structure are apparent: for example, the analogs of "Loneliness" show a marked similarity one to another—and to James Joyce's analog for Bloom, shown on page 96. "Excitement," "Bliss," and "Happiness" show agitated lines placed high in the format, "Playfulness" elicits circular forms spotted through the format, and so on.

Both for me and for my students, I believe these analog drawings have proved to be a very valuable exercise, for they demonstrate that there *is* a "vocabulary" of the visual language of drawing, a vocabulary that includes line, form, and structure—all of which can be "read" for meaning. Thus, I believe, the analogs do give objective existence to concepts—Orwell's requirement for making subconscious thought visible.

Confronting these thoughts-made-visual may require strength of mind. The analogs at times can be both unwelcome and right. Perhaps there is a parallel between analog drawings as a visual language and "free writing," sometimes used by writers to generate ideas and to overcome "blocks" to writing. Both methods apparently skim from the subconscious in R-mode fashion, skirting the rules and regulations, restrictions and censorship of L-mode thought processes, and, as such, can indeed be unwelcome—and right.

"An artist, then, expresses feeling, but not in the way a politician blows off steam or a baby laughs and cries. He formulates that elusive aspect of reality that is commonly taken to be amorphous or chaotic, that is, he objectifies the subjective realm."
SUSANNE K. LANGER
Philosophy in a New Key, 1942.

8 Drawing on Intuition

The main character of James Joyce's novel *Ulysses* is Bloom, who represents in many ways that mythical entity known as the average man. Bloom wanders through his day alone, ignored, barely tolerated, or rejected. Finally, late at night, his isolation attains cosmic overtones. He is alone, surrounded by infinite space. Bloom goes to bed, and our final glimpse of him is a graphic one.

In the early editions of *Ulysses*, a large dot represents Bloom, thus:

●

Excerpted from Robert S. Ryf, *A New Approach to Joyce*, 1962.

Now we come to the heart of the matter: the use of the parallel visual language in thinking—particularly the kind of thinking that results in First Insight, the initial stage of the creative process.

The analog drawings demonstrate that this visual language is there in the brain, accessible under certain conditions, and ready to be used right at this moment. Since creativity depends on the ability to perceive new solutions to old problems, or on new combinations of things or ideas already existing, or on seeing things in new ways, the first step in the process is to ponder a problem—to ask a question, to present an insight to the brain in a form that makes thought visible, for the eyes to *see*.

Portrait Drawing in Analog Form

Let's try an exercise designed to extend and deepen your use of the visual language. You will be drawing a portrait, but *please read the directions before you start your drawing.*

Several students' analog drawings for "Loneliness" echo Joyce's large dot for Bloom.

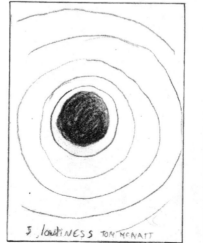

1. Concentrate your thoughts on a person—someone whose personality or character is important in your life now or in the past, but who perhaps puzzles you. You are going to draw this person not in the usual way of portraying a human being, but as an analog, a pattern of lines or shapes that *stand for* the person—as the dot stands for Bloom—with no realistic rendering whatsoever of outward appearance. In short, you will portray the personality and character of that person as you perceive them, using only the expressive visual language you practiced in the last chapter.

2. Once you have selected your subject, draw a "frame" for the portrait—that is, provide a format to work within (Figure 8–1). The format can be any shape you choose: rectangular (most usually chosen), square, round, oval, or irregular. Choose whatever seems right to you.

This drawing, like the previous set of analogs you drew, requires no previous artistic training or experience at all. As was seen in the last chapter, ability to use the power of drawn lines is already in place and available for this exercise. Remember that you will draw no recognizable objects at all and no symbols, letters, or words.

3. Understand that you need not know beforehand what the drawing will look like. In fact, you don't want to know, because the purpose of the drawing is to reveal aspects of this person that you may have sensed at some level of awareness but that are perhaps not accessible to conscious, everyday thought—again, to show you what you know but don't know you know.

4. Think, first, about this person, scanning the complexity of the personality without words, if possible. See the person in various situations. See the expressions on the face. Sense the underlying and unspoken messages. If, in your imaging, the person is speaking, try not to hear the words; watch the person but hear nothing, like watching a movie without sound.

5. Allow the pencil to draw, making its marks as they must be made. Censor nothing. This drawing is private and need not be shown to anyone. Know that the drawing will be true, at least in terms of your perceptions as they are sifted through your own personality, since the visual, perceptual R-mode of the brain must, even against its will, see what appears to be "out there." Allow the pencil to set down whatever you feel may be true about this person, even apparently contradictory or paradoxical truths. You need not be confined to a single period of time; the drawing can include different stages of time if you wish.

6. Keep in mind that the drawing will show you, when you have finished it, what is in your (right) mind about this person. Again, you cannot know beforehand—that is, before the drawing is done—because what you know is in a part of your mind that is often inaccessible to ordinary thought. The purpose of the drawing is to *make visible* what

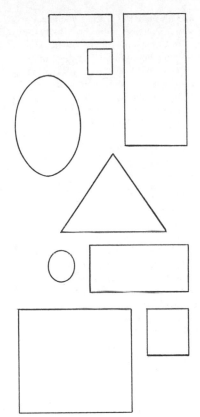

Fig. 8–1
A variety of formats.

In *Portrait of the Artist as a Young Man*, written between 1904 and 1914 by the Irish writer James Joyce, the hero, Stephen, identifies three "nets" that threaten him: "When the soul of a man is born in this country there are nets flung at it to hold it back from flight. You talk to me of nationality, language, religion. I shall try to fly by those nets."

"Line mediates a silent conversation between the draftsman and the currents of his experience. The draftsman attempts to maintain a condition where the senses meet directly with reality. . . . He seeks the structure of appearances, relatedness, and order."
EDWARD HILL
The Language of Drawing, 1966.

is there already in your mind—not to learn new things, in a sense, but to "fly by" the net of language and *see.*

Begin now to draw.

When you have finished, regard the drawing. In a strict sense, this is not a "portrait" drawing; you have drawn your insight—your "seeing into"—the person, not the person. Naturally, your insight and perception may be at variance with the perceptions of others, or with the self-perception of the person you drew. But this is not the issue at this point. The purpose of the drawing, remember, was *not* to draw out what you *think* you know, or what someone else knows, but to practice finding out what perceptions are in your mind that you don't know about at a conscious level of awareness.

Your drawing can now be "read" for meaning. The marks you made are intelligible to you because they represent ideas that were already in your mind. Can you perhaps finish one of these sentences?
"What I didn't realize is . . . . . ."
"I see now that . . . ."
"I'm surprised by . . . ."
"I didn't really understand before that . . . ."
"I found myself drawing . . . ."

Since one of the requirements for creative thought is the ability to bring insight up to a level of conscious awareness, try now to state in words what you have learned—to "tag" the drawing and capture the fleeting and fragile insight in words. I must caution you again that facing the insight and seeing what the drawing can show you may require courage. On the other hand, the drawing may show you some lovely aspect of the person which may have remained outside of conscious awareness. If you find yourself shrugging off the drawing, saying, "It doesn't look like anything to me," I recommend either taking a new, fresh look at the drawing or trying another drawing of the same person.

You can "tag" the drawing either by writing down the insight (or insights), or by telling yourself (or someone else) about the drawing.

Portrait Analogs by Students
Allow me to show you some "portrait" drawings by my students, along with their comments (Figures 8-2 through 8-7).

I'll begin by pointing out first the fresh, unstereotyped quality of these drawings—and I daresay yours as well. As with the previous analog drawings, once the requirement to produce recognizable images is removed, individuals, even though untrained in art, produce inventive, expressive drawings. Also, as with the previous analog drawings, these portrait analogs are absolutely unique, yet often contain similar struc-

98

tural forms that are part of the visual language that conveys meaning to the viewer.

Now, the portraits.

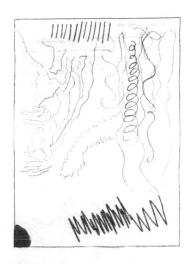

Fig. 8-2
First, "Portrait of D" by Janan Guyan. Janan's written comments:
"I see more clearly how emotionally detached he keeps himself. There is some anger that he hasn't dealt with and when he gets angry over something, it is very intense and comes out with no warning.
"He has a very solomn, serious, withdrawn personality at times, and at other times he is very silly—a lot of fun—but sometimes he is sarcastic and teasing.
"I have a much better handle on him than I did, but I would like to know more. I don't understand why he can't love me."

Fig. 8-3
"Portrait of SK" by Pamela Cremens.
"Angry, she hates someone before she gets a chance to know them.
"She's a true friend to the end, yet a fierce enemy.
"She's a good person and fun to be with. She wears her feelings on her sleeve; if she doesn't like you, you are the first to know about it.
"She's a very complex person.
"I found out that I like her more than I thought I did. I felt a need to fill up every space on the paper."

Fig. 8-4

"Portrait of a Friend" by Chuck Carroll.
"I see now that this person is confused with many emotions running through his mind—sometimes very anxious and trying to get his act together.
"I learned something new from this drawing: that he is lonely and home-sick."

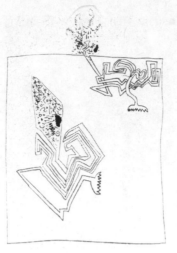

Fig. 8-5

"Portrait of A" by Natasha Joiner.
"Dancing, nearly every night—six days a week. Turned out to be his *backbone—what holds him together.* This placement, this part of the drawing was totally unintentional!
"The dark side is the part I can't get close to, but now I realize that maybe even he can't get close to it either. Yet the drawing shows that his beautiful personality radiates to touch every part of his life."

Fig. 8-6

"Portrait of JS" by Evelyn Moore.
"He can be very confusing. He is very self-absorbed and can be closed-mind-ed about things that don't directly concern him. His life is very habitual. He tries hard to be what he thinks he should be without taking into account who he is.
"The new thing I see is that maybe there is less inside than what appears on the surface. Or could it be that there are areas about him that I know nothing about?"

Fig. 8–7
"Portrait of JMB" by Barbara Paul.
"I meant to draw someone withdrawn (around the edges) but nevertheless easy to get along with and predictable, *except* occasionally when overt personality barbs intrude.
"Instead I seemed to draw a block of granite or *ice*."

Drawing Together Some New Ideas

Along the lines of my students' comments, what did your "portrait" drawing reveal to you? Do you "see" something now that you had not seen before? Is that person less of a mystery than before? Were you surprised about some insight into the personality? And were you surprised at yourself—at how easily you accomplished this drawing, using the visual language with ease and facility to make your inner thoughts and perceptions visible?

One important last step in the Portrait Analog exercise remains: take a long look at your drawing and put it into your visual memory—rather like making a mental snapshot and storing it, ready for easy access. When you are with that person again, or when you think of him or her at a later time, "take out" the analog. You will remember it, probably with great clarity. Thus, using the visual language of drawing, you have created an image that is *useful* in understanding personal relationships, an image far richer than anything you might be able to put into words, an image that provides access to "thought-about-feelings." Again, you have made this thought visible.

9

Drawing on First Insight to Find the Question

The American psychologist J. W. Getzels said in a footnote to an address on "The Psychology of Creativity" that he had found the sentences below "... under the name Gertrude Stein in a notebook I kept years ago; I no longer know where the sentences are from, but they must have pleased me, as they still do.
" 'The whole question of questions and not answers is very interesting. Suppose no one asked a question. What would the answer be?' "
From Carnegie Symposium on Creativity, 1980.

Creative endeavors often start when one simply "looks around" with curiosity and interest, perhaps searching specifically (either casually or intently, depending on your involvement with the subject at hand) for parts that are missing, that don't fit, or that "stand out" in some way.

In the last chapter, there was something about the person whose portrait you drew that you didn't quite understand, and you may have achieved some measure of understanding, an insight, by making your thoughts and perceptions visible in the Portrait Analog. Here we will attempt the same technique to examine an aspect of your own personality or life, something that seems missing or that doesn't fit. Something that you don't quite understand. Again you will make your thoughts and perceptions visible in an analog drawing which will bring the problem to a conscious level of awareness. You will "see" the problem, and something in the drawing will perhaps jog your mind and you will ask a question. It can be a beautiful question.

In the creative process, beauty, and the esthetic response to beauty, are deeply involved. Saint Thomas Aquinas, the Italian philosopher of the thirteenth century, said (in the quotation on page 103) that three things are needed if beauty is to be achieved: wholeness, harmony, and radiance. Aquinas linked beauty with truth, and held that faith and reason constitute two harmonious realms in which the truths of the heart (faith) complement those of the mind (reason). The drawing you are about to do can be thought of, then, as having an esthetic goal: to be a work, no matter how slight, that comes from the heart and therefore presents a beautiful truth which can later be comprehended in the realm of reason.

Drawing a Problem in Analog Form

Please read all of the directions for this exercise before you start your drawing. Following the exercise, I will show you some sample drawings by my students—but, again, don't look ahead at the drawings. It's important that you have no preconception about what your drawing will look like.

1. Scan in your mind's eye various aspects of your current situation, and select one that seems to be causing a problem: something that doesn't fit, or that you don't quite understand. The situation can be a personal one, involving only you, or a situation concerning someone else, or a group of persons, in relation to you. The problem can be related to your career or business, or to a social situation that is of concern to you. It should be a problem, however, whose solution would be a benefit to you and to others in some significant way—in fact, the more important the problem is to you, the better. You will be doing an analog drawing of the selected problem.

2. Do not *name* the problem before you draw. The time will be right to name the problem *after* you have drawn: our aim is to "fly by" the net of words in order to see, and premature naming of the problem may draw in the net of words too closely, perhaps excluding something that is in fact part of the problem. If you say something to yourself in words, try to limit the words to "What I know about this situation is . . ." or "What's bothering me is . . ." or "At this point, the way I see it is . . ."

3. As with the Portrait Analog, understand that you *need not* know beforehand what the drawing will look like. Again, the purpose of the drawing is to *find out*. Understand also that you will not solve the problem with this drawing—that is not its purpose. The purpose is to see the situation in a new light, to put it into a new perspective, to "see the picture."

4. Use a pencil for the drawing, and keep an eraser handy.

5. Draw a boundary line as the first step. This is to provide a *format* for the problem—to draw a line around it. The format can be any size or shape you wish, and can be roughly drawn, carefully hand-drawn, or carefully measured and drawn with a straightedge or ruler. This boundary will serve to separate the problem from its immeasurable surroundings and will allow it to be apprehended as one thing, one unified whole—the *integritas* of Aquinas, the first esthetic requirement.

6. Do not censor what you draw. Again, this drawing is private and need not be shown to anyone. Summon courage and let the drawing emerge on the paper. Make sure that you draw no objects, no recognizable symbols whatsoever, no words, no pictures, no rainbows, no question marks, no daggers, no lightning bolts—nothing but marks on the paper, the *evidence* of visual thought.

Thomas Aquinas (1225–1274) stated his philosophy of beauty in the exact and simple language that was characteristic of his writing:

"Art, then, is the human disposition of sensible or intelligible matter for an esthetic end. This esthetic end will be served if the matter is arranged satisfyingly. Beauty will be achieved. . . . *Ad pulcritudinem tria requiruntur integritas, consonantia, claritas.* I translate it so: 'Three things are needed for beauty: wholeness, harmony and radiance.'

"These qualities correspond to the phases of apprehension of the esthetic object. First, the mind draws a boundary line about the object to be apprehended, separating it from its immeasurable background of space and time. It is apprehended as one thing, one whole. This is *integritas*.

"Second, the apprehender passes from point to point of the esthetic object, perceiving the relationship of part to part balanced within its limits, and thus experiences the rhythm of its structure. The synthesis of immediate perception is followed by the analysis of apprehension: 'You apprehend it as complex, multiple, divisible, separable, made up of its parts and their sum, harmonious. That is *consonantia*.'

"Finally, the object is perceived to be the thing that it is and no other thing. This synthesis, the only logically and esthetically permissible one, now reveals the radiance [*claritas*], the *quidditas* or whatness of the thing. The contemplative instant at which it is apprehended by the mind, which has been arrested by its wholeness and fascinated by its harmony, is the luminous silent stasis of esthetic pleasure."
ROBERT S. RYF
A New Approach to Joyce, 1962.

If one drawing seems not to be enough, or if you want to make changes without erasing large areas of the drawing, take another piece of paper and start again—and another, if necessary—as many as you need. Some individuals like to define the problem progressively.

7. *Begin now to draw.*

When you have finished your drawing, hold it at arm's length and look at it. You have stepped into the first stage of creative problem solving. You have stated the problem in the visual parallel language. You have set it out so that you can *see* it.

The Message from out of the Blue

Regard this drawing as a message from the visual, perceptual part of your mind—an R-mode perception. Your task is to apprehend the message, to *read* it. This is the *consonantia* of Aquinas, the second requirement for beauty. You—as the apprehender, the viewer of the message—must pass from point to point of the drawing, perceiving the relationship of part to part within the boundaries of the format. Attempt to see the image as a whole and at the same time to see the parts. You are looking for your own thoughts, which will perhaps appear as unexpected or surprising forms. You may have drawn something you didn't expect you would draw. Yet subconsciously, you know the vocabulary of the visual language—its lines, forms, and structures. You know how to read them, and what the drawing *tells*. You know all this because . . . you know it. You can see it. When student Barbara Paul, for example (Figure 8–7, page 101), found that she had unexpectedly drawn "a block of granite or *ice*," that was the information she needed—not necessarily that the person she drew *is* like a block of granite or ice, but that Barbara Paul *felt* that way and didn't know it.

Search your drawing now for new information.

The Meaning of the Message

The next step is to grasp the information or the message by capturing the analog in words. Along the lines of André Breton's statement in the margin, we must connect the visual (R-mode) language of the analog to the verbal (L-mode) language by putting the analog into words. Remember, however, that words can serve only to "tag," or title, the analog—barely to grasp it—and cannot even begin to encompass its complexity.

But grasp it we must, or the fragile message from Robert Musil's* "other condition" will disappear. The trick is to hold the two statements—the visual *and* the verbal—in mind at once as a dual representation of the same thing, equally valid and equally valued, one complementing the other.

To complete this exercise, then, consult your drawing again, seeing what is there, and then capture its message by stating it in words, either silently (in writing) or out loud to yourself or to someone else.

If you write out the words, I suggest that you use another sheet of paper or write on the *back* of the drawing. This is in order to allow the drawing to continue to stand alone and communicate its complex message without interference from the verbal mode, which tends to overpower and limit the visual language. You may write at length and in some detail if you wish, or you may be as brief as one word. Remember, however, that words can only *barely begin* to represent the infinitely more complex drawing, and since you have the dual representation, you actually do not need a lengthy description in words.

Now, as the next step, again memorize the analog. Practice holding the drawing and the words in mind at once. Look at your drawing. Imagine that you are taking a mental snapshot of it: *remember* the look of it. Close your eyes and try to call up the image in your mind's eye. If you cannot, look at the drawing again, take a mental snapshot, close your eyes, and *see* the image. In your mind's eye, set the words you have written alongside the drawing. Can you read them? See both the drawing and the words side by side. If any part is unclear, look at your drawing/words again and repeat the process. This should not take long; a moment will often suffice to embed the images in your mind, because they came from your (right and left) minds in the first place.

Finally, perceive your drawing as "the thing it is and no other." This is Aquinas' third requisite for beauty—the *quidditas*, or whatness, of the thing. These slight drawings that, in the philosopher's terms, "come from the heart" have a wholeness derived, I think, from the *trueness* of their content, which is spontaneous, harmonious, and unstereotyped. As you confront your drawing now, perceive its wholeness and its harmony, and respectfully bestow on it for a moment the "luminous silent stasis of esthetic pleasure."

"Perhaps the imagination is on the verge of recovering its rights. If the depths of our minds conceal strange forces capable of augmenting or conquering those on the surface, it is in our greatest interest to capture them and later to submit them, should the occasion arise, to the control of reason."
ANDRÉ BRETON
from *Le Manifeste du Surréalisme*, 1924.

*Austrian writer Robert Musil's formulation of "two main conditions of human experience" seems to apply here. A brief review of Musil's ideas is on page 106.

Drawing from Life: Student Analogs of Problems

Let me now show you some examples of students' Problem Analogs. The problems they chose naturally reflect their interests and concerns at their particular stages of life, concerns that may be different, perhaps, from yours. Nevertheless, the analogs illustrate a stage in the process of creative thought or problem solving which, I believe, is applicable to everyone.

I am also including (on page 109) one example from the business world, a visual form—actually itself an analog—used by the management team of a large advertising company. The analog is called simply the "Grid," and though it uses only a very small portion of the vocabulary of visual language, it has apparently proved to be an extremely powerful tool for problem solving and communication. I believe it draws its power from the R-mode cognition it generates, and it demonstrates, I think, the potential use of the analog images for business problem solving.

In his writing, the Austrian novelist and essayist Robert Musil (1880–1942) grappled with the problem of reconciling human needs for both intellect and feeling in relation to the often conflicting requirements of civilized life in the twentieth century. His mature formulation of the structure of human experience postulated two main conditions of human experience in modern life, termed by Musil the "normal" condition and the "other" condition. He described the "normal" conditions as follows:

"We have evolved—if one were to describe this condition in relation to the other—by means of the *sharpness* of our intellect to what we are: lords of an earth on which we were once a nothing within the vastness of space; activity, boldness, cunning, deceit, restlessness, evil, a talent for the hunt, love of war and the like are the moral qualities for which we may thank this ascent."

The "other" condition Musil described as "no less demonstrable historically, even if it has left a less powerful imprint on our past." The "other" condition is that "of contemplation, of envisioning, . . . of escape, of will-lessness, of turning inward. . . . This condition is that in which the image of each object does not become a practical goal, but a wordless experience." Musil realized that the fleeting nature of the "other" condition made it seem illusory, without substance, irrelevant, uninteresting, even pathological from the viewpoint of the "normal" condition. Its inaccessibility to language made it difficult to mix itself with the "normal" condition.

But Musil argued that the "normal" condition was by no means more real, more objective, more rational or unfeeling than the "other" condition. Each condition, Musil stated, had its own substance, reality, objectivity, rationality, and feeling, but *different* one from the other.

The major problem that Musil set for himself in his writing was to clarify in what way the exceptional "other" condition of being could be brought into a more harmonious, productive, and ameliorating relationship with the "normal" condition.

In his essays and his best-known work, the novel *A Man Without Qualities*, published in three volumes dated 1930, 1933, and 1943, Musil explored the perplexing tensions between these two modes of perceiving the world.

From David S. Luft's biography, *Robert Musil and the Crisis in European Culture, 1880–1942*, 1980. The quotations cited are from Musil's essay "Ansätze su neuer Aesthetik: Bemerkungen über eine Dramaturgie des Filmes," 1925.

106

Fig. 9–1
A Problem Analog by Pam Folan. Her accompanying L-mode statement: "Where do I go? One part of me wants to go into business or law and be someone powerful; another part wants to go into fashion design. Another part is just confused!"

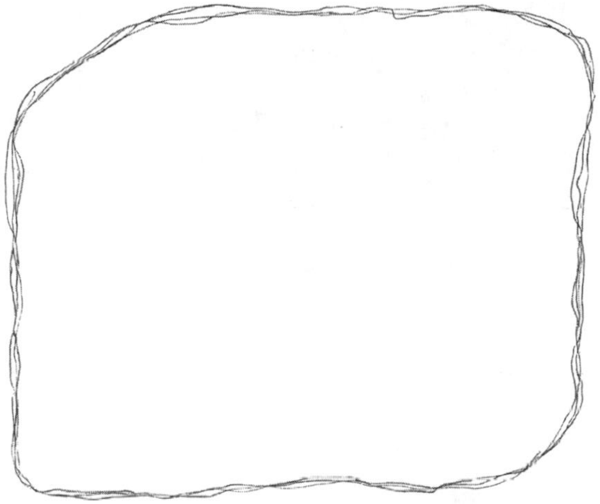

Fig. 9–2
A Problem Analog by Judy Stasl. "Problem: Career going nowhere. Life heading nowhere, in no one direction."

Fig. 9–3
Problem Analog by Craig Albert. "Problem: computer program." (Craig Albert later told me that his drawing had enabled him to solve the problem and complete the program so that it worked effectively.)

Fig. 9-4
An unsigned Problem Analog.
"Overweight—it seems as if it encompasses every part of my life—it shades and darkens all other parts of my life."

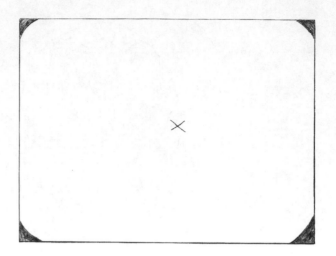

Fig. 9-5
An unsigned Problem Analog.
"Trying to fit in, find my own 'niche,' connect with other people."
(Note that the student carefully designated the *top* of the drawing. He was right to do so, because the location of the small isolated form relative to the large form is crucial to the meaning of the analog. If you turn the book upside down, you will find the meaning changed.)

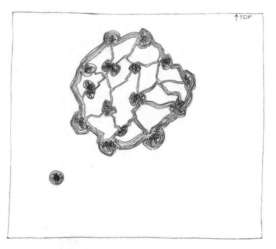

Fig. 9-6
A Problem Analog by Ruth Von Sydow.
"There I am at the top with all my complexities. Things and ideas coming at me from all sides. The main problem is that I can't decide between *careers*—actually, *ways of life.*
"One side is the scientific degree-oriented side; the other, the artistic, language-oriented, creative, joyful side. The answer to happiness lies somewhere in the middle, but it is getting harder and harder—more complicated—to decide. I feel lost."

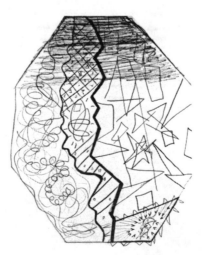

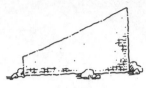

The Inclined Plane
c. 300,000 B.C.

The Wheel
5,000 B.C.

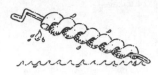

Archimedes' Screw
300 B.C.

The FCB Grid
1978 A.D.

The most useful tools are often the most simple.

An example of a use of R-mode visual language in business is the so-called Grid, first developed in 1978 by Richard Vaughn, a research director of the worldwide advertising corporation Foote, Cone & Belding.

The Grid, shown in Figure 9-7, is a simple, powerful image that condenses large amounts of complex data. To quote Dan Fox of FCB, "What the Grid did for us was to help to literally put lines around our thinking." David Berger, Corporate Director of Research said, "The Grid provides insight—and a way to communicate . . . it is a conceptual tool. It is not a formula. It is not a straightjacket. It is a tool with which to think and to communicate."

The Grid essentially depends for its effectiveness on *placement within the format*, one component of the parallel language demonstrated in the first analog exercises in Chapter Six (high and low placement, as in "joy" and "depression," and left/right placement, as analyzed in relation to the "anger" analogs).

"High" on the Grid is reserved for perceptions of important or costly products such as cars, "Low" for less costly, less crucial products, household items, for example.

"Left-side" placement (contralateral to the usually dominant right eye, largely controlled by the left hemisphere) is (correctly) reserved for verbal, numerical, analytic "cognitive"-type products for which purchasers prefer information and data—for example, automobiles and cameras. "Right-side" placement, on the other hand, is reserved for products that appeal to emotional needs and wishes, such as travel or cosmetics (see Figure 9-8 on the next page).

Placement of a particular product on the Grid is determined by researching a product and its potential customers in usual ways—surveys, questionnaires, previous sales records, etc. These data are computed according to particular formulas, and the product is subsequently *placed* as a dot on the grid—high or low, left or right, with infinite possible variability. As Berger said, the Grid is not a straitjacket.

Fig. 9-7

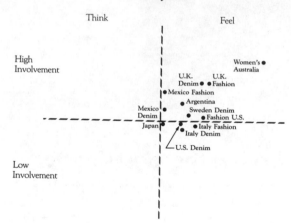

Bluejeans

Think   Feel

High
Involvement

Women's ●
Australia

U.K. ● U.K.
Denim ● Fashion
● Mexico Fashion
● Argentina
Mexico ● ● Sweden Denim
Denim ● ● Fashion U.S.
Japan ● Italy Fashion
● Italy Denim
└ U.S. Denim

Low
Involvement

Fig. 9–8

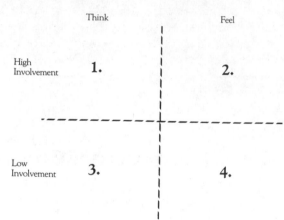

Think   Feel

High
Involvement   **1.**   **2.**

Low
Involvement   **3.**   **4.**

Fig. 9–9

Once placed, the simple, powerful visual image forms a basis for advertising strategy, and, perhaps even more important, provides the agency with a means to effectively communicate that strategy to clients: clients can *read* and understand the Grid immediately, because the parallel-language component, *placement* in the format, is intuitively understood.

An interesting aspect of the Grid is that correlations of agreement about placement of a particular product on the Grid are very high, estimated at higher than +.80. Blue jeans all end in the same general area of the grid—the middle of the High/Low continuum, and on the Right side (Figure 9–9); insecticide in the Low/Left quadrant; life insurance in the High/Left quadrant. These placements hold true for countries as diverse as Britain, Italy, Japan, the United States, and Puerto Rico.

FCB's successful and purely intuitive use of only one component of the powerful visual language gives promise that the language, when used more completely, will be useful in solving business problems.

"Our work with the Grid has of course been a creative process, and in any creative process you find simplicity emerging. Some of the speculation in Vaughn's first version didn't stand the test of experience. Some of it has been superseded. And most importantly, the tool works best when people load their own thinking into it. So we use the simple diagram."
DAVID BERGER
Address to an FCB management group, 1984.

Student Reactions to Analog Drawing

A number of students expressed to me their reactions to this exercise. The most frequent comment was that "drawing the problem changed it, made it seem more objective, as though it was now *outside* whereas before it had been *inside*." Another frequent response was one of surprise at what the problem "looked like," or surprise at some unexpected part of the problem that had been outside of conscious awareness.

Thus, by means of drawing, we can unlock a door not otherwise open to consciousness. Recall from my review of the journal notes of creative thinkers that elements of creativity have always been mysterious and outside of conscious awareness. As the great Russian artist Kandinsky wrote in 1910, we must "speak of mystery in terms of mystery." In our search for First Insight, the initial stage of the creative process, the function of the analog drawings is to objectify the mysterious subjective realm. And that, as philosopher Susanne K. Langer says in the quotation on page 95, is a function of art itself.

"Just as an explorer penetrates into new and unknown lands, one makes discoveries in the everyday life, and the erstwhile mute surroundings begin to speak a language which becomes increasingly clear."
WASSILY KANDINSKY
Point and Line to Plane, 1947.

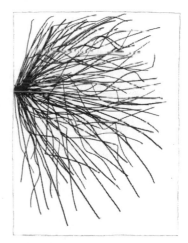

A Problem Analog, "The Problem of My Father," by J. J. De Moss.
"I see in this drawing intense pain. I never realized before I did this drawing how much my father has hurt me—not just made me angry, or offended me, but actually *hurt* me."

10 Drawing Meaning from the Inside Out

A number of years ago, on an assignment to tutor adult college students in remedial reading, I had an experience that has stayed with me. I watched a man comprehend *meaning* from printed words, apparently for the first time in his life. He was about thirty and had never learned to read. We were using an elementary-school primer, working on the sentence "The boy climbed up the hill." Laboriously, his finger marking the line, the man pronounced the words aloud, one by one, with long pauses between. When he finished the sentence, I asked him what he had read. "I don't know," he replied. I asked him to read the sentence again, and again he could not say what he had read. I suggested that he close his eyes and imagine that he was watching a boy walking along a path that led up the side of a hill, and that the boy climbed up the hill. I asked him if he could see that, as a picture in his mind. "Yes," he said, "I can see that." After a moment, he opened his eyes, looked at me, and said, questioningly, "Well?" I said, "That's what you just read: 'The boy climbed up the hill.'" Over his face came an expression I have never forgotten. He had suddenly understood that the printed words had meaning, that they could be understood and linked to experience and to mental images. Up to that moment, apparently, he had been looking at the words as *words* only—printed letters, grouped together, to be identified and pronounced—not *seeing* that they had meaning.

Working with drawing students, I often recall that experience when they suddenly *see* that drawings (and other works of art) have meaning. I am not, of course, referring only to drawings of things—portraits, landscapes, still-life subjects. That kind of meaning—what a drawing is *of*—can be summed up in a few words. But meaning is also expressed in the parallel visual language of a drawing, whether it represents recognizable objects or is completely nonobjective. This different kind of meaning requires a different kind of comprehension, just as my remedial-reading student had to use a different mind-set—triggered by a picture in his mind—to comprehend the meaning of a series of words.

In the same way, a drawing, to be comprehended for meaning, must be read by means of the language used by the artist, and that meaning, once comprehended, may be beyond the power of words to express. Yet, in its parts and as a whole, it can be read.

In your analog drawings, you have created pictures by using the language of the artist, and as you have already discovered, you are able to read them intuitively. It may be your first experience with this different kind of comprehension. But it is a skill, comparable to the skill of comprehending the meaning of words, that can be improved with training and practice, once the *different mind set* has been experienced.

To that end, I believe it will be useful to guide you in "reading" a few analog drawings—mainly to improve your skills in reading your own analog drawings and to increase your confidence that your own insight into drawings is valid.

This is risky business, I admit, given the very personal nature of analog drawings. But in art, certain basic compositional fundamentals hold true, whether for drawings by the great masters (as demonstrated by Nathan Goldstein's analysis of Rembrandt's drawing *The Mummers*, page 86, or your own analog drawings which pursue a personal insight. Meaning is embedded in the parallel visual language of the drawings, in the vocabulary of its lines, forms, spaces, and structures. That meaning may have originated in the subconscious mind of the viewer. But again, let us try to put it into words—to objectify the subjective.

A surprisingly modern view of drawing instruction was presented in a small textbook written for elementary-school teachers by Walter Sargeant and Elizabeth E. Miller in 1916:
"Two uses of drawing have been emphasized: first, its use as a means of intellectual expression which differs essentially from verbal language and therefore offers a unique method of analyzing and dealing with subjects and showing them in a new light; second, its use as a form of aesthetic expression, a means of developing artistic appreciation, and an avenue to the sources of aesthetic enjoyment."
From *How Children Learn to Draw*.

Fig. 10–1
Problem Analog Drawing by A.G.,
titled "The Broken Relationship."

"Reading" Problem Analogs

I have chosen three Problem Analogs for my analyses. Two were briefly "tagged" in words by the students who did the drawings, so at least their subjects are known. The third is "untagged," and I will attempt to "read" the drawing without the help of a title.

The first drawing, by student A.G., is titled "The Broken Relationship." My "reading" of the drawing is as follows:

A certain heavy, blocking form (the dark area on the right) presents an obstacle that holds in and contains the events of this relationship. (The "vocabulary meaning" of the placement of this form—on the right-hand side—was discussed on page 74.) Two groups are involved in the relationship, perhaps family or friends (the central, diagonal triangular forms and the opposing square forms), and these groups are quite different from each other. In both groups, however, repetition and a certain rigidity of the forms may "speak" of conformity. Events occur (the forms floating in the space between the "family" groups and the dark barrier), events that are separate and unique, yet somewhat ordinary and repetitive—all contained within a formal structure (the deliberate, evenly spaced, diagonal lines just above "family" groups; these lines form a new kind of barrier, layered and dense). But the "person" (the flower-bud-like form in the center) escapes, and in escaping, experi-

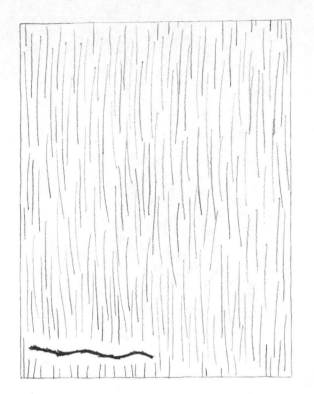

Fig. 10–2
Untitled Problem Analog Drawing by
J.D.M.

cnces a sense of renewed energy and personal power (the exploding form: recall the analog drawings for "Human Energy" or "Power"). "He" escapes into freedom (the empty space in the upper left, which about equals the "territory" of the problem in the lower right-hand half).

"The Broken Relationship" is a happy and confident drawing (the lines are definite and clear, strong and vigorous), and the upward-springing flower form is reminiscent of the analogs for "Joy."

The second drawing has a quite different aspect. In the vocabulary of drawing, recall that forms placed low in the format delineate "low feelings" or "Depression." In this drawing, by student J.D.M., the "person" is placed low in the format, almost as low as possible, and occupies minimal space. "He" is horizontal—that is, inactive (recall the analog-vocabulary form for "Tranquillity"). All the "others" (the vertical lines) are active and moving, but they do not intersect with the horizontal person. That person remains isolated, avoided, and somehow *lowly*, like a worm. Yet the drawing has a strange sense of confidence and clarity, as though the person were saying, "Yes, this is the way it is. Isn't it terrible? But I find it interesting, even agreeable!"

On the back of the drawing, J.D.M. wrote: "The problem is that I feel lonely and alienated. I feel as though I don't fit in." This "reading" of the drawing is perfectly consistent with the image. Yet somehow I can't

Fig. 10–3
Untitled Problem Analog Drawing
by S.K.

ignore the other message embedded in these marks: the care with which the image is drawn. The format is beautifully squared up, and the vertical lines representing "the others" are drawn with great delicacy and artistic precision. The wormlike form also is quite beautiful, with its little branching, outreaching marks. This precision, enjoyment, and artistic self-confidence is in strange contradiction to the message of the forms— and both messages are no doubt valid.

The third drawing, by student S.K., is very mysterious and very beautiful. If anyone doubts the ability of "non-art students" to produce work of artistic quality, this drawing will allay those doubts. But what does it mean? What problem does it communicate? What insight does it provide? The central vortex is compelling, even hypnotic in its intensity. The central form is contained, enclosed, is without an opening, is relentlessly encapsulated. And what is contained? An eyelike form, implacable, inward, seeing but unfeeling. Layers surround the eye (the spiraled lines, alternating light and dark). But the eye remains unmoved and uninvolved. This image is terrifying, like some terrible obsession or dread. Surely you feel it, as I do. You are looking at another person's reality. I think you will understand when I say it must have required courage to confront this drawing.

Pulling myself away from the hypnotic central vortex is difficult—

how beautifully drawn is the layered spiral! But *all* of the drawing is significant. The finlike forms seem defensive, a huge protective device to guard the central form, and the repeated figure-eight patterns reinforce the message of defense, seeming almost like the chain mail of ancient armor. Because the form is placed on the left-hand side, there seems to be a "wish" to move forward. But the movement is blocked by the very same forms that protect the central vortex.

This drawing immediately reminded me of a work by the French artist Odilon Redon, *The Eye, like a Bizarre Balloon, Drifts Toward Infinity*, shown in Figure 10–4. In the vocabulary of the visual language, the meaning of this dreamlike eye may simply be too complicated to put into words, as Redon himself indicated in the margin quotation. One interpretation might be that it has to do with the inner self, but the ambivalence remains. In the Redon image, the eye is the focus of a dreamlike fantasy. My student's drawing has the same dreamlike quality, but fearful, protective, and remote.

My interpretations of these Problem Analogs are included only as suggestions of possible ways to look at the drawings. Indeed, you may have entirely different interpretations of the same drawings. And perhaps the only truly valid reading is by the maker of the drawing, the person's *own* reading, the brain talking to itself. But I hope that my

Fig. 10–4
ODILON REDON (1840–1916)
The Eye, like a Bizarre Balloon, Drifts Toward Infinity (to Edgar Poe).
Lithograph, 1882.

Odilon Redon said about his work: "The essence of the mystery is to preserve a state of ambivalence, through double and triple possible interpretations, through mere hints of interpretations (images within images), through forms that will materialize, but will do so only in the consciousness of the spectator."

interpretations will help you read the message (or messages) contained in your own Problem Analogs. It is not difficult to do, once you grasp the idea that the lines, the shapes, the structure all convey meaning.

Thinking Upside Down

It is hardly necessary to say that when the letters of a word are re-arranged, the result is an entirely new word with a different meaning. Similarly, the words in a sentence, or the sentences in a paragraph: in each case, by altering the structure of verbal language, you have altered its meaning. Not surprisingly, the same is true of the visual language of drawing. Alter any of its lines, shapes, or structures and you alter its meaning. And the most dramatic and convincing proof of that is to turn your Problem Analogs upside down.

We are, remember, in search of First Insight, that largely subconscious R-mode awareness that something is puzzling or missing or doesn't quite fit in a personal problem or situation, the perception that propels the thinker to seek a creative solution to that problem. You have captured that perception in your Problem Analogs. What purpose is served in turning them upside down? Wouldn't they convey an entirely different visual message? Yes, of course. But reading that message, I believe, can reveal meaningful elements of the drawing that you might have missed. You are, in essence, looking at the same problem from a different perspective. And that perspective can be useful when the drawing is returned to its original orientation.

Upside-down orientation, as you learned in Chapter Two, is an effective way to trigger an R-mode response. It enabled you to both see *and* draw. But how effective is this upside-down "trick" in the process of creative problem solving? It's obvious that while we can turn a drawing upside down, we can't turn the world upside down in order to view a problem in a different perspective. And if you asked, "Why not just visualize something upside down, and then draw it (or work out a problem) from the mental image?" I would have to answer, "That's too hard." Correctly visualizing and then drawing an inverted image is extremely difficult, even for an experienced, trained artist. I certainly can't do it, though I have known a few artists who can accomplish such a feat. It is fun to try, but I would not have a lot of confidence in the outcome. I much prefer to try to see what is "out there" in actual fact—in reality! Now, if we could just get the models to stand on their heads . . . or the landscape to turn upside down.

But we cannot, and the difficulty of such complex visualizations perhaps illuminates a problem I see in many recommendations for creative thinking by writers in the field. For example, A. F. Osborn, a well-known expert in the field of invention, proposed a long "checklist of original thinking" in which he suggested a series of manipulations of

"Psychologists point out that most of us have mind sets. That is, we tend to fall into ruts that limit our thinking. "Turning the problem upside down may provide a novel solution. It is said that Ford's invention of the assembly line was achieved by this type of inverted thinking. Instead of the usual "How can we get people to the material to work on it?" Ford asked, "How can we get the work to the people?" With this fresh approach the assembly line idea emerged."
AUREN URIS and JANE BENSAHEL "On the Job: Quick Solutions to Job Problems," *Los Angeles Times*, 1981.

the object under consideration: "Can it be made larger, smaller, split up? Can it be reversed, turned upside down, turned inside out?" These suggestions sound easy, but then, the recommendation "Be more imaginative!" also rolls off the tongue with ease. Performing these manipulations is *not* so easy, though perhaps one can visualize a hazy picture, and perhaps that is enough to get started on a new approach to a problem.

Generally, however, I believe that R-mode works best with concrete material. Certain creativity exercises seem to fit this R-mode preference for real things from the real world. One example is the technique called "Random Wordplay," in which the problem solvers build connotations around a chosen word. Another technique is "Bioheuristics," which centers thinking around a picture of a creature or a natural object—an animal, bird, microbe, plant, shell, stone—that can be related to the problem at hand. Still another example is the ancient *I Ching*, a 4,000-year-old Chinese aid to intuition based on a set of sixty-four hexagrams consisting of six lines each in all possible combinations.

In my approach to creativity, the concrete objects used as aids to thinking are, of course, drawings. As I see it, one advantage of drawings over techniques described above is simply that the drawings come from within the problem solver and represent thought made visible. And drawings *can* be turned upside down. Held in the hand and looked at in different ways, drawings can yield up information sometimes not immediately apparent on first view.

Let's try it out. Turn back the pages of this book to the first analog drawings (pages 70–73), and please take out your own analogs: the Emotional State Analogs, the Portrait Analog, and the Problem Analog of a situation you are currently working on. Turn your drawings upside down and regard them from this new point of view.

You will notice that the Emotional State Analogs shown in the book, when viewed upside down, convey a different nonverbal message. "Anger" seems to "move" in a different direction. "Depression" becomes mania—a sort of high frenzy. "Peacefulness" is less quiet, more akin to "Happiness" or "Joy." "Joy" itself becomes slightly melancholy. Regard your own drawings now, and read this new information. What you are seeing is the *reversal* of the emotional state— its opposite, or the possibility of its opposite. Just as you were able to "read" your own analogs right-side up, so you can "read" them upside down, and the message you receive can enhance their meanings when they are again viewed in their original orientations.

Reading the Analogs Upside Down

Again, I would like to make a few comments on my own "reading" of the visual language in students' drawings, now viewed upside down. And once more, a cautionary note: my reading is only *my* interpretation—not necessarily accurate by any means, given the personal nature of these drawings.

Now look at the Portrait Analogs starting on page 99, and turn the book upside down. You will find that when viewed this way, the portraits present a "What if . . . ?" question. What if the subject's traits, as perceived by the artist, were inverted? What if the characteristics viewed as being at the bottom, or base, of the portrait were instead at the top?

The inverted image presents the person from a different perspective, a different point of view. The perception hasn't actually changed—the lines are the same after all—but you may notice something that was not apparent before: how much space is taken up by anger, perhaps, or how lighthearted the person is most of the time. In the "Portrait of JS," by contrast (on page 100), what Evelyn Moore termed the "self-absorbedness" of JS becomes very much more apparent upside down.

Now read your own Portrait Analog for new information from a new point of view, asking the question "What if . . .?" To "tag" this new perception, I recommend that you write in words on the back of the drawing or on another sheet of paper the insight derived from this new point of view.

Turn next to the Problem Analogs, starting on page 107, and again turn the book upside down. You will see that when the image is inverted these drawings also seem to yield new insight. Even the seemingly symmetrical image (Judy Stasl: "Career going nowhere," page 107) takes on a *slight forward* movement when viewed upside down—a small rise at the lower right-hand corner, a slight leaning to the right. It was only when I looked at this drawing upside down that I was able to see, paradoxically, the down-and-backward, self-defeating quality of the original right-side-up perception. That is, when I saw the slight forward movement, viewing upside down, only *then* could I see the reverse.

Another symmetrical drawing, unsigned, titled "Overweight" (page 108), yields a small bit of information upside down: the cross in the middle (representing perhaps the inner person, the will, thought, or whatever) is (in upright orientation) slightly forward-moving—a positive sign. Again, I had not been able to see that until I turned the drawing upside down.

In Chapter Nine (page 108) I mentioned how different the unsigned drawing captioned "Trying to fit in" appears in upside-down orientation. When it is viewed upside down, a "What if . . .?" question becomes apparent: What if, though still outside the group, "Unsigned" had a different, more buoyant feeling (attitude, position, view, mind-set, outlook, orientation, aspect, etc.)? In upside-down orientation, the small shape seems to draw the large shape toward it. After seeing this orientation, I could more clearly see the feeling of rejection and sadness in the drawing as originally oriented.

And finally, the three Problem Analogs analyzed at the beginning of this chapter:

First, "The Broken Relationship," when viewed upside down (Figure 10–5 below), reveals another aspect of the problem: its sharp and piercing character. What is joyful and confident right-side up now reveals itself as somewhat aggressive and contentious—thus perhaps also revealing A.G.'s contribution to the breaking of the relationship.

About the second drawing, J.D.M. himself wrote, "When I turn my drawing upside down (Figure 10–6), it seems as if everyone is drawing toward me, or going toward me, and I am the one that is keeping myself isolated. I wonder if I do that?" A beautiful question!

The third, S.K.'s drawing, to me is absolutely transformed upside down (Figure 10–7). It becomes animated, lively, and dancing. The enclosed, spiraled form seems buoyant, tenderly held up by the gentle touch of a loving structure, which protects but does not hold back the form. True, the eye form remains inward and remote, but carried along in such a tender way, it loses its foreboding quality. What if the person who drew this drawing could reverse the feelings, turn the problem upside down?

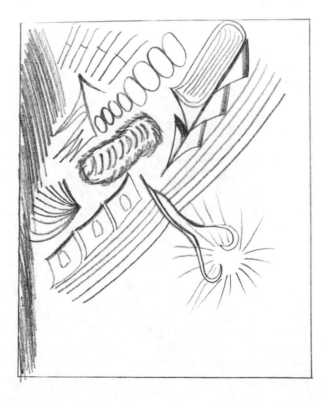

Fig. 10–5
Problem Analog Drawing, "The Broken Relationship," by A.G. shown upside down.

Fig. 10-6
Untitled Problem Analog Drawing by
J.D.M., shown upside down.

Figure 10-7
Untitled Problem Analog Drawing by
S.K., shown upside down.

122

The Analogs Are Mirrors, but Not Magic Mirrors

Of course, the information in analog drawings is *only* information; it is not magic. Seeing something doesn't make it any easier to change attitudes or habits of thinking. But the drawings do provide concrete images, dredged from the subconscious, on which to hang conscious thoughts and actions—a metaphor or analog around which to organize random thoughts and actions and to imagine possible solutions.

One additional thought on Upside-Down Drawing and Upside-Down Problem Solving. I believe its main contribution to the creative process is to relieve anxiety. It seems that L-mode decrees that anything upside down cannot be important and, bowing out, allows perception, intuition, and the playful creativeness of R-mode to occur.

As a result of perceiving your original Problem Analog upside down, you may wish to do a new analog, incorporating these perceptions and carrying the first Problem Analog to a further stage. Alternatively, you may wish to start an altogether new analog. Many creative problem solvers work on a number of problems simultaneously. Remember that the problems may be large or small, important or relatively trivial, societal or personal. The analogs will show you what is in your mind that you are not aware of at a conscious level.

Keeping an Eye Out for the Beautiful Question

While looking at (your) reality in the form of "problem" drawings, be on the lookout for parts that puzzle you, that seem out of place or missing, or that "pop" into focus by changing your point of view, as in an upside-down orientation. Be alert to questions: "I wonder why . . .?" "What if . . .?" "How come . . .?" "But where is . . .?" or "But what is that?" or "What could that mean?" Among these questions, one may "stand out" as a beautiful question.

If the answer to this question doesn't come easily, but seems very important to *find out*, you have probably entered the initial stage of the creative process: First Insight. R-mode, in its mysterious way, has jogged L-mode into asking a question it can't turn down, and suddenly the search is on. To find the answer, L-mode *must* know more, learn as much as possible, saturate the brain with information, explore every facet of this question now in mind to find the answer.

Part III

New Strategies for Thinking

"If we were face to face, you and I, and you should ask, 'Can I learn to draw?' my unhesitant reply would be, 'Yes.' For anyone with normal intelligence can. There is not the slightest doubt about it."

ARTHUR L. GUPTILL
Freehand Drawing Self-Taught, 1933.

11

Drawing Up
the Rules of the Game

"It seems, then, to be one of the paradoxes of creativity that in order to think originally, we must familiarize ourselves with the ideas of others."
GEORGE KNELLER
The Art and Science of Creativity, 1965.

The biographies of creative individuals make it clear that creative solutions come more easily to a mind prepared with knowledge. If the researcher is already an expert on a subject, all the better, because the goal of Saturation, the second stage of the creative process, is (ideally) to learn everything possible about a problem. Naturally, most problem solving requires a less rigorous approach, but even for small problems one must gather enough knowledge to make headway toward a solution.

The process of Saturation is, I believe, mainly an L-mode function. The qualifier "mainly" is an important one. Simply to gather information probably would not produce a creative solution to the problem at hand. Something more has to come into the picture: a way to choose from the great mass of available information that which *fits* the First Insight you have achieved, information that at least offers some potential for solving the problem.

Looking Inward, Looking Outward

I have proposed that "looking around" for information crucial to such a search requires knowledge of *how* to see—not in a literal sense, but rather in the sense in which an artist uses the term. The rules or heuristics for this kind of seeing are brief. Not surprisingly, they correspond to the basic requirements for realistically drawing a perceived object or person—something "out there"—since in this stage of the creative process one must look outward, in contrast to the first, inward-looking stage.

As you found in the last chapter, First Insight often takes the form of a speculative question. In an attempt to find an answer to that question, Saturation, on the other hand, usually takes the form of statements: "So-and-so says that . . ." or "History shows that . . ." or "In 1972, a certain event occurred . . ." Thus, First Insight gives purpose and direction to the second-stage exploration of existing information, providing a kind of guiding light for the search. Though it may change or even be transformed during the research, First Insight usually persists throughout the five stages of the creative process as an organizing principle—the *inspiration*, which by definition "breathes life into" the pursuit of a solution.

The Basic Strategies of Saturation

To saturate your mind with information about a problem, I suggest that the following heuristics will help you *see* whether it fits within the boundaries of the problem, how it fits, where it fits, and why it is important (or unimportant). To achieve that perspective, you will have to be able to:

1. *Perceive the edges* of a problem. Where does one thing end and another begin? Where are the boundaries of the problem (the edges that separate the problem from what surrounds it)?

2. *Perceive the negative spaces* of a problem. What is in the space (or spaces) around or behind the objects (or objectives) of the problem? Since the edges of the spaces are shared with the objects, can the spaces help define the objects?

3. *Perceive the relationships and proportions* of a problem. Relative to your point of view, what is the state of the problem in relation to the constants of the situation—the things that don't change (or can't be changed)? What are the relationships of the parts to each other and to the whole?

4. *Perceive the lights and shadows* of a problem. What is visible—in the light—and what is in shadow? What parts can't be "seen into" at this moment?

5. And finally, *perceive the Gestalt* of the problem. What is the unique set of qualities, the "thingness of the thing"—the *quidditas* of Aquinas—that makes the problem what it is and none other?

Paradoxically, these verbal questions can best be answered not by means of language, but by skillful *seeing*.

The questions form a *strategy*, or more properly, a set of strategies, five in number, for looking at the available information "differently." And to use these strategies—the heuristics of seeing—requires that you understand, in a real sense, the meaning of the terms: for example, the term "negative space." I believe that the most efficient way to attain that understanding is to learn to see by learning to draw, just as the most efficient way to learn to do library research on a subject is first to know how to read.

Seeing as a Teachable, Learnable Skill

There is an old saying in the art business: "If you can teach a person how to see, that person will be able to draw." It's not *drawing* that has to be learned, it is *seeing*.

"One should not think slightingly of the paradoxical; for the paradox is the source of the thinker's passion, and the thinker without a paradox is like a lover without a feeling: a paltry mediocrity.... The supreme paradox of all thought is the attempt to discover something that thought cannot think."
SØREN KIERKEGAARD
Philosophical Fragments, 1844.

> "If brains work by representing, as we believe that perceptions are representations, then we need to know the code—the rules of representation. On this account, physics is almost entirely unimportant, just as the physics of chess is unimportant."
>
> R. L. GREGORY
> *Mind in Science*, 1981.

> "The arts are neglected because they are based on perception, and perception is disdained because it is not assumed to involve thought.
>
> "In fact, educators and administrators cannot justify giving the arts an important position in the curriculum unless they understand that the arts are the most powerful means of strengthening the perceptual component without which productive thinking is impossible in every field of academic study.
>
> "What is most needed is not more aesthetics or more esoteric manuals of art education but a convincing case made for visual thinking quite in general. Once we understand in theory, we might try to heal in practice the unwholesome split which cripples the training of reasoning power."
>
> RUDOLF ARNHEIM
> *Visual Thinking*, 1969.

Seeing is a paradox in itself. Despite reams of evidence that human perception is fraught with error, the notion persists that seeing is "natural" and no more requires teaching or learning than does, say, breathing. One result of this notion is that visual perception is generally ignored as a possible school subject, if one discounts incidental learning of perceptual skills in sports or sewing, drafting or woodworking classes. Even in art classes, teachers seldom directly instruct children in perceptual skills.

It is probably safe to say that no schoolchild is taught how to *see* with anything approaching the rigor of systematic reading instruction. For most children, learning to read and write occupies years of study and effort, but seeing is simply taken for granted. Though children's schoolbooks usually have pictures, it is the *words* that really count. If the pictures have a function, it is to support the reading instruction. That the child will understand the pictures without instruction is usually just assumed.

And for ordinary seeing, this assumption is obviously right. Children and adults perform amazingly complex and difficult feats of visual perception without any instruction whatsoever. For example, infants at a very early age respond to individual faces—a perceptual feat requiring delicate and precise discriminations. Unlike reading, no child has to take lessons to learn how to watch television. And an adult of my generation, looking at a group photograph of, say, a particular West Point graduating class, could very likely pick out the *young* Dwight D. Eisenhower.

Curiously, computers are now playing a role in increasing our respect and admiration for human visual skills that have always been taken for granted. For computers, even the most rudimentary kinds of recognition or discrimination require extremely complicated programs. And perceptions human beings can make in an instant, seemingly without effort, are at present absolutely beyond the capability of machines. Human-level visual perception is simply too complex.

PROJECTED TECHNOLOGICAL EVOLUTION TOWARD RIGHT BRAIN AUGMENTATION ERA

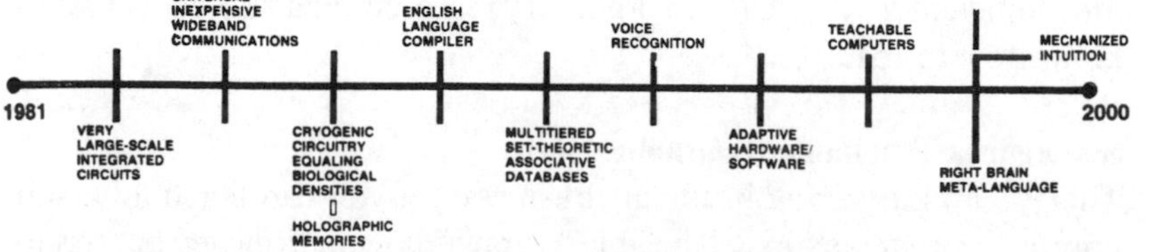

Fig. 11-1
VINCENT RAUZINO
"Conversations with an Intelligent Chaos," *Datamation*, 1982.

Granted, then, that human visual perception is already a marvel of natural ability, what can one gain by learning how to see "differently," in the artist's way—a way of seeing that *does* require instruction?

One important reason (in addition to my conviction that perceptual skills enhance creative thinking strategies) is to give the silent brain half training in its own special function—visual, perceptual processing. Fortunately, the training is not difficult, given proper teaching techniques. The skills are few in number and can be readily learned by any individual who has been able to master other complex skills such as reading.

I came to understand the nature of the basic visual strategies of drawing by an odd experience. One day, about six months after my book *Drawing on the Right Side of the Brain* had been published, I suddenly realized what the book was about. It dawned on me that the subject of the book, its content, was different from what I had thought I was writing. This was a very strange experience, but apparently not unknown among writers, as I have since heard other writers describe similar experiences of comprehension that occurred long after publication.

The book I thought I was writing, exploring the relationship between brain-hemisphere modes of information processing and learning how to draw, contained within it another content of which I was unaware. That content, in fact, was knowledge that I didn't have at the time I wrote the drawing book—or, better stated, something that I didn't know I knew.

Five Fundamental Skills of Seeing

The hidden content defined the basic skills of drawing. In providing exercises designed to cause (presumed) cognitive shifts in brain mode to help beginners learn to draw, I had inadvertently selected from many aspects of drawing the few fundamental perceptual skills that seem to underlie all drawing. I had spelled them out, the five basic-component skills, without ever stating—or realizing—what they were.

Now I realize that for the basic *seeing* necessary for drawing a perceived object, five particular skills (the five listed at the beginning of this chapter) are needed. Mind you, I am again speaking of simply the ability to match with a drawing what is seen—that is, the ability to draw objects or persons realistically. I am not speaking of "Art with a capital A." Comparable ability in language would be basic reading and writing, say at high school level, or in music, the ability to read music and play a tune on the piano.

I was elated about this discovery. Over the following weeks and months, I discussed it at length with colleagues and searched through the available texts on drawing. My colleagues and I have not found

Vincent Rauzino proposed in 1982 that "the goal of a truly right-brain augmentation computer would be to harness the complex set-associating, pattern-synthesizing, gestalt-processing right-brain machinery into coherent and predictable equations."

Rauzino stated that the qualities of association, inference, and extrapolation, often identified as higher-order intellectual traits than computation and correlation—the province of computers—are as yet largely out of range of today's computers.

From "Conversations with an Intelligent Chaos," 1982.

that any additional *fundamental* perceptual skills are needed adequately to process visual information for basic realistic drawing.

Obviously, there are many other skills beyond the basic perceptual skills, ultimately leading to great art, just as skills with language extend far beyond fundamentals of reading and writing and ultimately lead to great literature. Also obviously, ability to draw realistically does not guarantee that the ability will lead to artistic creation any more than ability to read guarantees unusual literary or poetic prowess.

But for the person who wants to use the "other half" of the brain to complement language and analytic processes, who wants to learn how to see and draw in order to use visual perceptual heuristics as strategies for problem solving, five perceptual skills will do it. And this presents the exciting prospect that most individuals can learn to draw within a reasonably short period of time—and to apply their seeing/drawing skills to every phase of the creative process.

Drawing as a Parallel to Reading

The key insight, I believe, was that drawing is very much like reading. In reading, the fundamental illumination—that words on a page have meaning—is ideally achieved in early childhood. This illumination then provides the motivation to learn the basic *component* skills of reading one by one (letter sounds, word recognition, spelling, grammar, and so on). Gradually, the components are integrated into an almost automatic set of strategies used in meaningful, logical, verbal, sequential, analytic thinking. And when that has been accomplished, the global skill of reading is there in the brain, ready to be used for the rest of one's life.

Once I had glimpsed the parallel strategies of reading and drawing, my ideas about teaching drawing, and about thinking in general, changed. I viewed drawing in a new way: I saw that the first requirement was the fundamental illumination that drawings have meaning, and that this illumination provides motivation for acquiring the basic component skills of drawing—a limited set of integrated visual-perceptual strategies. These skills could be learned at a young age and be used to structure thinking—in short, drawing as cognition training rather than (or in addition to) artistic training.

I believe that this idea had previously eluded me because the components of any global skill, once learned, become so melded and integrated that they almost seem to disappear into each other. The separateness of individual skills, so clear during the learning process, somehow becomes lost in mind, no longer to be seen at the conscious level.

Conventional art programs may help obscure the global nature of drawing. Students take courses called "Life Drawing," "Landscape Drawing," "Portrait Drawing." And this separation into courses often

Designer Joe Molloy views *designing* and *writing* as parallel strategies. In teaching graphic design students, Molloy recommends applying the ideas expressed in the famous little book by Theodore Strunk and E. B. White, *The Elements of Style*, a guide used by countless writers since its first publication in 1935.

Some of Strunk and White's rules for writers that Molloy applies to design are the following:

Omit needless words.
Place yourself in the background.
Revise and rewrite.
Do not overwrite.
Do not overstate.
Do not affect a breezy manner.
Be clear.
Write in a way that comes naturally.
Work from a suitable design.
Make sure the reader knows who is speaking.

encourages them to think that drawing becomes different if the subject matter changes. If asked about their drawing skills, for example, art students often respond in this way: "Well, I'm pretty good at drawing still-life setups, and I'm okay at landscapes. But my figure drawing is not so good, and I can't draw portraits at all."

These responses reveal that one or more of the basic drawing skills may be shaky, since drawing is *always* the same task, requiring that all of the basic component skills be available simultaneously (though the person who is drawing may choose to emphasize, say, *line* in one drawing, *negative space* in another, *light/shadow* in a third, as shown on page 133).

The need to master all the component skills becomes clearer when one thinks of other global skills. To illustrate, suppose you asked about a person's driving ability, and the answer was "Well, I'm pretty good on paved roads, and I'm fair on freeways, but I'm not so good at dirt roads, and I can't drive on hills at all." One would guess that some component or other of the basic driving skills must be missing.

Or if you asked about a person's reading ability and the answer was "Well, I'm pretty good at books, and I'm okay at magazines, but my newspaper reading is not so good, and I can't read encyclopedias at all," one would conclude that the basic reading skills might need work.

The point is that drawing a portrait requires precisely the same perceptual skills as drawing a figure, a landscape, a still-life—or an elephant, or an apple. It's all the same. And each component skill must be readily available for use as putting on the brakes in driving or recognizing words in reading.

From Component Skills to Global Skills: Putting Things on Automatic
A look at other global skills may also illuminate the point previously made about integrating component skills into smoothly melded global skills. Again, driving a car is a good example. Driving is a global skill made up of component skills: one learns to steer, to use the brakes, to signal, to use the rearview mirror, and so on. At first, a new driver consciously thinks of the components, often with mental reminders: "Now I must turn the steering wheel (don't forget to signal!); now I'd better accelerate; quick, step on the brake!" and so on.

Once learned, however, driving becomes an integrated global skill with the various movements, thoughts, actions, and adjustments melded into a smooth, effortless whole. An experienced driver no longer needs to think consciously about the components of driving, and in fact can drive while thinking of other matters. And, obviously, the same skill, made up of the same components, is used no matter what the destination of the driver, or, with slight variation, no matter of what different make the car.

Another example is dancing—first learned as components, which are then integrated into a global skill. Psychologist David Galin's famous funny remark about this global skill is "The reason I could never learn to dance is that I could never get beyond '*One*, two, three; *One*, two, three.' "

So it is with drawing/seeing/R-mode thinking. When a person has learned, one by one, the five basic components of drawing, they soon become integrated into *one* skill. At that point, you can draw anything at all—that is, anything seem with the eyes. (Drawing imagined or visualized images, I believe, requires imaging skills just beyond the very basic five components we are dealing with right now.) And when one has learned the rules of the game, they can become almost automatic, operating smoothly, almost out of conscious awareness.

Of course, a person's mastery of component skills can be at various levels, whether in reading, dancing, drawing, tennis, bicycle riding, playing a musical instrument, or any other global skill. But at some point of assimilation and integration of components, one says, "Yes, I can read," or "Yes, I can draw."

Strategies for Saturation and Beyond

In the Saturation stage of the creative process, *seeing* what is "out there" is just as important as information presented to your mind in any other way. In learning the component skills of drawing, you will embark on a new way of presenting information to your mind: arranging and manipulating it by means of visual strategies, always keeping the organizing principle—the purpose of the search—clearly in view. This is a different method of research, as valuable, I believe as the more usual methods.

In learning the component skills of seeing/drawing, you will also be able to build on the illumination of the analog drawings—that drawings have meaning. And you will discover, happily, that the lines, shapes, and structures you so readily and intuitively used for the analog drawings are the *same* components, already existing at a subconscious level, that you can develop and use at a conscious level of awareness. Thus, you will attain a visual vocabulary and a set of conscious visual strategies that you can use with maximum effectiveness. The time is right for you to draw power from your perceptions.

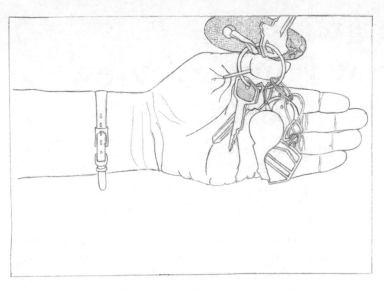

Fig. 11–2. A drawing by student Kuroyama emphasizing negative space.

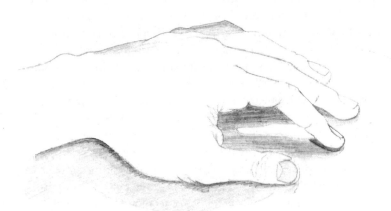

Fig. 11–3. A drawing by student Abdel Hamid Sabry emphasizing light/shadow.

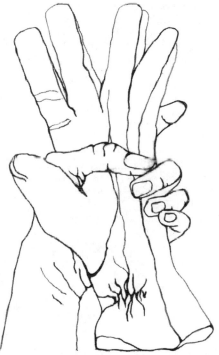

Fig. 11–4
Student Diane Hahn's drawing, "Hand Holding a Glove," emphasizes edges.

Drawing on
New Points of View

"In my opinion," says James L. Adams, "the optimal situation in problem-solving is to be able to use a clean-minded approach to a problem, even though your mind is stuffed with information. . . . The more information I have about the problem and previous attempts to solve it, the better I do. . . . However, this abundant information can often prevent you from seeing very elegant solutions."

Adams goes on to quote J. J. Gordon in his *Synectics*:

"Learned conventions can be windowless fortresses which exclude viewing the world in new ways."

The reason for maintaining an open mind, of course, is so that no information derived from seeing what is "out there" will be overlooked, rejected, or revised because of prematurely drawn conclusions.

Conceptual Blockbusting, 1979.

Drawing is full of paradox, as is creativity itself. And dealing with paradox requires that one be able to hold in the mind simultaneously two diametrically opposed ideas and, as novelist F. Scott Fitzgerald put it, "not go mad."

The paradox we must deal with here is the following: the second stage of creativity, Saturation, requires finding out as much as possible about the problem—ideally, a thorough research of the chosen subject. At the same time, one must maintain a "clean-minded approach to a problem," to use James Adams' phrase, a state of mind in which one *knows nothing*, so to speak. One must sift, absorb, arrange, and re-arrange incoming new information along with previously known "old" information without ever drawing conclusions. One must be alert for misinformation or misinterpretation, yet at the same time be willing to risk taking chances. One must search outside oneself for whatever is related to the First Insight, testing confidence in the rightness of the initial question or insight by constantly checking information for *fit*. But at the same time, one must acquiesce to being completely unsure of the next move, or in fact of the whole process. A paradox.

Seeing What *Is*

Drawing requires just this kind of approach. The artist must avoid at all costs making verbal decisions about the subject of a drawing, whether a person, an object, or a landscape. In drawing a portrait, for example, the ideal situation is to know nothing, almost in a Zen sense, about that person, even if the artist and the model happen to be friends. Somehow, the subject must be seen as though never seen before. If the artist—or the thinker—plunges in with conceptions, labels, ideas, or conclusions, trouble lies ahead, and the subject or the solution to the problem may remain forever out of reach.

"How should you start [a drawing] then? Look at the subject *as if you had never seen it before*." (Gollwitzer's emphasis)

GERHARD GOLLWITZER
The Joy of Drawing, 1963.

Fig. 12–1
JEAN-SIMÉON CHARDIN (1699–1779)
Hare with Game Bag and Powder Flask.
Oil on canvas.

Eighteenth-century French artist Jean-Siméon Chardin is quoted: "Here," he said to himself, "is an object to be rendered. In order to paint it as it is, *I have to forget all I have seen* and even these things as they have been painted by others."
From a manuscript written shortly after Chardin's death by Ch. N. Cochin, "Essai sur la vie de Chardin," 1780.

Seeing What *Isn't*

An example: a woman student was drawing a portrait of a male model whose head, in its bony structure, was somewhat unusual and interesting. Walking past the student as she worked on her drawing, I saw that she had misdrawn the proportions of the model's head. I stopped and suggested that she check the proportions again. She did, then erased part of the drawing and started to redraw.

I walked away, thinking the correction would be made, but when I came back, to my surprise, the same error had been redrawn into the portrait. I again suggested that she look for the proportions, which she did, but again the error was redrawn, just as before.

At this point, I asked the student, "Are you saying something to yourself about this model? Something about the head?" "Well," she said, "he does have a very long face." We both laughed; she knew at once what had happened. Her preconception had momentarily blinded her to what was in front of her eyes and caused the error in the drawing; she had drawn a "very long face" by distorting the proportions of the model's head. Later, paradoxically, when she drew the model's head just as she saw it, the "very long face" was there in the drawing, but subtly delineated.

Naturally, artists often intentionally revise and distort information from "out there" for emotional and expressive effects, and such distortion can make drawings very interesting—look again, for example, at the Ben Shahn drawing on page 63. But for a student in a beginning drawing class, where the purpose of drawing is to train the eye to see what is "out there," so-called "interesting errors" are not in order.

And for a person working in the second stage of creativity, gathering relevant information and trying to see the context of a problem, "jumping to conclusions" prematurely can drastically narrow and impoverish the search. New information which perhaps contradicts the premature assumption may be subconsciously rejected, just as the drawing student subconsciously rejected what she saw with her own eyes. And in problem solving, it may be just *that* bit of rejected information which is needed during the next stage of creative problem solving, Incubation.

On the other hand, again paradoxically, an artist or a creative thinker must not be afraid of error. Error can be very useful if one keeps in mind the goal of the search, always trying each new bit of information for *fit* with the problem at hand. Errors can show you what doesn't work (Thomas Edison tried 1,800 different substances in his search for an electric light-bulb filament) and they can help guide the search.

A Precarious Balance Between Two Modes

How, then, can one keep an open mind while at the same time focusing on a specific problem? How can one seek the *correct* answer, and at the same time intentionally risk error? That can be accomplished, I suggest, by a sort of double-tracking of the brain: L-mode gathers and sorts information into categories, translating perceptions into language, while at the same time, R-mode regards both the subject of the search and the information "out there" with its innocent eye (that is, without preconceptions). R-mode manipulates the information in a visual space, always looking for *fit* with the problem at hand—where does a new bit of information fit into the whole picture?—and tries to see *more* of what is really "out there." In the meantime, L-mode tries to link ideas to words and memories of previous conceptions.

I must state here again that one mode is not better in any way than the other. Their functions are simply different. R-mode, because it cannot convert its perceptions into verbal statements or judgments, must in a sense stick to what it sees. It gulps in vast amounts of visual data, searching for patterns, seeking to form bits and pieces into a congruent whole.

On the other hand, L-mode must do its own thing, as we say, which is to abstract details in order to name, analyze, categorize, and converge on a solution. If new details crop up that contradict a decision or judgment, L-mode is likely to say, in effect, "Don't bother me with more details. I've already decided," while R-mode protests, "I don't care what you've decided. I'm telling you it's out there. Let me show you where this new information may fit in."

Tweedledee and Tweedledum Agree *Not* to Have a Battle

Somehow, for creative thinking to progress through its successive stages, we must keep these two, this Tweedledee and this Tweedledum, from having battles. We don't want either/or—either this conception or that perception—but *both*, intertwined and interlocked, as Tweedledee and Tweedledum are, in fact, when they are not battling.

But L-mode and R-mode are *not* identical twins, and in the battles that do occur, L-mode usually dominates. How, then, to give R-mode

Fig. 12–2
Tweedledee and Tweedledum prepare
for a battle.

Fig. 12–3
Tweedledee and Tweedledum when
they are not battling.
Courtesy of the British Museum.

a better chance to do *its* thing.

In order to gain access to the subdominant visual perceptual brain mode, it is necessary to present the brain with a task that the dominant verbal analytic mode will turn down.

Put another way: It's no good trying to go up against the strong and dominant language mode of the brain, saying, "Now you stay out of this for a while because I need to take a different point of view and see things in new ways." L-mode would answer, in effect, "Oh, *I* can do that. Now, let's see: where was I?" and it would continue its linear, verbal, analytic dominance. Therefore, to gain access to R-mode, one must find a way to prevail on L-mode to bow out of the task.

Tricking L-mode out of the Task

However resistant, L-mode is susceptible to being *tricked* out of the task. And it never seems to learn how *not* to be tricked out of the task. (I always feel as though I should say that very softly.) The trickery can take many forms—upside-down drawing, of course, is one.

Artists are familiar with this type of trickery, because in order to do art at all, an artist must have access to what the American artist/teacher Robert Henri called "the higher state." Some forms of artists' trickery: boring, repetitive acts (drawing the same line or form over and over); thumbnail sketches (tiny, rapid sketches); long periods of solitude; simply holding the brush in hand (as Henri suggests); or taking the pen in hand (a method recommended by the English writers Thackeray and Southey). An artist or writer *without* trickery can experience so-called "blocks," possibly a result of L-mode's refusal to let go of its dominance.

Similar blocks can occur in the Saturation stage of the creative process, when, in effect, L-mode refuses to "see" what is really "out there." Might not, then, the kinds of trickery that enable an artist to see serve the same purpose in creative thinking? And might not the basic component skills of seeing, invaluable in learning how to draw, be invaluable as well in creative thinking? I have already stated my conviction that they are. It now remains to show you how.

Some more familiar forms of trickery from business-management expert F. D. Barrett:
"Managers report to us that many of their important thoughts come to them while driving to work. Others tell us that shaving is a good time. Others find that their best thoughts flow best while in the shower. Some find the golf course is a good place, or when quietly sitting in a boat on a lake or while puttering tranquilly in the garden." Barrett speculated that "When the body is distracted by a simple repetitive activity the mind is freed to think."
"How to Be a Subjective Manager," 1976.

"A well-known physicist in Britain once told [the American psychologist] Wolfgang Kohler, 'We often talk about the three B's, the Bus, the Bath, and the Bed. That is where the great discoveries are made in our science.'"
JULIAN JAYNES
The Origin of Consciousness in the Breakdown of the Bicameral Mind, 1976.

13

Beaux Gestes: Drawing on Beautiful Gestures

Poet and artist William Blake (1757–1827) told his artist friends, "You have the same faculty as I [the visionary], only you do not trust or cultivate it. You can see what I do, *if you choose*." On one occasion he said to a young painter, "You have only to work up imagination to the state of vision and the thing is done."
From A. GILCHRIST
Life of William Blake, 1880.

Our goal is to provide ways to extricate parts of the thinking process from verbal trappings, thus enabling you to follow poet William Blake's advice to "work up imagination to the state of vision." Rosamond Harding, in her book *An Anatomy of Inspiration* (1948), remarked of Blake's words, "Fantastic as this advice appears, there can be no doubt that working up the imagination to the state, or at all events almost to the state of vision, is a definite practice with creative thinkers."

Vision (in my terms, R-mode perception) occurs when L-mode can be persuaded to bow out of the job. But for the stage of Saturation, the vision must be captured in words, and therefore we need the two modes working together: verbal thought guided by the heuristics of visual thought.

It is, however, an uneasy alliance, for confronted with information that appears contradictory or hopelessly complex, you are tempted to stick with what you already "know" or "think" you know. The same situation occurs in drawing, where the temptation is to draw what you "think" you see rather than what is actually there. Again, L-mode is the culprit, and it must be tricked into bowing out of the job.

In Blake's "state of vision," one parts the veil for a fleeting moment, the veil that separates us from the complex, profound, multilayered real universe existing largely outside of human consciousness. The ecstatic imaginative vision of the artist, paradoxically, often derives, as writer Arthur Koestler suggests, from perceiving *reality* in new ways. Many artists have spoken of "seeing differently," of parting the veil, however briefly. As Blake said, this faculty of artistic vision is there for the taking, as a matter of choice, if only one trusts and cultivates it. Let's try it with "gesture" drawing, an exercise that will both confound L-mode and demonstrate the first basic-component skill of drawing.

Drawing Up a Storm

"Gesture" drawing is a technique of very rapid drawing, one drawing after another, perhaps fifteen scribbled drawings accomplished in fifteen minutes or less. It works, I believe to "set aside" the strong, verbal left-hemisphere mode, perhaps in the following way. L-mode, which prefers a rather *slow* (relatively speaking), step-by-step linear, sequential, analytic procedure for drawing, preferably using familiar namable forms, says, in effect, "First, we'll draw the head, (let's see, that's sort of an oval); then the neck (two lines); then the shoulders (two slanty lines from the neck) . . ." But in gesture drawing, L-mode finds you drawing helter-skelter, all over the page, saying to yourself, "Just get it down! Faster! Faster!" And L-mode objects, "If you're going to draw that stupid way, count me out! I like to do things the sensible way—my way! One thing at a time, the way . we . . always . . . do. . . . ." And L-mode bows out. Perfect! Just what we want!

The component skill you will learn in gesture drawing is the *perception of edges.* In drawing, an edge is defined as the place where two things meet: where a space meets an object; where a space or an object meets the boundary line; where one thing ends and another begins.

Please read all of the instructions before you begin:

1. Count out fifteen sheets of typing paper and put them in a stack. You may use pencil or pen; felt-tip pens are good for gesture drawing. You won't need an eraser; you won't have time to stop and erase.

2. If possible, use some sort of timer; a kitchen timer is fine. Someone could keep time for you, though it's really better to work alone.

3. Place a magazine, a book, or any publication that has pictures on nearly every page near your stack of typing paper. Open the publication at random—any page that has a picture will do.

4. Each drawing will have the following sequence:

a. Set the timer for one minute.

b. Look at the magazine page. Whatever picture your eye lands on, *that* is your subject.

c. Quickly draw a format (the boundary line that separates your drawing from all the rest of the world), making sure that the *shape* of the format matches as nearly possible the shape of the picture you are going to draw.

d. Draw what you see, using *edges* as your primary source of information. Draw quickly, scribbling almost, never allowing the pencil to stop, trying to *match* the edges and shapes, line directions, curves. Don't bother with details—facial features, for example; you won't have time for that. Just get it down! Faster! Faster! And when the minute is up, stop!

5. Reset the timer. Look at a new picture, draw a new format on a

Laurence Wylie states in his 1977 book *Beaux Gestes*:
"Like ideas and words, gestures have a life of their own."
Wylie describes gestures as a "channel of communication that makes up what linguist Edward Sapir called 'that elaborate and secret code that is written nowhere, known by none, and understood by all.' "
Beaux Gestes, 1977.

"Form, in the narrow sense, is the boundary between one surface and another: that is its external meaning. But it has also an internal significance, of varying intensity; and properly speaking *form is the external expression of inner meaning.*"
WASSILY KANDINSKY
Concerning the Spiritual in Art, 1947.

According to California artist and teacher Howard Warshaw:
"The great Spanish painter Francisco Goya (1746–1828) is supposed to have said that an artist, seeing a man fall from a third-story window, should be able to complete a drawing of him by the time he hits the ground.
"Such a drawing," Warshaw says, "could not be made by analysis, measurement of thumb, or application of the laws of perspective . . . understanding comes in the drawing of the lines, not before or after."
H. WARSHAW
Drawings on Drawing, 1981.

Fig. 13–1
EDGAR DEGAS
Mounted Jockey. Black crayon.
Bibliothèque Nationale, Paris.

Fig 13–2
EUGENE DELACROIX
Tiger and Alligator. Pen.
Louvre, Paris.

Fig. 13–3
HENRI MATISSE
Nude, Semi-abstract.
Pen and ink on paper.
The Metropolitan Museum of Art,
New York. The Alfred Steiglitz
Collection.

new piece of paper, then draw what you see—for one minute only. Stop. Then another, another . . . fifteen drawings in fifteen minutes.

I think you'll find your first few gesture drawings are not much fun. L-mode, protesting as usual, says, "This is really stupid. A real waste of time. Forget this! Turn over to the next chapter! Maybe this author will come up with something that makes more sense than this idiotic stuff! Let's just skip this!" And so on.

Pay no attention. Keep on drawing. L-mode will soon be quiet—tricked again! The truth is, you are working too fast for L-mode to keep up with. And the gesture drawings, like upside-down drawing, will soon become fun and interesting. They may even become good, power-ful, expressive, cogent. Look at the drawings by master artists shown in Figures 13–1 to 13–4; they were done in a flash, a gesture—an intuitive insight recorded by a rapid line.

Finally, try not to think while you are drawing. R-mode can handle this job without your monitoring and, in fact, works better if you simply let go. *Start your drawing now.*

Fig. 13–4
PABLO PICASSO
Study for Guernica, 1937.
Pencil on blue paper. 8¼ x 10⅝″.
The Prado Museum, Spain.

Picasso's initial studies for his master-work, *Guernica*, were small rapid sketches. As you see, this small sketch contained the major conception that was later elaborated and refined.

Fig. 13–5. PABLO PICASSO. *Composition Study for Guernica*, 1937. Pencil on white paper. 9½ x 12⅞″. The Prado Museum, Spain.

Fig. 13–6. PABLO PICASSO. *Guernica*, 1937. Oil on canvas. 11′6″ x 25′8″. The Prado Museum, Spain.

Beaux Gestes: Drawing on Beautiful Gestures   141

Some good advice:

"A curator I used to know in London liked to hide his aesthetic sensibilities behind a kind of off-hand, slangy praising or scoffing. His advice for anybody standing in front of an unfamiliar picture . . . was simply to have the courage of your own perceptions. I've always been grateful for the guidance, and I've found, in the relatively unfamiliar realm of art, that the good work, as against the merely clever or slick, makes itself felt because it carries a kind of emotional weight."
CHARLES CHAMPLIN
Los Angeles Times, 1984.

If self-criticism tends to inhibit your freedom of expression in drawing, the following brief visualization exercise suggested by art therapist Betty J. Kronsky is helpful (once you make your way through the she/he's and him/her's):

"One method I have found helpful for contacting the inner critic is a fantasy exercise. The artist is encouraged to fantasize herself/himself pursuing an artistic project in a space which she/he imagines as ideal for the task . . . there is a knock at the door; it is her/his critic. When she/he opens the door in fantasy, she/he sees her critic standing there. He or she speaks to him/her; he/she answers the criticism, however he/she can.

"This exercise points up the nature of the internalized criticism. Is it benign and constructive, even encouraging? Or is it negative, cruel, and destructive? Who is the person at the door? Is it a member of one's family, a teacher, someone from one's current life? The healthy part of the personality may find a way of standing up to the critic and perhaps of putting its energies to work."

"Freeing the Creative Process: The Relevance of Gestalt," 1979.

When you have finished, close the magazine and look back over your drawings. Also close the door on criticism, if possible, and review the drawings one by one. Call up in your mind's eye the original magazine picture for each. You will find that your recall of the pictures will be exceptionally clear, because you were *seeing* in the artist's mode.

Choose the drawings you like best and pin or tape them up on a wall where you will see them. Trust your judgment! You will like the *best* drawings. You know much more than you know you know! Put the other drawings aside for one day, then review them again. Discard any that do not please you on this second review. (Most artists keep about *one in twenty* drawings, sometimes fewer than that—a little-known fact, I believe. But that twentieth drawing will have something: a record; perhaps just a single line that feels right; a true response to something truly seen or felt.)

Drawing on Brainstorms to Open the Gates of Thought

Gesture drawing is similar in some ways to a problem-solving technique called "brainstorming." In brainstorming, a group of experts, at most a dozen, works for a prescribed period of time on a specific problem by spontaneously voicing any ideas that come to mind, no matter how bizarre or absurd they may seem. Judgment or evaluation of the ideas is banned for the allotted time period. The atmosphere of the meeting ideally is unrestrained and anxiety-free. All suggestions are written down, usually on a blackboard, for subsequent evaluation. The main purpose of brainstorming—*and* of the second stage of creative thinking, Saturation—can be stated as follows:

For a project that will be costly in terms of money or time or energy, it is advisable to gather all available information and possible general conceptions of solutions of the problem, and to evaluate them carefully.

Brainstorming has been fairly successful as a thinking technique for diverse groups such as educators, songwriters, business executives, and scientific teams. Recent investigations, however, have shown that the technique is even more effective when *individuals work alone*—for reasons that are fairly obvious. First, it takes more courage than most of us can muster to shout out bizarre and absurd ideas in a competitive business setting, especially if the boss is present. Second, brainstorming depends heavily on the language mode of the brain and therefore stacks the deck *against* the very mode of the brain that is needed, the elusive, playful, visionary, pattern-seeking R-mode.

I suggest a different technique: visual brainstorming by means of gesture drawing. Let's try it out.

Fig. 13-7
"Funny Business" by Roger Bollen, reprinted by permission of Newspaper Enterprise Association.

1. From your folder of drawings, take out your Problem Analog. Look at it once more to set it firmly in your memory. Think about any insight you derive from the drawing. Then close your eyes and visualize your analog in your mind's eye. Do this several times until you can "see" the drawing clearly in your mind. Then put the Problem Analog back in your folder.

2. Think next about your reseach on the problem or the situation that you brought to conscious awareness in the analog, reviewing in your mind any questions, new information, possible relationships or patterns, or gaps in your knowledge of related information. The checklist in the margin, reviewed *before* you start drawing, may gently jog your memory of relevant bits of information relating to the problem.

Remember, we are dealing with the perception of *edges* and using lines to define edges: where one thing ends and something else begins. Think of your Problem Analog. Think of the lines as edges. Which edges are clear and which not clear? Where are the largest areas with no lines at all? Does something from your recent research fit into the empty areas? Should the forms be different—larger, smaller, more complex, differently shaped, etc.—now that you know more about the subject at hand?

3. Get set to draw; use pencil or felt-tip pen, and have ready fifteen or more sheets of ordinary bond paper or typing paper. Number each sheet, 1 to 15, in the upper right-hand corner. Again, use a timer if possible. For each page, draw for one minute.

A. F. Osborn, an American expert in the field of invention, proposed a "checklist of original thinking." A few of his ideas:

"Are there other uses? Modifications?

"Change in color, motion, smell, form, shape?

"What could be magnified? Made stronger? Multiplied? Made smaller, lower, shorter, stronger, larger, thicker, in miniature, in duplicate, split up, exaggerated?

"A different arrangement, layout, sequence, pace, ingredient, material, power, place, approach, tone of voice?

"What could be reversed, transposed, combined, streamlined?

"What are the bottlenecks, intersections, surprises, goals, inefficiences, vital needs?"

Applied Imagination, 1957.

4. You will be making analog drawings, as rapidly as possible, one after another, all on the same problem, over and over again, trying to find out how the new information fits in. Again, avoid recognizable images, words, symbols, shooting stars, lightning bolts, unless the analog seems to urgently call for a certain symbol—an arrow, a question mark, etc. Remember that the language of line is infinitely expressive, whereas symbols, closely linked to L-mode words and concepts, may narrow your focus.

Note that this is not mindless doodling, but an attempt to express thought in visual form. You will understand the marks you make; the language of line is readable. And since your brain is communicating with itself, you need not be concerned that anyone else understand the marks you make.

5. On each page, the first line you draw will be a format—a boundary for the analog—quickly drawn freehand. The format lines needn't be exactly straight or the corners exactly square. The format can be any shape you wish and can change from drawing to drawing. This boundary separates the problem from the surrounding, unbounded world, or one part of the problem from another part.

6. Keeping your mind fastened to the problem, begin to draw the first analog, the pencil moving rapidly, as fast as thoughts can fly. Censor nothing. Do not stop to erase. Ignore the protests of L-mode ("This is stupid stuff," and so on). Just keep drawing. As you draw, ideas will come to you . . . from out of the blue. *Start your drawing now.*

When you have finished, review your drawings, just as you reviewed your gesture drawings. This time, however, you are looking for the visual notations of thoughts that may help organize and clarify your research of the problem. These thoughts can take many forms: new approaches to the problem; recognition that certain bits of information may not *fit* within the boundary of the problem; conversely, a part previously thought to be peripheral might be seen in a new light.

Review the drawings one at a time, in order, calling to mind for each drawing what the thoughts were: what bits of information or what ideas were in your mind. As with the magazine pictures, you will find that you will *clearly* remember what your thinking was for each drawing, and this memory will stick in your mind, ready for use as a *visual* image.

An important next step: on each drawing, back or front, write in words the main idea. These notations can be as brief as one word, or they may be more detailed. For the moment, discard no thoughts, and reject no ideas. The very fact that you connected them with the problem may prove to be significant.

144

Again, separate the drawings, pinning up a chosen group. Do not discard the remaining drawings, however, until you have reviewed them again the following day.

The Saturation process requires preparing the brain with information that is *ordered* in visual, perceptual relationships. Viewing the chosen drawings, now pinned up and in clear sight, commit them to visual memory: look at them; take a "mental snapshot"; close your eyes and test whether you can *see* the drawings in your mind's eye, linked to the words you have written for each drawing. Repeat this until you *know* the drawings as visual images. This is an important step in the thinking process: along the lines of Blake's advice, you are saturating your mind with words and images relevant to the subject, making all possible connections, fitting together as many puzzle pieces as possible in preparation for the stage of Incubation.

14

Drawing at a Snail's Pace

"Contour" is defined as the *edge* of a form. A contour line, in this definition, is different from an "outline," which generally refers to the *outside* edge only. Contour lines can describe *any* edge, inside or outside the form.

The next step is to reverse the process—still perceiving edges, but this time tricking L-mode into bowing out of the job for a while by *boring* it. You will be drawing very, very slowly.

The process is called "Pure" Contour Drawing, sometimes termed "Blind" Contour Drawing. For this drawing you will need just one sheet of paper, taped down at the corners to your table or desk (so that it won't shift around while you are drawing).

Please read all of the directions before you begin.

1. Set a timer for ten minutes, and put the timer where you can't see it.

2. Sit in the following position: your drawing hand holding the pencil is ready to draw on the taped sheet of paper, but you are turned completely *away* from the paper so that you cannot see it. (Figure 14–1 shows the position.)

3. Look at your other hand, specifically focusing on the wrinkles in the center of the palm, or where the thumb joins the hand, or the heel of the thumb where it joins the wrist—anywhere that you see complex

Fig. 14–1
The position for "Pure" Contour Drawing. The important thing is to *not* be able to see your drawing.

patterns of wrinkles. You'll be drawing just a small section of lines and wrinkles—to practice "seeing differently" and drawing what you see. In a later chapter, you will draw the whole hand.

4. Focus your gaze on *one* wrinkle (where two sections of the skin meet, the meeting place is represented by a single line—an *edge*). Begin to draw that one wrinkle, recording with your pencil every bit of perceived information that your eyes gather as your gaze moves slowly, slowly, millimeter by millimeter, along the wrinkle. Imagine to yourself that your fate hinges on seeing and recording everything possible about that wrinkle. Imagine that your eyes and your pencil are moving at exactly the same speed, and that the pencil is a recording device (like a seismographic stylus) that necessarily records every minute perception, every undulation of the line, every slight change in direction.

5. When you have seen and drawn every detail on that wrinkle, proceed to an adjacent wrinkle, and begin to exactly record it *and* its relationship to the first wrinkle. Then proceed to the next adjacent wrinkle. And so on.

6. Do not turn around to look at your drawing. Never shift your gaze from the palm of your hand until the timer sounds. *Most important: continue to draw without stopping until the timer sounds.*

7. Ignore the protests from L-mode that this is "Too slow, too boring, too ridiculous, too useless for words." Just keep on drawing, and soon L-mode will fade away—to take a little time off. At that point, you may find yourself *seeing differently.* You may find yourself wanting to see more, and then even more. The information, the complex patterns of tiny edges and lines, may begin to seem strangely, intensely *interesting.* Allow this to happen: this is the shift in vision we are looking for.

As you feel yourself entering a somewhat different mood, or state of consciousness, do not resist it. The R-mode state is pleasurable and satisfying; one feels alert, interested, self-confident, and concentrated on the task at hand. Nevertheless, some individuals find this mental shift fearful, even alarming. It need not be feared, because the state is so ephemeral, so fragile that the slightest interruption can break the spell, or you yourself can easily break the mood if you wish.

What is the fear? A speculation, partly in jest: L-mode may fear that if you get "over there" deeply enough, you may not want to "come back." More seriously, if the fear is one of "losing control," there is nothing to worry about. When the timer sounds, you will be back all too completely to your "normal" L-mode state. As every creative person knows, the *real* problem is to sustain the elusive R-mode state long enough to finish the job at hand.

Begin to draw now.

Fig. 14–2
Two examples of Pure Contour
Drawings by students Mahendra Patel
and Mike Suriko.

When you have finished, regard your drawing. You will see a very strange set of hieroglyphic marks, fresh, unstereotyped, and, in artistic quality, quite deep, even profound. One of my favorite memories is of a remark made by writer Judy Marks Howard on seeing Pure Contour Drawing for the first time. She said, "No one in their left mind would *do* a drawing like that!" And that is a true observation. L-mode simply can't or won't deal with such complex visual information.

The question is, of course, "What good does it do?" This is not a new question. For forty years, since publication of Kimon Nicolaides' famous drawing book, *The Natural Way to Draw*, American art teachers have used Pure Contour Drawing, knowing that it helps students to draw better—to see better—but why it works so well has always been puzzling. I offer the following speculation as a possible explanation.

First, Pure Contour Drawing causes L-mode, which usually "sees" the details of a form—fingers, fingernails, wrinkles—as symbolic abstractions to bow out of the job. L-mode says in effect, "I've got it; that's a wrinkle. Why keep on looking at it? I've named it already. They're *all* wrinkles. I've got a little mark that I always use for wrinkles. Here it is! They're all alike; we'll just make a few of these marks—that'll tell the story. Let's move on . . . this is too boring," and so on.

Second, Pure Contour Drawing may also change R-mode's usual way of operating. Perhaps in the "normal" sharing of functions, R-mode sees the whole hand as its main perception, while L-mode deals with the details as abstractions. But deliberately focusing R-mode's attention on a detail (a wrinkle, a fingernail) perhaps forces it to see that detail *as a whole configuration*, while at the same time it seems to retain its simultaneous perception of the *relationship* of the detail to the whole configuration. Apparently, R-mode can go deeper and ever deeper, seeing details of details of details, like a set of Chinese boxes, one inside another, and still never lose sight of the whole configuration with its complex relationships. This is the mind-set necessary for drawing a perceived form, and thus Pure Contour Drawing may, in a sense, be a kind of shock treatment for *both* modes, bringing to both a realization that something different is going on and perhaps accounting for the stress many students experience with this technique.

In short, Pure Contour Drawing sets up conditions in which R-mode does not share the visual information-processing job with L-mode, but instead deals with the whole, all the details and configurations locked into relationships to each other. These relationships which make up the whole image are enormously complex (recall Mondrian's *Chrysanthemum*, page 44), far beyond the capability or inclination of L-mode to deal with. But this global perception of the forest *and* the trees provides *unity* of vision, the rock-bottom nitty-gritty of art and of creativity—the *integritas* of Aquinas (page 103)—the first of the three esthetic requirements for a beautiful drawing or an elegant solution to a problem.

Summing up, then, the end results of doing Pure Contour Drawing are, first, to experience (as nearly as possible) perception that is purely *relational* rather than partly linear-sequential, perception that is relatively uninfluenced by verbal concepts; and, second, to produce a drawing which records that experience. In your Pure Contour Drawing, as in your analog drawings, you have made perceptual thought visible.

Drawing Analogies from Perceptual Thought

In the next exercise, we will use the technique of Pure Contour Drawing to define further the *edges* of the problem at hand, and to saturate the mind with metaphorical-analogical connections between the problem and a real object.

Please read all of the instructions before you begin.

1. Have close at hand several random objects: a leaf, a crumpled piece of cellophane or foil, a shell, a pencil, a flower, a scrap of wood— or, taking Aldous Huxley's lead, you may observe the wrinkles and folds of the clothing you are wearing. Any object will do, the more complex the better. (A book of photographs of objects will work nearly as well; photographs of complex natural forms, as shown in Figure 14–3, are excellent.)

2. Tape a piece of paper to your table or desk.

3. Set a timer for ten minutes. Make sure that you will not be interrupted. If necessary, lock the door!

4. Place your hand, pencil ready to draw, on the paper; then turn away so that you cannot see the drawing.

5. Call to mind your Problem Analog. See it in your mind's eye. Call to mind the Gesture Analogs. See them also in your mind's eye, one by one, as you review your research on the problem at the same time. The mind can do this very rapidly, in a flash.

6. Then focus on one aspect of the problem, something that perhaps stands out a bit in your mind's eye as a detail of slightly special puzzlement or interest.

7. Choose one of the objects. (Actually, any of the objects will do; R-mode is extremely flexible and agile in finding analogic similarities.) Say to yourself, "In what way is the problem I am working on (or a detail of a problem) *like* this object?" Don't be impatient—let your (right) mind play with the idea. Try to regard the problem and the object as if they were linked together, the object a metaphor for the problem. (The somewhat frivolous example in Figure 14–4 will demonstrate this analogic-metaphoric linkage.) Focus on what puzzles you. Focus at the same time on the real object at hand. Then direct your

"The ability of the average person to make metaphorical-analogical connections between very unlike areas of experience was entertainingly demonstrated many years ago by Wolfgang Kohler, the Gestalt psychologist: he asked subjects to match two nonsense words, 'maluma' and 'tuckatee,' to the abstract figures shown (below). Without fail, Kohler's subjects connected maluma to A and tuckatee to B."

MORTON HUNT
The Universe Within, 1982.

In his 1954 book, *The Doors of Perception*, the English author and philosopher Aldous Huxley described effects of the drug mescalin on his perception of ordinary things—in this instance, the folds of his gray flannel trousers. He saw the folds as "living hieroglyphs that stand in some peculiarly expressive way for the unfathomable mystery of pure being. . . . The folds of my gray flannel trousers were charged with 'isness.' "

Fig. 14–3
Epiactris prolifera, the brooding sea anemone.
Photograph by Eugene Kozloff, 1973.
From *Seashore Life of the Northern Pacific Coast*, 1973.

Fig. 14-4
Object analogy is a process of making ordinary objects give us answers to our problems. Sometimes the insights for solving problems lie right under our noses. The pencil is an example of how object analogy works to produce creative thinking.
From KURT HANKS and JAY PARRY
Wake Up Your Creative Genius, 1983.

Problem: How can I improve my marriage?

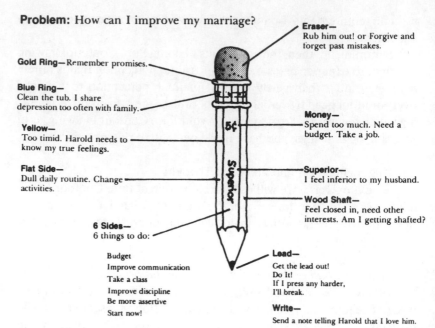

Gold Ring— Remember promises.

Blue Ring—
Clean the tub. I share depression too often with family.

Yellow—
Too timid. Harold needs to know my true feelings.

Flat Side—
Dull daily routine. Change activities.

6 Sides—
6 things to do:

    Budget
    Improve communication
    Take a class
    Improve discipline
    Be more assertive
    Start now!

Eraser—
Rub him out! or Forgive and forget past mistakes.

Money—
Spend too much. Need a budget. Take a job.

Superior—
I feel inferior to my husband.

Wood Shaft—
Feel closed in, need other interests. Am I getting shafted?

Lead—
Get the lead out!
Do It!
If I press any harder, I'll break.

Write—
Send a note telling Harold that I love him.

"In finding resemblances between remote objects or ideas, metaphorical-analogical thinking opens new pathways of thought and thus of creative problem solving.

"If the unlike things are really alike in some ways, perhaps they are so in others; that is the meaning of analogy. We pursue the thought, and find new meanings, new understanding, and often, new solutions to old problems."
MORTON HUNT
The Universe Within, 1982.

focus to one actual detail of the object. Focus on the edges of that detail—the edge of a petal or the pattern on the shell, some part of whatever you are gazing at.

8. As you begin to draw, again without ever looking at the drawing, slowly move your eyes and your pencil at the same speed, recording everything. In the meantime, keep your mind absolutely focused on what puzzles you about the problem: don't let your thoughts stray. Follow up on any leads, any connections that occur to you during the drawing. Your aim is to attain even a slight insight into some aspect of this puzzlement, this detail that stands out in your mind. Be sure to continue drawing until the timer sounds.

You will note that at first nothing will seem to happen, and L-mode again will protest and deliver its logical arguments that this is "Too time-consuming, a waste of time, absurd," and so on and on. Ignore these protests and keep drawing. We are hoping *not* for a large insight, which will come later with Incubation and Illumination when all your perceptions are put together, but instead just a bit of advance, a minor gain in setting a puzzlement into a new relationship to the whole problem. While your hand is occupied, you will find your mind at work on the detail as a whole configuration, which is in a relationship to the whole problem, the global concept.

Begin to draw now.

150

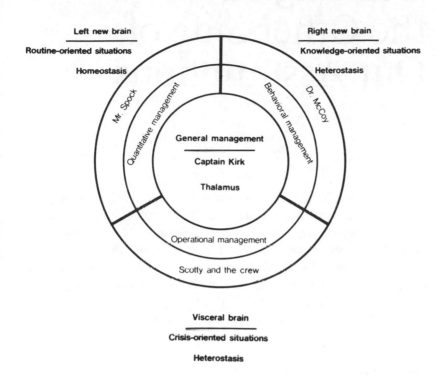

Star Trek, Management, and the Brain

Left new brain
—————
Routine-oriented situations

Homeostasis

Right new brain
—————
Knowledge-oriented situations

Heterostasis

Mr. Spock

Quantitative management

Behavioral management

Dr. McCoy

General management

Captain Kirk

Thalamus

Operational management

Scotty and the crew

Visceral brain
—————
Crisis-oriented situations

Heterostasis

Fig. 14–5
A business-management metaphor. The "Star Trek" management theory is by Waino W. Suojanen, "Management and the Human Mind," 1983.

After you have finished, turn and regard your drawing. You will see again the strangely beautiful, detailed marks of Pure Contour Drawing. To someone else, of course, the object may not be recognizable because of the special procedure of Pure Contour Drawing—the object, after all, was out of sight, but not out of mind! But the drawing is of particular value nevertheless, because it becomes a visual link, a metaphor, a sort of talisman, signifying your insight into the *edges* of the problem at hand. To fix it firmly in memory, write whatever insight you have dredged up as a *title or statement* underneath the drawing, linked with the name of the object you drew.

For example: "Sycamore leaf: I see now that . . ." or "I realize now that I must look further into . . ." etc. Alternatively, you may wish to add several notes to the drawing itself.

Next, gaze at your drawing with its verbal notations and remember it. Look away or close your eyes; call up the memory in your mind's eye. If you find any detail hazy, look again at the drawing and repeat the process. Remember that during this Saturation stage, the aim is to store a visual record of images linked with the words for later use in the Incubation stage.

15

Drawing on the Other Side of Our Assumptions

In teaching people how to draw, one of the most difficult things is to convince them that objects are not all-important—that the spaces around the objects are of *at least* equal importance. There is, in fact, a saying in art that "If you can solve the negative spaces, you will have solved the drawing (or painting or sculpture)"—"solved" meaning that the painting, drawing, or sculpture works as a total, unified image. The concept most difficult to grasp, perhaps, is that the *spaces unify the objects*. Or better said, the spaces and the objects link together to form a unified image.

Seeing Spaces as Shapes

The *perception of negative spaces* is the second basic component of the global skill of drawing. As you broaden your research during the Saturation stage, you will be adding this second skill to the first—your ability to perceive edges, the skill you used in Upside-Down Drawing, Gesture Drawing, and Pure Contour Drawing. In those exercises, you were seeing and drawing the shapes of objects and persons mainly by delineating the edges. In the exercises of this chapter, you will use edges to draw the shapes of *spaces*. You will recall that in art, an edge is defined as the place where two things meet: that is, a line delineates a *shared edge*.

In perceiving negative spaces, you will shift away from the objects and persons (in art terminology, the "positive shapes") and focus on the edges of the spaces between (in art terminology, "negative spaces"). Note that the term "negative" has no *negative* connotations in art terminology; it simply means those areas generally not perceived as namable objects—for example, the spaces between the railings on a stairway. In drawing, these spaces become important, as you will see.

The term is usually used in the plural—negative *spaces*—because in drawing, spaces are usually bounded by the edges of objects, or by the boundary edge of the drawing. If used in the singular, the term "space" would seem to refer to unbounded three-dimensional space, usually thought of as edgeless, which cannot be directly captured in drawing (though, paradoxically, by capturing bounded space the artist can "portray" by inference unbounded space).

Not Empty, but Full of Nothing

The idea that "nothing" could be important goes against the grain in our culture, and against the preference of L-mode for "real things" that can be named and categorized. Interestingly, however, the concept that empty space is important permeates Oriental cultures. The following Tao verse from Witter Bynner's *The Way of Life According to Lao Tzu* presents the idea:

> Thirty spokes are made one by holes in a hub
> Together with the vacancies between them,
> They comprise a wheel.
> The use of clay in moulding pitchers
> Comes from the hollow of its absence;
> Doors, windows, in a house
> Are used for their emptiness:
> Thus we are helped by what is not
> To use what is.

Moreover, Oriental thinkers are willing to allow nothingness to be ambiguous and unknowable, in the sense that it need not be named or otherwise specified. Emptiness or nothingness is simply allowed to be what it is, as Richard Tanner Pascale, professor of management at the Stanford Graduate School of Business, points out in the quotation in the margin.

In his article, Pascale describes a number of ways in which Japanese executives operate within the "empty" spaces of business problems, in contrast to American business practices, which tend to focus on *objects*, or, as we say, "objectives." For example, if merging two departments appears desirable, American executives most often "make an announcement," thus objectifying and naming the new situation. They then proceed, also objectively, to deal with any anxieties and difficulties that may result among employees who are directly affected.

In a similar situation, Japanese executives often quietly shift into the "negative spaces" of the situation, informally merging certain procedures, increasing the flow of information across the boundaries of the two departments, leaving the situation ambiguous until the employees involved become accustomed to the new composition with its shifted spaces and shapes. Only after they have grown used to the change is the situation formally recognized or announced—that is, named in an L-mode sense.

Fig. 15–1
A negative-space drawing of a chair by student John Mato.

"Ambiguity may be thought of as a shroud of the unknown surrounding certain events. The Japanese have a word for it, *ma*, for which there is no English translation. The word is valuable because it gives an explicit place to the unknowable aspect of things.

"In English we may refer to an empty space between the chair and the table; the Japanese don't say the space is empty but 'full of nothing.' However amusing the illustration, it goes to the core of the issue. Westerners speak of what is unknown primarily in reference to what is known (like the space between the chair and the table), while most Eastern languages give honor to the unknown in its own right."
RICHARD TANNER PASCALE
"Zen and the Art of Management," 1978.

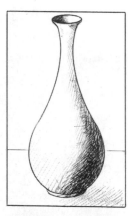

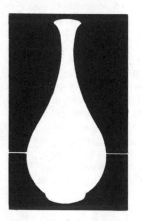

Fig. 15–2
Two Views of an Object:
1. A view of the object.
2. A view of the spaces that *share edges* with the object.

Or, confronting a problem of production, Japanese executives would take a different perspective on the problem than would American executives: the Japanese would be more likely to focus first on the spaces around the problem—the context of the difficulty—rather than zeroing in, "defining the problem," "identifying objectives," "making decisions" in the manner of the Americans.

Additionally, Pascale points out that in the West we select leaders who are "outstanding," while Eastern cultures value leaders who stand "in" rather than "out." To the Oriental mind, the unifying function of standing in the "space between" is of greater value than being in the spotlight. Since that point of view is largely shared by both leaders and those who are led, getting credit for outstanding work is less valued than being seen as one who promotes the implicit wholeness of the organization.

Pascale recognizes that Western technology and business methods have been enormously successful and productive. He proposes, however, that the Eastern outlook provides a new perspective that assigns "a particular human value to human needs." Significantly, he warns against simply co-opting the ideas. (One can imagine L-mode saying, in effect, "Right! I've got that! First, we'll do a little—what do you call that, now? Oh, yes! Negative space. . . . Okay. Well, that takes care of that. Now, where was I?") For Pascale fears that if wedded to Western assumptions, Eastern business practices might become only superficial techniques.

Professor Pascale ends his article with the recommendation "I submit that a nontrivial set of management problems might be better understood if viewed from the other side of our Western assumptions. Undoubtedly, a very high degree of personal development is necessary to embrace both of these outlooks, to know when each is appropriate and to acquire the skills which each requires."

A Mind-set for Both Outlooks

That is precisely our goal: to embrace both outlooks, no matter what the field of creative endeavor, and to acquire in some small measure, at least, the mind-set that viewing from the other side of our assumptions requires. Learning to apprehend and to deal with negative spaces is an interesting experience, different from merely talking about it. I believe that it can help one to edge closer to the viewpoint of Eastern perspective. Just as important, it can also help provide a fresh look at things as well as ensure the unity of vision essential in the Saturation stage of the creative process.

To demonstrate the power of negative space in creative thought, try the following brief exercise.

154

Fig. 15-3

Please read all of the instructions before you begin.

1. Tape down a piece of paper just a practice sheet; a scrap will do—and have a pencil ready to draw. In this exercise, in contrast to Pure Contour Drawing, your drawing will be in view, so that you can glance at it to check on how it is going. The sketch in Figure 15–3 demonstrates the drawing position.

2. Hold your left hand (or your right, if you are left-handed) up in front of your face. Close one eye, to take a single-eyed view as opposed to a binocular, or two-eyed, view of your hand. (Closing one eye produces a "flattened," or two-dimensional, view, with clear rather than blurred edges. Most artists frequently close one eye when drawing; this helps in transforming the three-dimensional world out there into a drawing on flat, two-dimensional paper.) To test the difference, gaze at your hand with one eye closed, then with both eyes, then again with one eye closed.

3. Next, arrange your hand in a position that provides at least *one* enclosed space—more than one if possible. Figure 15–4 demonstrates one possible position.

4. Focus your gaze on one of the spaces; keep gazing until the space pops into focus *as a shape.* This popping-into-focus-as-a-shape takes an increment of time—why, I don't know. Perhaps, in that small space of time, L-mode is saying, in effect, "Why are you looking at nothing? I do not deal with nothing. Nothing carries no weight with me! I deal with *real* things—namable things! And if you're going . to keep on . . with this silly stuff, I'm . . . getting . . . . o-o-o-o-u-u-t."

Perfect! Tricked again! And now, let's have a closer look.

5. Hold your hand steadily in the chosen position. When looking at your hand, keep your head in a steady position as well. This is to ensure that you see only one pose, one position for drawing. Recall that

Fig. 15–4

I asked artist Mark Wethli, "When you want to see a negative space, can you see it right away, the very instant you look at it?"

Wethli's answer:

"There's always a little time lag before a space pops into focus as a *shape.* But the lag gets shorter all the time."
In conversation, August 1981, Long Beach, California.

I mentioned in connection with Piet Mondrian's drawing *Chrysanthemum*, on page 44, that if the flower were changed in position only slightly, an entirely new set of edges would be presented to the artist. Likewise, if Mondrian had changed the position of his head (and thus his eyes), he would have been looking from a new point of view and seeing a new set of edges.

Advanced art students in life-drawing classes can become very upset if the model moves; one student complained that the model was "breathing too deeply." The rest of us (even the model) thought that was amusing, but it does point up the need to hold your hand in a constant position as you draw it. If the position changes, the edges (and the spaces) will change and can cause problems in the drawing.

6. Now, look at your hand, focus on the one enclosed shape you have chosen, and begin to draw the edges of the shape on your practice sheet of paper—just that one shape, making sure that the shape you draw matches as nearly as possible the shape you see. Use the slow-drawing technique of Pure Contour Drawing, recording as much information as possible about the edges of the negative space, occasionally looking at the drawing to monitor the proportions and the directions of the lines. (To differentiate this monitored contour-drawing technique from "Blind" or "Pure" Contour Drawing, I have called it "Modified" Contour Drawing.)

7. Do not change the focus of your gaze. Forget about your hand! Stay focused on the space. Try not to think about what you are doing, and try not to talk to yourself.

Do not name the space! Don't say to yourself, "It's shaped like a duck (or a fish, or whatever)." Try for the other mind-set, a mind-set that can accept not needing to have a name for the space, not needing to categorize, analyze, characterize, anatomize. Allow the shape to be what it is, with its particular relationships of width, length, complexity. Whatever it is, that's what you see and draw. You want to *match* the shape of your drawing.

8. If you see another enclosed space, draw that also, placing it in proper relationship to the first. Figure 15–5 demonstrates. Draw as many spaces as you can see, then stop drawing. Let your hand relax, but try to remember the pose (the position of your hand) so that you can resume it if you wish.

Begin your drawing now.

When you have finished, regard your drawing. You will see one or more oddly shaped "pieces" of space, shapes that you thought were empty, but can now be seen as being "full of nothing." You may darken in the shapes with your pencil, if that will help you to see that *spaces are real.*

Fig. 15–5

156

Imaging Shapes by Means of the Edges of Spaces

The next step is to see that negative space and the forms share edges. Focus your eyes now on your drawing. Create an image in your mind's eye of the finger and thumb, or the fingers of your hand, between and around the negative space/shapes you have drawn. If you can't quite see the fingers, put your hand back into the position—then look at your drawing again until you can visualize the fingers (see Figure 15–6). Notice the sense of surprise that you experience when you find that you *can* "see" your fingers, though you haven't drawn them at all. Notice also how "well drawn" they seem.

Now we confront another example of the paradox I have mentioned before: it's much easier to draw what you don't know than to draw what you know. In this instance, the edges of the space become the edges of the fingers and thumb. It is the same edge. But because you know nothing about the space, you were able to see it with fresh eyes, and therefore you drew it as you saw it. About hands, fingers, and thumbs you know too much. About spaces, your mind is clear and open. Having drawn the edges of the negative spaces, which share edges with the hand, you have inadvertently also drawn the hand. You have drawn the fingers correctly by *not* drawing them!

This is the main use of negative space: it makes drawing easy. Wasn't it? Didn't the shapes seem easy? If so, it was because you simply saw them without fighting a mental battle about how hands and fingers "should" look—and you've experienced a little of the magic of drawing.

Shapes That Are Strangers

Another brief preliminary exercise. Again, *please read through the instructions first.*

1. Tape down another piece of paper.

2. Hold your hand so that the fingers point directly toward your eyes and you can barely see the tops of your fingernails. Close one eye and focus on one fingernail. Again, wait a moment for the shape to pop into focus. (Yes, I know, this is a "positive shape" that can be named; but remember that R-mode is not hemmed in by L-mode rules! Any shape can be *imagined* as a negative space and used as such, *if the mind wills it.*)

As you see, this shape you are focused on is not fingernail-shaped! It is a shape that simply is what it is. Your job is to draw the shape just as you see it, not as you know it "should" be.

Ah! now the mind rebels. How can I call that a fingernail when it isn't the "right shape"? Don't think! Don't call it by its rightful name. Just draw what you see—a shape full of nothing.

3. Next, shift your gaze to the negative space above the finger.

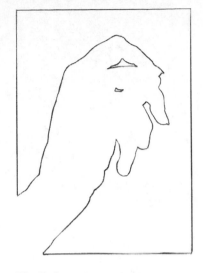

Fig. 15–6
Try to see the edges *not* drawn (of the fingers and the thumb).

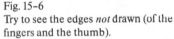

"Sometimes it is actually easier to draw the spaces and let the objects take care of themselves."
ARTHUR L. GUPTILL
Freehand Drawing Self-Taught, 1933.

King Henry to Lord Salisbury, before the battle of Agincourt:
"All things are ready, if our minds be so."
From WILLIAM SHAKESPEARE
Henry V, Act IV, Scene III.

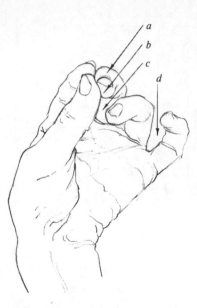

Fig. 15–7
Using *shapes* as negative spaces.
Focus on:
a. the space above . . .
b. below . . .
c. any other shape . . .
d. the space between.

Draw that shape. Look underneath the top of the finger. Find a shape to focus on. It will be part of the hand, but we can *call* it a negative space/shape. Draw that shape. You can, if you wish, continue to draw, one negative space/shape after another, or you may stop at any point. Figure 15–7 demonstrates.

Begin your drawing now.

After you have finished, regard your drawing. Notice that by simply shifting your mind-set, you can see either your finger pointing toward you in space *or* a set of negative spaces.

This is the second major use of negative space: it gives you power over space. In the exercise just done, you drew *foreshortened* fingers, a three-dimensional view of the hand in space. Foreshortening has always been difficult, for reasons that have to do with paradox: how can the strange shapes I draw on the paper be at the same time the fingers as I know them? Once more, by drawing the "easy" negative space/shapes, you have drawn the "difficult" position of the hand.

Putting It Together: Spaces and Shapes

In the next exercise, you will do a "real" drawing, a complete drawing of your own hand using the first two component skills of the global skill of drawing—the perceptions of edges and spaces. You will also experience a small start at the third skill as well—perceiving relationships and proportions.

The main purpose of doing this drawing is the opportunity it provides for you to observe your own reactions as you experience the different mind-set that the exercise requires. Try to notice as much as possible, without letting your observations interfere with the drawing. If your mind slips out of the mind-set, observe what you do to return to it. Observe any uneasiness or distress. Observe delight, satisfaction, pleasure. Observe, if possible, your concentration. If an interruption or distraction occurs, observe your reaction. All these observations will help train your mind to be able to shift at will to the different mind-set required by drawing. Again, of course, you are tricking L-mode into bowing out of the job of "seeing" what is really there. Thus, R-mode will assimilate information that might otherwise be missed and present it to the mind in the unity of vision essential in the Saturation stage of the creative process.

Before you start your drawing, read all of the instructions:

1. Arrange for a full half-hour (more if possible) of uninterrupted time. Work without a timer and simply take whatever amount of time you need to complete the drawing. The best condition for this drawing is to be without time pressure or even awareness that time is passing.

2. You will need two sheets of paper—plain bond paper is fine—and a pencil. An ordinary yellow writing pencil, No. 2, is fine, or you may want to use a softer pencil, a No. 4 drawing pencil. And you should have an eraser handy in case you want to use it.

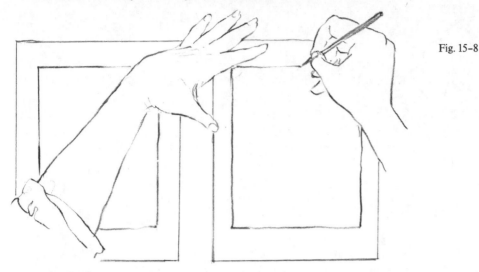

Fig. 15-8

3. Draw format boundaries on both sheets of paper, either freehand or with a ruler. The formats should be the same, as shown in Figure 15-8. You will hold your "model" hand on one sheet of the paper, and you will draw the model on the other. Figures 15-9 and 15-10 show the arrangement. When you are in a comfortable position, tape both sheets of paper to the table so that they won't shift about and distract you.

Fig. 15-9
Your "model."

Fig. 15-10
Match your drawing with your "model."

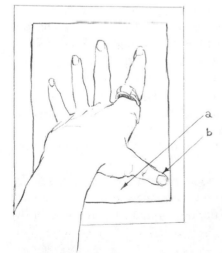

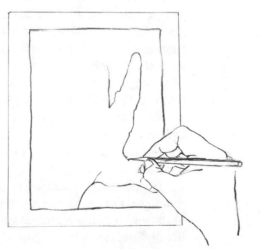

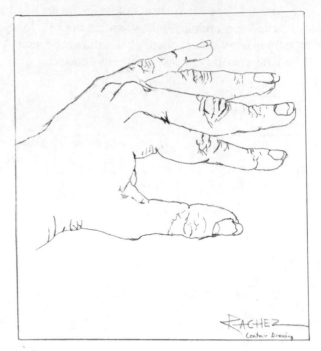

Fig. 15–11
A Modified Contour drawing by student Mark Gray.

Fig. 15–12
A Modified Contour drawing by student Rachez.

4. Arrange your "model" hand in a position that is interesting, preferably one involving some foreshortening (fingers or wrist coming toward you), and with interesting negative spaces. (Remember that you will have to hold your hand in that position steadily, so it should be reasonably comfortable.)

5. Take a moment to observe the negative spaces created by the position of your hand and briefly focus your eyes on one of them. This will start the shift to R-mode perception.

6. Observe that the format lines on the paper on which your "model" hand rests provide guides for checking angles. You can say to yourself, "Relative to that vertical edge of the format, what is the angle of the edge of my hand?" Or conversely, looking at the negative space (marked "a" in Figure 15–9), "What is the shape of the space bounded by the format and the edge of my hand?" You will notice that the negative spaces around the fingers can also be seen more easily because of the format lines that bound the model hand and the spaces around the hand.

In addition, you can begin to assess proportions. Ask yourself, for example, "How long is this finger relative to the width?" Or, "Relative to the width of the thumb at the tip, how wide is it at the heel of the thumb?"

160

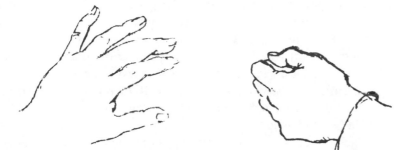

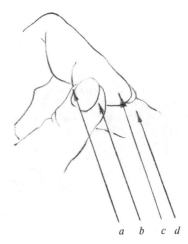

Fig. 15-13
PABLO PICASSO
Two drawings of the left hand of the artist, 1919.
Lead pencil. Private collection.

7. Notice also that any shape whatever can be regarded as a negative space. For example, the shape marked "d" in Figure 15-14 is part of the hand, but is more easily seen if the mind regards it as a negative space/shape. Since that shape shares edges with the fingers and the thumb, you will inadvertently have drawn that part of the fingers and the thumb, but it will be easy to see and draw.

Another example: the shapes around the fingernails ("a" and "b" in Figure 15-14), perceived as negative spaces, will give you better information than will the fingernails themselves. Why? Because the concept of "fingernail" is very strong, and as you have seen, known shapes are more difficult to see and draw when they are in unusual orientations that change the known shape. And since the shape *around* the fingernail shares edges with the nail itself, you will inadvertently have drawn the fingernail by drawing the shape around it—but you will have gotten it right!

In fact, if you come to any part of the drawing that seems difficult, shift immediately to any adjacent shape that can be regarded as a negative space. This is a key point, one of the magical tricks that make drawing enjoyable and easy.

8. Prepare your mind to find that these "jigsaw-puzzle" pieces will all fit together, locked into connected relationships in which each

Fig. 15-14
The shapes *around* the fingernails are easier to see than the fingernails themselves.

"piece" plays its role. Your job is to perceive these relationships and to record them as they are, without questioning why they are as they are. If you see it, believe it.

9. Proceed from edge to edge, space to space, always trying to see clearly the connecting relationships as you put the parts together. As the parts go together, you will find that they will "check out." Two lines will come together just where you expected them to, or two shapes will fit together just as you knew they would. This provides a little "kick" of pleasure, one of the joys of drawing.

10. If a line or shape "comes out wrong," don't panic. Check back on one or two previous shapes or spaces or edges to find the reason, looking for shapes or angles or proportions that don't match what is "out there." Correct any misperceived shapes, and proceed with the drawing. Remember that drawing has its own kind of logic, its own heuristics. It is not a mystery. The relationships are rational—beautifully, elegantly, esthetically logical and rational. They *fit* together.

11. Last, trust what your eyes perceive. Remember, all the information that you need is right there, right in front of you.

This is a Modified Contour Drawing, one you accomplish by drawing edges of shapes and spaces. Therefore the line will be very slow and you will record as much as possible of the detailed visual information along the edges—ideally, everything. Take your time; you will truly *enjoy* this drawing.

Begin the drawing now.

It would be interesting at this point to retrieve your Preinstruction Drawing of your own hand (the third of the set of three Preinstruction Drawings) and compare it with the drawing you have just finished. You will probably see in your Preinstruction Drawing how much perceptual information you were unaware of at the time.

After you have finished, take a moment again to bestow on your drawing a luminous moment of respect for its wholeness and harmony and for the trueness of your perceptions.

162

Reviewing Negative Space with Creative Thinking in Mind

Review now in as much detail as possible the changes in your state of mind during the drawing period. Did you lose awareness of time passing? Do you recall consciously shifting from positive shapes to negative spaces? Do you recall shifts in mind-set, where you looked at something one way, then made a conscious shift so that you perceived it in a new light? Did you experience something at first not seen, which then popped into focus *as a clear perception*? Did you experience a sense that the drawing became like an intensely interesting puzzle, whose pieces you were putting into "correct relationships"? Did you experience that small kick of pleasure when something "came out right"?

All these questions, I believe, apply to creative thinking. The point, of course, of doing the negative-space drawings is to experience these "different" modes of perception, these changes in mind-set, so that you *know* what the changes are and what they feel like. I really believe that it is impossible to actually see negative space in drawing and ever return completely to former ways of perceiving. Even the brief foregoing exercises may change your mind forever in some slight but significant way. And once experienced, perception of negative space can be used as a heuristic for thinking. Let's try it out.

Turning Now to the Problem under Investigation

In this next exercise, first take out the analog drawings you have done so far that relate to a situation or problem. If you are not working on a specific problem, you may regard your drawings as separate areas of investigation. Now looking first at your Problem Analog, regard the areas that are enclosed by lines or shapes which could be regarded as empty. Focus your thoughts on these spaces. To set them clearly in mind, you might even want to *redraw* the Problem Analog, this time drawing the shapes of the spaces *around* the problem. Or you might prefer simply to visualize the Problem Analog as a photographic negative, with the positive and negative reversed. Then, with both the "positive" and the "negative" analogs in front of your eyes, or visualized in your mind's eye, center your thoughts on the negative spaces of the drawing. Regard them as being full of information which may be easier to see and read than the positive shapes. Once you have focused your thoughts, you are ready to start asking some questions.

Question One: What is the proportional relationship of the negative spaces to the positive shapes of this Problem Analog drawing? Fitted together within the format, the parts make up a unified whole; the whole format is "occupied." How much is occupied by the problem, how much by the space? (I realize that in drawing the Problem Analog, you were not consciously drawing the spaces around the "problem." Nevertheless, by bounding the drawing with a format and then drawing

Fig. 15–15
Elizabeth Layton at her work table.

Fig. 15–16
ELIZABETH LAYTON
Stroke, 1979.
In a powerful drawing, Layton
portrayed the right side of her face,
affected by her 1979 stroke, as a
negative space.

the "objects" within, you subconsciously delineated the negative spaces. As part of the visual language of drawing, they can be "read" now in the same way you can read the problem itself. For example, you may have drawn the "problem" very large, leaving very little space around it. "Reading" this configuration might tell you that the problem is very close to you, fills your mind, and looms large in your "field of vision." Conversely, if the negative spaces around the problem are larger than the shapes of the "problem," this might indicate that the problem seems remote, perhaps unreachable.)

Question Two: Is there any positive shape within the drawing that could function as a negative space? Shifting that part of the problem to the role of a negative space may also allow you to see information presently distorted beyond recognition, just as your fingernails in fore-shortened view were changed in shape.

Question Three: What would be the result of changing the negative spaces (thereby changing the positive shapes, since the two share edges)? Can you make them larger or smaller? Can you shift the spaces from one side to the other, from top to bottom? What information about the spaces do you gain by turning the drawing (or drawings) upside down?

164

Question Four: Are there any clues for new directions of research on the problem? Have you achieved new insights? If so, as with previous drawings, bring your insights up to verbal level by titling or "tagging" the drawing.

Finally, take a mental snapshot of each of your drawings, storing them in memory as visualized negative-space images, tagged with verbal ideas, ready to join with previous images in this process of saturating the mind with information on the problem. With each new procedure, you are adding to the heuristics that will guide Incubation.

16 There Is More to Seeing than Meets the Eyeball

"Seeing is an experience. . . . People, not their eyes, see . . . there is more to seeing than meets the eyeball."
N. R. HANSON
Patterns of Discovery, 1958.

Anthropologist Edward T. Hall discusses preprogrammed closure: "There is an underlying, hidden level of culture that is highly patterned—a set of unspoken, implicit rules of behavior and thought that controls everything we do. This hidden cultural grammar defines the way in which people view the world. . . . Most of us are either totally unaware or else only peripherally aware of this.

"This was brought home to me recently while discussing Japanese [cultural differences] with a friend, a brilliant man with an unusually fine mind. I realized that not only was I not getting through to him, but nothing of a substantive nature that I had said made sense to him. . . . For him to have understood me would have meant reorganizing his thinking . . . giving up his intellectual ballast, and few people are willing to risk such a radical move."
EDWARD T. HALL
The Dance of Life, 1983.

Human beings expend great quantities of brainpower on deriving meaning from the constant jumble of incoming sensory data. The mind seems to long for conclusion, for termination, for closure—closure that most often consists of naming and categorizing, of identifying a stimulus. Each of us yearns for the moment of identification, of "Now I see it!," of the unspoken "Eureka!," whether the incoming data are important or trivial. And often closure is accompanied by some sense of relief, the degree depending on how important the identification.

Perhaps partly because of this incessant need to identify events and objects, human perception is not the receptive "Let-me-just-have-a-look-and-see-what-is-out-there" approach that we assume it to be. The visual information that falls on the retina of the eye is not necessarily what we "see." Research in perception suggests just the opposite: "Our minds are made up before the fact." Carolyn M. Bloomer in her 1976 book *Principles of Visual Perception* states the situation:

"If this view is correct, your mind does not interpret stimuli with anything like an open-minded approach. Instead, you can see things only in relation to categories *already established* in your mind. Closure does not represent objective knowledge about a stimulus but rather the confirmation of a preexistent idea. It means that on a perceptual level our minds are made up before the fact: we have the closure programmed before the stimulus happens! . . . The result is that you encounter reality with an enormous number of preconceived notions."

Obviously, these perceptual hypotheses ("perceptual prejudices," in Bloomer's term) make life simpler. If everything had to be figured out from scratch, and we paid full attention to each stimulus as if seeing it for the first time, we could never make it through the day.

The problem is that the brain's preprogramming is so all-encompassing, so ready to "jump the gun," so bent on avoiding the anxiety of "not-knowing" that it is almost impossible to turn off the program at will in order to "really" see when perception of a different kind is appropriate and useful.

Setting Aside the Brain's Programs

I am convinced that this is the chief reason drawing seems difficult: drawing requires a major effort to set aside the programs in the brain.

Let me show you some examples:

As an experiment before starting instruction in one of my classes, I requested that the first drawing of the semester be of an American flag that happened to be hanging in the classroom. The flag was on a staff, set on an angle on the wall. I asked the students to "Draw the flag, just as you see it there." Student R.F.'s drawing is shown in Figure 16–1.

"... knowledge is important for perceiving objects, that is for handling the information from the eye, but the knowledge is kind of built in—stored—and most of it is not available to consciousness. We can't juggle with it with our intellect very much to affect perception. They're almost separate processes."
RICHARD L. GREGORY in a dialogue with Jonathan Miller, "Visual Perception and Illusions," in *States of Mind*, 1983.

Fig. 16–1. "The Flag, No. 1" by student R.F., February 8, 1978.

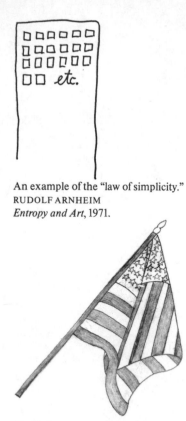

An example of the "law of simplicity."
RUDOLF ARNHEIM
Entropy and Art, 1971.

Fig. 16–2
"Flag, No. 2" by R.F., February 15, 1978.

Fig. 16–3
"Flag, No. 3" by R.F., February 22, 1978.

First: A Preprogrammed Response

R.F.'s first drawing, I believe, represents an L-mode, preprogrammed, conceptual response to the assignment. His drawing of the flag, with its simplified, rapid notation, indicates that R.F. "got it" immediately. "Flag?" he might have said to himself. "Yes, I've got 'flag.'" (One could translate that into the language of an educational psychologist: a language-linked symbol for the concept "flag," developed during the language-acquisition preadolescent period of childhood and subsequently programmed into the brain.) R.F. might have continued his internal discussion: "Here it is. Some stripes, a block of stars. Here's the staff. And an arrow at the end of the staff. There, that's it, an American flag." (Note that only six stripes are drawn, three "red" and three "white." This is consistent with the law of simplicity: just enough information to identify the concept, and no more. The stars are simplified to dots, the staff a single line.)

When the class met again the following week, I said to the students (many of whom had produced similar symbolic drawings of the flag), "Please take another look, a *closer* look at the flag. I realize that you know the stripes are really straight. They start at one edge of the flag or of the field of stars, and they go straight across to the other side. But if you really look at the stripes and the stars as the flag hangs there, what do you see?"

Second: Conception Versus Perception

I observed that student R.F. looked at the flag for a long time, and I could see that he was grappling with two conflicting views: how can stripes that are known to be straight and parallel actually cross each other at right angles? To resolve his puzzlement, R.F. must *accept* the paradox and allow his R-mode visual perception of the flag to prevail over his first, L-mode response. Looking intently at the flag, he struggled with the conflict. Then, at last, I could see "the light dawn" by the change in his facial expression. He immediately started to draw, and produced a second drawing (Figure 16–2) that was much closer to the reality of the *retinal* image—the incoming stimuli actually hitting the eyeball.

Third: Letting Reality Slip Through the Gate

The third week, I said to the students: "Fine—you've been able to let in part of the information. Now we'll try to see more. I realize that you know the stripes are all the same width—that is, from one side of the flag to the other the width of the stripes doesn't change. And I also realize that you know one star is exactly like all the others. But if you really look, what do you actually see?"

Again, R.F. looked at the flag for a long time, grappling with this new paradox, trying to set aside his conceptual "knowing" for a moment.

168

This perception took longer for R.F., and for others as well, because the information, though clearly visible, was paradoxical in a subtler and more elusive way. But R.F. finally *saw*, and again his face "lighted up" with his discovery. "They change!" he said. "The stripes change width, and the stars change shape."

Even as he said this, I could see his nerve falter, and L-mode preprogramming come rushing back to correct matters. "How can that be?" he asked. Then, shaking his head as though to clear it, he said, "I must be wrong."

"No," I said, "You saw it right. The curved surface causes the stars and stripes to change visually. If you draw the changed forms just as you see them, then, paradoxically, you will have described the curved surface of the flag. And whoever views your drawing will not notice that the stripes change width or that some stars have 'funny' shapes. To viewers of your drawing, the stripes and stars will 'look right,' but they may wonder how you managed to make the flag look 'curved.' " Reassured, R.F. then drew the flag shown in Figure 16–3—not without difficulty, to be sure; the brain's programs are not easily set aside.

A casual observer viewing R.F.'s three drawings (Figure 16–4) might conclude that he had "learned how to draw" in the three weeks. But that wasn't it at all: R.F. had learned to *see* "differently"—that is, to "see" information which was out there all the time, but which was at first simply rejected because of quick closure and premature, preprogrammed conclusions.

Fig. 16–4. R.F.'s three drawings over a three-week period.

Fig. 16–5
"Hand Holding a Cup" by student Carol Frech.

Fig. 16–6
This is the cup as actually seen by Carol—a cup with a "rounded bottom," and a perception in conflict with the concept of a "flat-bottomed cup that sits on a flat surface."

The Surprising Strength of Concepts

A second example: a drawing by student Carol Frech of her own left hand holding a cup (Figure 16–5).

The class had been in progress for about four weeks, and Carol had learned to perceive and draw edges and negative spaces. With these component skills she was able to draw her hand, the fingers coming toward her in a foreshortened view, with gratifying success. She even included a bit of light logic ("shading"), which is well done. Because we had not yet worked with sighting proportional relationships, the hand's thumb is in one scale and the fingers in a slightly smaller scale.

But the top of the cup was also perceived and drawn quite well. Despite the fact that the cup is "known" to be round, the apparent change to an elliptical shape is "accepted," perhaps because the concept requires that the cup have an opening but at the same time be in an upright position.

A collision of L-mode conception versus R-mode perception occurred, however, when Carol drew the bottom of the cup. Perceptually, this is an elliptical curve approximately the same as the near edge of the top (as shown in Figure 16–6). Carol drew the bottom, though, as a straight line, because *the cup sits on a flat surface.* Had she drawn the shape she actually saw, she would have drawn a cup with a

170

rounded bottom—*a cup that would tip over* and spill its contents. This concept of flat bottom/flat surface is very strong, reaching back into childhood conceptions—perhaps even old memories of spilled milk. Carol's error, therefore, is very common, even with much more advanced students.

Walking past Carol as she drew, I noticed the problem and suggested that she look at the cup in her hand to check the shape of the cup bottom. At first, she couldn't see the elliptical curve. I suggested that she look at the negative space under the cup. After a moment she saw it, saying, "Oh, I see—it curves."

There was a moment's pause while she grappled mentally with the paradox ("How can a cup, flat on the bottom, a cup that sits on a flat surface, have a rounded bottom?"). She looked intently at the cup for several moments. Then she erased the line she had drawn for the cup bottom, and I walked away thinking she would make the correction. When I returned, however, I was surprised to see that she had drawn the same straight line.

Carol looked puzzled. I asked what had happened and she said, "I don't know. I'll try it again." She erased the line once more, then again looked intently at the cup in her hand. An odd expression came over her face, an expression I have seen so often when students are grappling with paradoxical perceptions: eyes alternately focused first on her drawing, then on the cup, then back again to the drawing; mouth slightly open, the lips held tautly, then the lower lip caught in the teeth. She was poised tensely over the drawing, as if trying to keep her mind very still. She started to draw the cup bottom, and I could see her hand, tightly holding the pencil, start to shake, the tremor increasing as she drew the line. As I watched, she *redrew* the same straight line.

She finished the line and sat back, deflated, shaking her head a bit.

"What is it, do you think, Carol? What is going on?"

"I don't know what it is," she said. "I can see it, but I can't make my hand do it right."

I saved the drawing—it's a lovely example of the unexpected power of conception over perception, which illustrates the point made by the noted perception expert Richard L. Gregory in the margin quotation. The episode was a key insight for Carol and enabled her to overcome the difficulty in her next drawings.

Dropping a Glitch into the System

Psychologists have developed a number of ambiguous images that throw a "glitch" into the brain's preprogramming system by providing not one but two equally valid interpretations. On perceiving such an image, the brain jumps to a conclusion but then finds it almost impossible to "stick" with that conclusion, because an equally compelling alternative

"I have been told by some friends that I have a special way of looking when indulging in mathematical research."
JACQUES HADAMARD
The Psychology of Invention in the Mathematical Field, 1945.

"I think a very important point [is] that what we *perceive* and what we *conceive* can be different.
"In other words we can know that we're wrong perceptually and yet we can't correct the perception in many cases."
RICHARD L. GREGORY, in a dialogue with Jonathan Miller: "Visual Perception and Illusions," 1983.

A "glitch," as the word is used here, means an odd, bogus, unexpected, or extraneous device or bit of information that disrupts a smoothly integrated, preprogrammed, or familiar train of thought.

hypothesis forces itself to be recognized. One finds, therefore, that one's brain shifts back and forth, first to one and then to the other closure.

Since most individuals find it nearly impossible to control these shifts, I believe that the ambiguous images provide experiences at a conscious level of the kind of shift necessary to grasp alternative perceptions in drawing (or creative thinking), as experienced, for example, by R.F. (the unchangeable/changeable flag stripes) and Carol Frech (the flat/rounded cup bottom).

Paradoxical Images: First, the Vase/Faces Illusion

Let's try confronting a few paradoxical images. First the Vase/Faces drawing (Figure 16–7), introduced by Edgar Rubin in 1915. Two images can be seen with equal validity: either two profiles facing each other or a symmetrical vase in the center.

Notice that though the shapes don't change, the image *seems* to change remarkably as your mind shifts back and forth between the alternative interpretations. Notice also that the shift can occur without your willing it, and can even occur against your will, if you decide, for example, to see the vase but not the faces. Try *making up your mind* (there's a curious phrase!) to see one and not the other. If you have a feeling you have tried this before, of course you are right; seeing negative spaces requires exactly that decision, also at *conscious* level. But with the illusion drawings, you are likely to find that your brain, of its own accord and outside conscious control, keeps changing its *own* mind. Here are shapes that can be perceived with equal validity as *both* positive and negative space/shapes. If you draw one perception, you have *truly* drawn the other as well. Thus, these illusion drawings provide a nice illustration of how negative-space perception *works* and why it is such an important component drawing skill. An interesting experiment is to try drawing the Vase/Faces pattern, as suggested in Figures 16–8 and 16–9.

Fig. 16-7
The "Reversible Vase" was introduced by Edgar Rubin in 1915 and is still a favorite demonstration of figure/ ground reversal. Either a vase or a pair of silhouetted faces is seen.

An interesting experiment (Figure 16–8 and Figure 16–9).
1. Draw two horizontal lines for the top and bottom of the pattern.
2. Draw one profile—on the left side for right-handers, on the right for left-handers. (This is to leave the first profile in view while you are drawing the second profile.)
3. Complete the pattern by drawing in the second, *reversed* profile, thus inadvertently also completing the symmetrical vase in the center.
4. While drawing the second profile, notice your "state of mind," particularly any confusion or conflict you may experience.

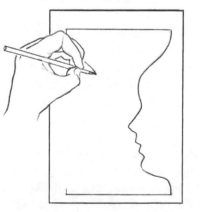

Fig. 16–8. For left-handers.

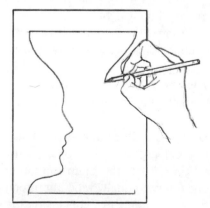

Fig. 16–9. For right-handers.

Second: The Reversing Necker Cubes

For another example of changeable perceptions, focus now on the well-known Necker Cube reversing image (Figure 16–10), which was introduced by a Swiss geologist, Louis Albert Necker, in 1832. Necker noticed that drawings of transparent crystals often seemed to change position in space in a manner uncontrollable by the viewer. As you gaze at Figure 16–10, you will see the cube change its orientation and reverse spontaneously, the inside becoming the outside, emptiness becoming solid, near becoming far, again with or without your willing it. Furthermore, the double Necker Cubes (Figure 16–11) will reverse spontaneously at random intervals, first one and then the other, or sometimes both at once, if you focus steadily on the central dot.

Third: The Duck/Rabbit Paradox

Psychologist Joseph Jastrow's ambiguous figure, Figure 16–12, drawn in 1900, can be perceived with equal validity as either a duck or a rabbit. Notice that when the identificaton shifts to "rabbit," you tend to see, in a way, a whole rabbit, even though nothing but the head is shown. Likewise, in seeing the duck, one sees, in a way, the whole duck. Remember, the lines don't change—that's obvious. And yet they *seem* different in each view. Again, note that the shifts in image can occur whether willed or not.

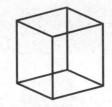

Fig. 16–10
The reversing Necker Cube.

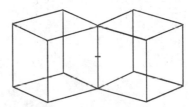

Fig. 16–11
The double Necker Cubes. Focus on the center mark.

Fig. 16–12
The "Rabbit/Duck" figure. This drawing was used in 1900 by psychologist Joseph Jastrow as an example of rival-form ambiguity. When it is a rabbit, the face looks to the right; when it is a duck, the face looks to the left. It is difficult to see both duck and rabbit at the same time.

Fig. 16–13
The "Wife/Mistress" figure.

Fig. 16–14
The "Husband/Lover" figure.

Austrian writer Robert Musil puts into words the mind-set necessary to accept ambiguous or paradoxical experiences:

"There are truths but no Truth. I can perfectly well assert two completely contradictory things, and be right in both cases. One ought not to weigh one's insights against one another—each is a life for itself."

Tagebücher, Aphorismen, Essays und Reden, 1955.

Fourth: Two Ambiguous Images

The ambiguous image in Figure 16–13 is usually called, I regret to say, the "wife/mistress" figure. (To balance matters, I sketched a second image, which I suppose in all fairness should be called the "husband/lover" figure, seen in Figure 16–14.) The original drawing, devised in 1930 by the American psychologist E. G. Boring, is a truly dramatic example of how perception can shift from one identification or closure to an altogether different one, given a cleverly constructed set of lines presenting two completely valid but very different images.

Watch what happens in your own brain as you "close in" on one or the other: either the young girl glancing back over her shoulder, wearing a necklace and a fur scarf, *or*, alternatively, an old woman—a hag, in fact—with her head sunk down into the fur collar of her coat. (I shall leave it up to you to decide which is the wife and which the mistress.) Having solved this first paradox, you will easily find the "husband/lover" images—the young man wearing a plumed hat and a ruffled shirt; the old man with a beard, wearing an old-fashioned nightcap.

On the other hand, you may experience surprising difficulty in seeing the alternative images. This may indicate that you strongly prefer unambiguous closure. Your mind, having prematurely closed on the first image, may resist further information that would invalidate the original identification. This resistance can be very strong indeed, as Carol Frech found in drawing the cup. If you cannot see the "other" figure, continue to gaze at the drawings; it will "come forward" sooner or later.

These images are strangely compelling. The mind, longing for closure, yet longing to grasp the alternative image, will search the information until it "gets it"—in the sense that R.F. "got" the changing width of the flag's stripes. When that happens, you will find yourself seeing the second figure, so to speak, *after* the brain has "found" it. What can be going on here? Perhaps R-mode is presenting L-mode with two images that can be conceptualized in two entirely different, but equally valid, ways and L-mode "can't make up its mind." In fact, even after L-mode "gets it," it can't accept the alternative images simultaneously—a very interesting phenomenon.

The Brain Yearns for Closure

In nearly every group I've worked with, a certain percentage of individuals are simply unable to "find" one image or the other, both of which are there, of course, right in front of the eyes. This is an almost-painful experience of the brain's yearning for closure. In these instances, if at last the "Ah-Ha!" occurs, the person nearly always gives an excited, irrepressible exclamation of delight and relief, shifts back to the first image, and then switches again, as though to clinch the validity of the alternative perceptions.

It seems to me that premature closure is one of the greatest roadblocks in both the process of drawing and the creative process itself. A prime requirement for the Saturation stage within which you are presently working is to keep an open mind, to go on seeking information and ideas without ever satisfying the brain's longing for closure. Just so in drawing: you must go on seeing without giving in to premature "knowing." How, then, to throw a glitch into the system to achieve an open, not a closed, mind and the unity of vision (L-mode *and* R-mode) necessary for Saturation?

Sighting: A Useful Glitch

As with the skills of seeing edges and negative spaces, the next basic component skill of drawing, the *perception of relationships* (mainly angles and proportions), helps bypass the brain's propensity to jump in with preprogrammed, premature closure. The technique for implementing this skill is simply called "sighting." It's a technique that dates back to the Renaissance and was notably illustrated by the great German artist Albrecht Dürer.

Sighting is, in fact, a telling strategy, to use Daniel Dennett's term from the anecdote in the margin on page 176. But it is the most difficult of the five basic component skills of drawing—difficult to explain

The idea of dropping a "glitch" into the system comes from philosopher Daniel Dennett. Dennett was discussing the difficulty of studying the brain's strategies of processing information:

"A nice analogy occurred to me recently. Suppose you've been given the task of catching spies. You've been told: 'We've discovered that information is getting out to our enemies about various matters, and we want you to plug those leaks; we want you to catch the spies. Well, how would you proceed?

"A telling strategy, which is also nicely analogous to many experiments in cognitive psychology, is to plant a little *mis*information at a particular place—deliberately put a little falsehood into the system.

"You casually drop in a bogus 'fact' of some sort . . . and then you see if, in a little while, the enemy shows signs of relying on that bit of information."
If that happens, says Dennett, "You're on your way to catching your spy."
DANIEL DENNETT in a dialogue with Jonathan Miller, "Artificial Intelligence and Strategies of Psychological Investigation," 1983.

Fig. 16–15
Using a paper tube to take a sighting on two objects, one close by and one at a distance.

because the process is complex, and mind-bendingly difficult to learn, at least at first. Sighting is complicated by requiring assessment of relationships and proportions, a process that *seems* more like an L-mode rather than an R-mode function. Thus, L-mode is more resistant to being persuaded out of the task. But although proportional relationships, for example, are often expressed in L-mode numbers such as 1:2—one part of this to two parts of that—they are processed mainly by R-mode, specialized as it is to deal with spatial relationships. Furthermore, sighting relationships of angles and proportions involves deep paradoxes that must be confronted and accepted—again a function better suited to R-mode, which seemingly is able to work within paradox.

Once learned, however, sighting provides a quick, simple, elegant method for putting aside the dark glass of preprograms in the brain, forcing it to give in to compelling new information and to see what is really "out there." Let's try one of the very simplest sighting techniques.

Catching Misperceptions with a Spyglass

If you happen to be in the company of friends or family, or you are in a classroom of students, or if you can walk out on a busy street, try the following. (If you are home alone, you can use two cups, or two apples, or two lamps—any objects that are more or less two of a kind.)

1. Arrange your friends or place the two objects as far as possible one from the other, one close by and the other across the room.

2. Compare the two persons or the two objects. Ask yourself, "Do they seem different in size? If so, how much different? Without measuring in any way, make a mental note of the difference by comparing the two.

3. Next, roll up a piece of typing paper and gaze through the paper tube (Figure 16–15) at the near object—a person's head, an apple, a cup, a lamp—and adjust the paper tube so that the object just fits within the circumference of the tube. (The tube, in this case, is the glitch.)

4. Not changing the size of the tube, shift your gaze to the far object. Compare the size of the far object relative to the near object as revealed by its relationship to the circumference of the paper tube. You are sure to be surprised.

5. Now, without the paper tube, regard the two objects and try, unaided, to *see* the size difference you just saw through the tube. You will probably find this difficult.

6. Then using the tube again, check the two sizes.

7. In a quick sketch, record the size differences seen through the tube, as in the example with apples set at a distance from each other in Figure 16–17.

You were no doubt surprised at the degree of size change and the struggle to "see through" the mechanism of the brain which interprets

176

Fig. 16–16
Two apples side by side . . .

Fig. 16—17
. . . and at a distance one from the other.

information to fit certain standard, or "normal," expectations, quite independently of the visual stimuli falling on the retina. Again, the brain "makes up its own mind." One aspect of this phenomenon is labeled "size constancy" by psychologists, meaning that we more or less perceive categories of objects as uniform in size, no matter how far away they happen to be. This is a useful and probably necessary perceptual mechanism for everyday life, saving us the need for attending to every slight change in apparent size caused by distance: an apple still looks "normal" whether close by or across the room.

But be prepared for another paradox: we are double-tracking all the time. While the brain is perceiving like objects as uniform in size, no matter how far distant, it also has a second track in operation which is simultaneously deciding how far away an object is by seeing how much smaller than "normal" it appears to be! Other cues contribute to this largely subconscious assessment of distance: changes in texture or intensity of color, comparison with sizes of other objects, and so on. But at a conscious level, size constancy (and color constancy and texture constancy) prevail.

At this point you may be giving a little shake of the head as did R.F. about the changing but unchangeable width of the flag's stripes. But stay with me! We'll break through this apparent contradiction just as Dürer did in his efforts to solve visual paradoxes, to gain power over space, and to achieve a bit of control over the brain as well.

Two Key Questions
Let me put the paradox another way. Apparently the human brain continually asks, among a myriad of others, two key questions: "What is it?" and "Where is it?" The first question, better suited to L-mode, requires ignoring perceptual size changes in order consistently to name and categorize objects; an apple a foot away from you is still an apple if twenty feet away, or fifty feet. You can imagine how complex life would be if

"Brains, we believe, construct predictive hypotheses of aspects of the world which are generally useful for survival. We now appreciate that most brain hypotheses, and especially perceptual hypotheses, are largely at variance with the realities of physics. Perceptions are, in any case, only approximations; there is always some error, which usually goes unnoticed."
R. L. GREGORY
Mind in Science, 1981.

In an insightful analysis, H. W. Leibowitz and L. O. Harvey pinpointed a seeming paradox in the study of size constancy and distance perception. What is the ostensible paradox? It is that size constancy demands *invariant size* over distance and yet *decrease in size* is used as a cue to distance.
HERSCHEL LEIBOWITZ
Visual Perception, 1965.

My daughter Anne, at about age 4, came with the family to take her grandmother to the airport. After saying goodbye, Anne watched her grandmother get on the plane, then watched intently as the plane flew away. Later, on the way home, she asked, "If Grandmother gets smaller when she flies away, does she get big again when she comes back?"

different names were required for apples of infinite numbers of sizes ("pinpoint-sized-apple," "apple-the-size-of-a-dime," "plum-sized-apple," and so on). Moreover, perhaps to reinforce consistency, the apples are *seen* as the same size, no matter how near or far: the actual size change is "cancelled out." The anecdote in the margin illustrates a child's puzzlement about apparent size changes which all too soon became invisible to her as well, as she grew older and the effects of size constancy took over.

The second question, better suited to R-mode, is "Where is it?" Answering this question requires perceiving size changes by somehow mentally comparing them with the known size of objects. R-mode apparently computes instantaneously and nonverbally, "According to the way that apple looks, and compared with apples as I know them to be, that particular apple is six strides away from me." This computation— and the size-change information that hits the retina—is somehow kept "secret" from conscious awareness, perhaps in order not to interfere with or complicate the language system. This hidden information comes to light only under special circumstances—a glitch in the system. The following example shows what happens when a glitch is inserted—in this case with detrimental results, because the glitch itself remained invisible for quite a long time.

First, the background (negative space!) of the situation. While you are driving at night, the headlights of oncoming automobiles all appear to be the same size, no matter how near or far a particular automobile happens to be. (Try that out, next time you drive at night.) This is the dominant, preprogrammed conscious perception—the one you are aware of, the one that is almost impervious to correction by willpower alone. Yet simultaneously, size-change of headlights (including how close together they appear) constitutes the "real" visual information hitting the retina that your brain uses at a *subconscious* level to decide how far away an oncoming car really is.

The glitch: when foreign autos were first introduced in this country, some puzzling night-driving accidents began to occur and were eventually attributed to their headlights, which were smaller and more closely set than those on domestic cars. Drivers of domestic cars, subconsciously noting small, closely set headlights on approaching cars, simply assumed (again, subconsciously) that the foreign cars were farther away! Because few people are aware of this subconscious double tracking, stunned drivers were at a loss to explain why, for example, they had caused accidents by making left turns directly in front of oncoming foreign cars.

In drawing, you are forced to grapple with problems and visual paradoxes of this kind. You cannot change the situation: your brain will continue its covert use of size-change information for distance assessment, but at the same time force you to "see" like objects as uniform in size.

British scientist and perception expert Richard L. Gregory has said that only trained artists are able to overcome the effects of size constancy (and the other constancies). I wish that were true, but I think that artists are just as susceptible as everyone else to perceptual "errors" that result from this otherwise useful brain mechanism. The difference is that artists of necessity have learned ways to gain access to the "real" information when, during drawing, the need is to see the retinal image *without change*.

Seeing and Believing: A Two-Track System

A mind-boggling example of how the brain tampers with visual information can be seen in Figure 16–18. It illustrates another apparent perceptual constancy, which could be called *concept* constancy. This constancy seemingly takes precedence, even over size constancy.

Fig. 16–18
The four figures are identical in size.

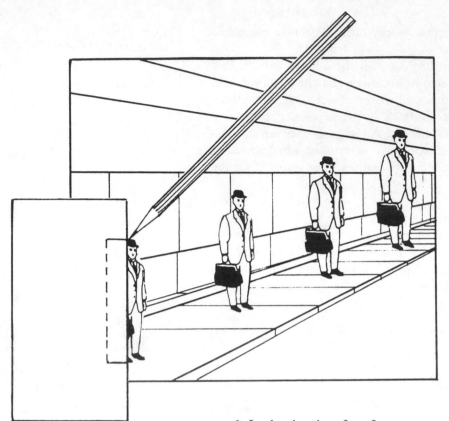

Fig. 16–19
Mark the size of one figure on a
piece of paper.

1. In the drawing, four figures appear to range in size from small to large, yet they are *identical* in size. Check that out for yourself by marking on a scrap of paper the height of the figure on the left, as shown in Figure 16–19. Then, using scissors, cut out a notch in the paper between your two marks, just the right size for the figure on the left to fit into (Figure 16–20). Now use this measuring device to check the size of the other figures. Double-check if you discover that you do not believe your own findings. You are using the device (a glitch) to put your brain into a logical box so that it can't "weasel out."

2. Next, turn the book upside down. Now—even without the measuring device—you will probably see more easily that the figures are all the same size.

3. But, turning the book right-side up again causes that farthest-away figure to grow again, *against your will*, and it is almost impossible for anyone—artist or nonartist—to overcome the effects of the brain's apparent fiddling with the "real" information. I presume that the brain's "thought" is something like this: a far away figure that appears to be as large as a nearby figure must be a great deal larger because things appear smaller as they move into the distance. It is a useful concept. The problem is that the brain, apparently, abandons its usual practice of seeing like objects (here, category "walking man") as uniform in size

Fig. 16–20
Cut out a notch the size of one figure
and measure each of the figures by
fitting it into the cut-out notch.

180

and decides to "see" the far figure as larger than it actually is in order, again apparently, to make the *concept* "truer than true." This is overdoing it!

Even *knowing* the true size of the figures doesn't help overcome the constancy effect of the concept. The converging lines that create perspective and the sense that you are viewing the silhouettes at different points in space prevail over size constancy, and in general, you cannot control these size changes. Easier by far to throw a glitch into the system—any glitch that works and enables you to "get at" the real information "out there." A measuring device, such as the one you just used, is very helpful (though the brain may ignore the measurements!). And upside-down orientation appears to be the most effective glitch of all.

But why? The conceptual clues are more or less intact in an upside-down orientation—that is, there are still four figures, and lines still converge as in a perspective drawing. Why, then, does the brain immediately stop fiddling with the visual information just because the image is upside down? This is a difficult question. And needless to say, it would be impossible to resolve the difficulty by turning the world upside down, or going through life standing on our heads. In fact, perceptual constancy is a necessity in everyday life to reduce complex visual information to manageable proportions.

But there are times when you must somehow push away what your own brain is telling you—ignore it, not give credence to its message—or you will see something that isn't really there, or fail to see something that is there. Attaining this control is essential for drawing and, I believe, for the Saturation stage of the creative process, in which information from both L-mode and R-mode, both conscious conceptions and subconscious perceptions, must be integrated into a unity of vision. The creative thinker, as well as the artist, must indeed see differently.

Another way to put it:
". . . he suffered from a hardening of the categories."
ERIN BOUMA
World Student Times, 1982.

"It begins to appear that we have, in Keith Gunderson's phrase, 'underprivileged access' to the goings-on in our own minds. We make mistakes even about what we are thinking."
DANIEL DENNETT in a dialogue with Jonathan Miller, "Artificial Intelligence and Strategies of Psychological Investigation," 1983.

17 Taking a Sight on Reason, Ratios, and Relationships

How is sighting useful in the third basic component skill of drawing, the perception of relationships and proportions? And in what ways is sighting helpful in the Saturation stage of the creative process?

In seeing relationships, sighting provides a method—a device, a glitch—that helps the mind accept competing information which may even contradict conceptual, often preprogrammed L-mode beliefs. Sighting accomplishes this by using *constants* in the environment (the parts that can't be changed), against which newly seen information can be compared and contrasted, and by providing a way to compare relationships, the relative differences of parts—to see things, as the saying goes, in proportion and in perspective.

In the Saturation stage of creativity, sighting of relationships and proportions, along with perceptions of edges and negative spaces, helps one to see beyond obvious information to other possibilities. These *other* possibilities, I believe, enrich the Incubation stage of creative thinking with original information—original in the sense that others simply may not have seen it, though it was there all the time. The history of creativity is full of instances of the one person who said, "Wait a minute! I see something different out there!"

The basic method of sighting is simply *comparison.* But for some, sighting will perhaps seem overly detailed and complicated. Drawing that has been fun and exhilarating may begin to seem more like *thinking* and *figuring out,* more like mental calculation and less like pleasurable pursuit. Let me assure you, however, that although learning sighting (that is, learning to see relationships) may seem slow and laborious, the doing of it, once learned, is as fast as lightning and as elegantly simple as an expressive gesture. Moreover, sighting is, in fact, great fun, because it endows you with the artist's repertoire of magical tricks to gain power over space.

© Field Enterprises, Inc., 1981.

The real problem is that sighting does not translate well into language. It is too complex, rather like trying to describe in words a spiral staircase or a high-wire balancing act. A complicated spatial, perceptual calculation that flashes in a split second through the brain of someone drawing could take six or eight pages of print to translate into instructions. And when *you* have learned the skill of sighting, the information will flash through *your* brain, also in an instant. But in learning this skill, as, for example, in learning a new dance step or how to play golf, you must first understand the underlying procedures, and then try it out.

Sighting *Is* Believing

I confess that in my early days of teaching, I reacted to my students' sighs and protests by passing lightly over sighting, hoping they would gain the skill somehow, by osmosis perhaps. It was a mistake, comparable in some ways to not teaching a driving student full use of the brakes or gearshift, simply because of complaints that braking or shifting was too hard to learn.

I see now that the global nature of drawing requires that none of the component skills be missing. Otherwise, the student will "crash out" and be forever plagued by inability to draw "in proportion," to draw "in perspective," or to draw "difficult" subjects such as foreshortened views. Among the basic component skills of drawing, sighting may be the most complicated, but it is also the most rewarding. And since we are transferring these skills to the Saturation stage of creativity, as well as to the process of creative thinking as a whole, the ability to grasp relationships mentally is extremely important—and, again, rewarding.

Fig. 17–1
Imagine a clear plastic grid, always held on a plane parallel to the eyes.

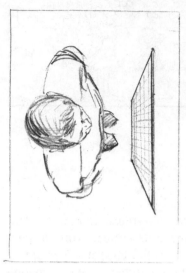

Fig. 17–2
The picture plane is aligned with your eyes . . .

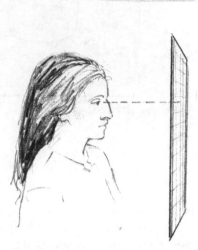

Fig. 17–3
. . . and is always perpendicular to your "line of sight."

Getting to Know the Picture Plane

A rock-bottom, basic mind-set of the artist is the first step toward grasping the skill of sighting. This mind-set concerns the so-called "picture plane."

In trying to explain the picture plane to a recent class, I said, "Imagine that wherever you go, whatever direction you turn your head, there is always a sheet of clear plastic out there in front of your face, always aligned with your eyes and always perpendicular to your 'line of sight.' Imagine further that on the piece of plastic is printed a grid of horizontal and vertical lines. Imagine one more detail: a small circle is superimposed on one of the crossbars in the center of the grid, providing a fixed point for sighting. To sight an object for drawing, imagine that you look through the piece of plastic and line up three points: your eye (the other eye is closed), the small circle on the grid, and a point you have chosen on the object. Now you have established your 'point of view,' a reliable three-point 'line of sight' relative to the object, to which you can always return during the time you are drawing."

Fig. 17–4
Eleanor's invention: a mobile sighting
device . . .

Fig. 17–5
. . . in use by student David Smith.

A wonderful exercise to help students grasp the concept of the *picture plane* was suggested by Arthur Guptill in his 1933 book on drawing:
First obtain a piece of glass about 9 x 12 inches. Facing the model (or still-life or landscape), hold the glass up with one hand and with the other draw directly on the glass, using a china-marking pencil or a felt-tip marker. When you have finished the drawing, lay the glass on a piece of paper and study the drawing with care. Then wipe off the glass with a damp cloth and repeat the entire process with another subject.
When you have tired of this somewhat limited and uncreative effort, lay the glass flat on your drawing board and slide a sheet of paper underneath it to act as a background for your marks on the glass. Place an object before you as a model, and attempt to draw its outline correctly on the glass, making your drawing a little smaller than the actual object. When you have drawn the main outlines, raise the glass to an upright position and look through it, with one eye closed, to see if you can make the drawing on the glass and the object coincide. Shift the glass if necessary. If your drawing is correct, the two images will almost exactly coincide. If not correct, errors will show plainly, and you can correct them.
By this method, you will firmly grasp that the image on the picture plane and your drawing are (or should be) *the same image.* This exercise is extremely helpful if you are working through the exercises in this book without a teacher.
ARTHUR L. GUPTILL
Freehand Drawing Self-Taught, 1933.

Eleanor's Invention: A Mobile Dürer's Device

I went on to say, half-jokingly, that an artist is a person who goes through life with an invisible plastic grid forever hanging in front of the face. One student, Eleanor McCulley, took me up on the joke and to my delight and surprise later presented me with the Rube Goldberg contraption shown in Figures 17–4 and 17–5.

Eleanor's contraption is actually a good idea and could be added to the literally dozens of similar devices recorded in the U.S. Patent Office starting in the late 1850s. All of the patented sighting devices are variations of those invented by the German artist and theoretician Albrecht Dürer in the sixteenth century. Dürer's devices, in turn, were based on previous work by earlier Renaissance artists Leone Battista Alberti (1404–72), Filippo Brunelleschi (1421–69), and Leonardo da Vinci (1452–1519).

Eleanor's device is particularly apt, however, in that the grid is held in a fixed position relative to the artist's face and eyes, thus remaining always aligned with the eyes and perpendicular to the "line of sight," a key requirement and a key concept in sighting. Her invention, therefore, is a kind of mobile "Dürer's device" and graphically demonstrates the concept of *picture plane,* the imaginary two-dimensional, transparent plane that hangs in front of the artist's eyes.

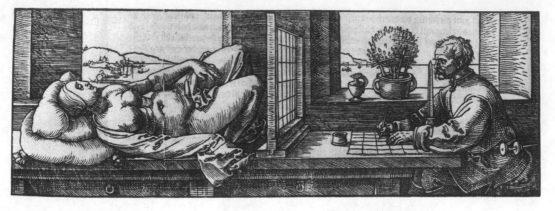

Fig. 17–6
ALBRECHT DÜRER (1471–1528)
Draughtsman Making a Perspective Drawing of a Woman, 1525.
Etching. The Metropolitan Museum of Art, New York.

Fig. 17–7
A perpendicular post guides Dürer's viewing eye.

Matching the Image Seen on the Picture Plane

The next key point is the following: what the artist sees "on" the picture plane (in our case, the piece of plastic) is what will be drawn on the paper. The image, of course, is seen *through* the clear plastic, but the word *on* fits the concept better. For the artist, in drawing the image, must imagine that it is no longer three-dimensional but is pressed flat and two-dimensional (like a photograph) on the back surface of the plastic. The artist now draws (in a sense, copies) that flat image on the drawing paper. Those two images—one the actual scene (transformed to a flat, two-dimensional image) as observed on the picture plane, the other a rendition of that scene on the drawing paper—are the *same* image. What the artist strives for is a *match* of those two images, while (paradoxically) trying to hold in mind at the same time the actual three-dimensionality of the scene.

Furthermore, the grid lines can provide some information about relationships and proportions. If you look at the Dürer woodcut, Figure 17–6, this last point may become clearer. Dürer regards his model through a grid (which could be glass with lines drawn on it, but was actually made of wires attached to a wooden frame). On the table before him is a sheet of paper, gridded in lines that correspond to the grid in front of him.

Notice the perpendicular pointed post (Figure 17–7) that guides the position of his viewing eye (the other eye is probably closed), thus ensuring a fixed point of view. (On the plastic grid described above, the small circle performs the same function as the perpendicular post.) Dürer will draw on the paper exactly what he sees through the grid, so that what he draws matches exactly what he sees, as if the figure had been pressed flat on the grid to become a two-dimensional rather than a three-dimensional image. For example, as Dürer looks at his model along his "line of sight," he might be checking to see where on the grid is the top of the model's left knee (Sighting *1* in Figure 17–8). Once he

186

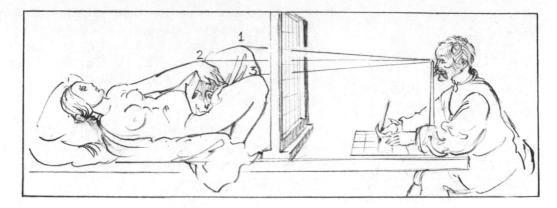

Fig. 17–8
Dürer matches sighted points on his
gridded drawing paper.

has checked that and drawn it on his paper, he can determine where, in relation to Sighting *1*, is the top of her left wrist (Sighting *2*). Then, relative to those two sightings, and, of course, relative to the grid lines, he will locate the top of her right knee (Sighting *3*).

One by one, Dürer transfers these sightings from the picture plane to his drawing without questioning why an edge is where it is, or wondering why the length of an arm or leg is so strangely different from the shapes he knows them to be. His aim is simple: to set down his direct perceptions—the information falling on the retina—without revision. At the same time, paradoxically, he retains his knowledge of the three-dimensionality of the image, but he holds that knowledge at arm's distance, so to speak.

Two Sets of Information, Locked into a Relationship

The grid provides answers to two crucial questions that recur throughout the drawing process:

1. "Relative to the constants, vertical and horizontal, represented by the grid lines and by the frame, what are the angles of (this edge, that form, that negative space)?"

2. "Relative to the size (width, height, length, etc.) of this form, as I see it from this viewpoint, how big (wide, high, long) is that other form?"

In assessing these relationships, the grid provides a glitch—an extraneous source of information—that helps (one could say, *forces*) the brain to accept perceptions *as they are* without revising them to fit preprogrammed concepts. Putting that another way: if a line slants (forms an angle relative to one of the grid lines), that's the way you draw it, even though the conceptual (L-mode) mind may protest, "How can that be? That must be wrong!" Or, seeing that in foreshortened view a forearm appears to be the same length as its width, "Come on, now! Everyone knows that forearms are always longer than they are wide!"

These protests must be pushed aside—ignored—and the perceptions accepted, even if they contradict what you *know*.

If you see it, you draw it. Then, paradoxically (and magically), the form that you drew merely as a set of lines on a flat piece of paper will be seen—that is, interpreted—by a viewer of your drawing as a "real" form in a three-dimensional space.

A Variation of Dürer's Device

A quick and easy way to try out a simple version of sighting is to look through a window with an interesting view of rooftops, a street, a row of trees.

1. Use a marker that will work on glass, such as a china-marking pencil or a felt-tip pen. First draw a fairly large format on the glass, say about 18 by 24 inches.

2. Stand in front of the window at a distance comfortable for drawing on the glass. The window will become your "picture plane" *as well as* the surface on which you will draw what you see on the "picture plane."

3. At about the center of the format, just at the level of your eyes, make a small circle to use as a fixed point (the equivalent of Dürer's vertical post.) This point establishes "eye level," also called the "horizon line," since eye level infinitely extended forward becomes at last the (horizontal) line of the horizon.

4. Choose any convenient point in the scene beyond the window, and line up the three points: your eye (with the other eye closed), the small circle on the glass, and the chosen point in the scene. This three-point lineup establishes a fixed "point of view" to which you can always return if you happen to move your head while drawing.

5. Regard the scene with one eye closed, the other at the fixed "point of view." Imagine now that the scene has been pressed forward and rests as a two-dimensional image on the outside surface of the glass.

6. Draw the scene directly on the glass, keeping your eye always at the same "point of view." Try to clear your mind. You need not think about what you are doing, in the sense of "figuring out" why a certain line slants thusly, or why the size of something seems so radically changed. *Trust* what your eye sees; it sees truly. Your job is quite simple—to draw the lines that match the image "pressed" on the outside of the glass. Don't make it difficult; it isn't. Draw the edges of forms and the edges of negative spaces, shifting back and forth from the forms to the spaces, giving equal attention to both.

7. When you have finished, step back to look at the drawing. (If you aren't three stories up, it may be possible to tape a plain sheet of paper over the outside of the window, so that you can see your draw-

In 1435, the great Renaissance artist, architect, and mathematician Leone Battista Alberti wrote a brief essay on art, usually referred to as the *della Pittura*. In his essay, Alberti pursued the idea or problem of space, one of the central issues on which rests much of the subsequent history of physics, philosophy, art, and mathematics. Alberti attacked the perspective problem from a strictly practical point of view, and experiments he called his "demonstrations" were simplicity itself.

"The basic idea is that when a man sees something through a window he can get a correct image of it by tracing its outlines on the window pane, provided that while he does this he uses only one eye and does not move his head." From *Art and Geometry: A Study in Space Intuitions* by William M. Ivins, Jr., of the Metropolitan Museum of Art, 1946.

ing more clearly.) You will see that you have drawn the scene "in perspective," without actually using the principles of scientific perspective at all. (Most artists learn the principles of perspective, then lay them aside to draw just as you have drawn, by a method called, significantly, "eyeballing.")

8. Now we come again to Dürer's device. If you wish to transfer your drawing to paper, you can draw a grid of evenly spaced lines within the format on the glass, then draw a second grid on a piece of paper (not necessarily the same size but necessarily with the same relationship of width to length). The final step is to copy the drawing from the glass to the paper, locating the shapes according to the grid, just as Dürer "copied" what he saw through his wire grid onto the paper in front of him.

Is This Really Drawing?

You may be saying to yourself, "But this isn't really drawing; this is just copying down lines." Yes, in a way. But in some sense, that's what learning to see and draw means. Through drawing, one gains a means of seeing with *direct* perception, and through seeing directly, one learns how to draw—to "copy down" what is seen. The two are interlocked. Mechanical aids simply demonstrate seeing and drawing processes that are later accomplished *without* mechanical aids.

Note that I am still speaking of realistic drawing—recording of perceptions. Ability to draw an imagined scene comes later and depends on first learning the basic skills, just as reading and writing follow learning to talk, and are in turn followed by expressive poetry and prose. Self-expression in drawing is largely manifested by the personal quality of your marks on paper, as shown in *all* your drawings, but perhaps shown most clearly in your analog drawings. This is your unique "signature," which no one can duplicate. In time, the personal expression melds with visual skills and imagined or invented forms to produce truly expressive art. After that, the goal to express the self through art can absorb a lifetime, as artists' biographies attest. Edward Hill's statement in the margin is an eloquent plea for training the eye to see as a prerequisite for expressive drawing.

If It Was Good Enough for Holbein . . .

Returning to the use of drawing aids by artists, allow me to quote from a recent catalog of an exhibition of drawings by the great sixteenth-century Dutch artist Hans Holbein the Younger, official portrait artist to the court of King Henry VIII of England.

The author of the catalog states that many of the portrait drawings reflect ". . . Holbein's use of a device for tracing the outlines of the head on a piece of glass placed between the artist and the sitter (Figure 17–9) and, though there is no proof that Holbein actually followed this

The term "eyeballing" in drawing means to draw without any mechanical or perspective aids—to simply see and draw, without quarreling with the perceptions. The opposite of "eyeballing," I suppose, would have to be called "braining," or some such term—meaning drawing what you (conceptually) know to be "out there." In between is a whole range of combinations of the two extremes.

"The student must set understanding as his goal, not self-expression; the latter will arise naturally from the former. In this light we can see that the value of the study of drawing goes beyond training professional artists. There is not one of us who could not profit from the education of our vision."
EDWARD HILL
The Language of Drawing, 1966.

Fig. 17–9
HANS HOLBEIN
Queen Jane Seymour. Black and colored chalks, the outlines reinforced with pen and ink. The Royal Collection, Windsor, England.

practice, the idea is convincing, as the method was described by Dürer in detail and was certainly current in Holbein's time. Dürer recommended its use to artists who felt unsure of their skill, but in Holbein's case the reason is more likely to be that he was in a hurry because his models were reluctant to sit for long periods. To modern minds the idea is slightly suspect as being an unfair short-cut, analogous to the use of photography."

The author goes on to say, however, that present-day audiences are not as disapproving of the use of such devices and remain somewhat unaffected by ". . . the Romantic heresy that the employment by the artist of any 'mechanical' device was a sort of *dérogation de noblesse*, and apology is perhaps no longer necessary."

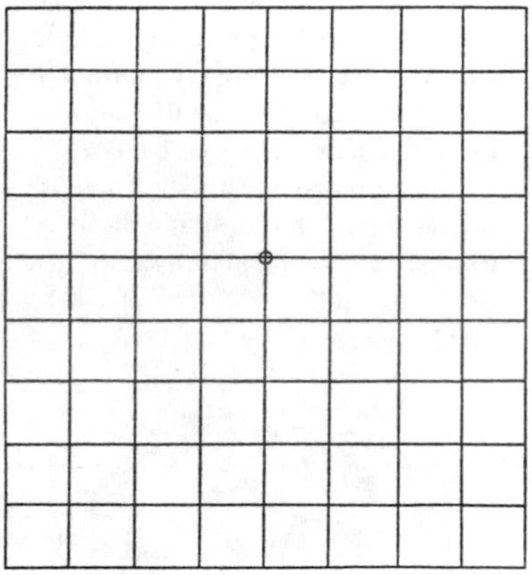

If It Was Good Enough for Dürer . . .

For a person learning perceptual skills, the main lesson gained from using a grid and drawing on glass is the concept that *the image perceived on the flat picture plane is identical with the image on the drawing paper*. A second main lesson is that drawing is easy when you set up conditions that enable you simply to see and draw what is "out there," without quarreling with your conceptual ideas about how things "should" look. Let's try it out.

You will need a plastic grid for the following exercise. It's quite easy to make a grid from a sheet of plastic, about 9 by 12 inches, heavy enough to stay upright when held by one hand in front of the eyes. The horizontal and vertical grid lines should be measured with a ruler and can be drawn with a felt-tip marker or a china-marking pencil; they should be drawn about an inch to an inch and a half apart to form squares. At the point where two grid lines cross in the center, make a small circle, as in Figure 17–10. Clear plastic report covers often sold in stationery stores make good grids. Or you may prefer to draw a grid on plain bond paper and have a transparent copy made by a photocopier. In either case, you will find the cost of a grid is minimal.

You will be using your plastic grid to draw the corner of a room, or some other view in your surroundings that you find interesting and challenging—perhaps a hallway or a corner of the kitchen. Your drawing will help you learn a skill that has two interlocked parts, each equally important: first, to see things "in proportion" or "in perspective"—meaning to see things as they really are, undistorted by conceptual ideas; and second, to see things in relation to *constants*. In drawing, the constants are vertical and horizontal, against which angles can be compared and therefore ascertained. The grid will help you to transfer the image from the picture plane to the paper. The grid supplies: (a) the format or boundary line; (b) the constants (vertical and horizontal); (c) a means of measuring relative proportions; and (d) a glitch to prevent the

Fig. 17–10
A pattern for a plastic sighting grid. The size of the grid squares is a matter of personal choice. Some individuals prefer small squares, some large, and some prefer simply one vertical and one horizontal line.

190

brain from changing or misperceiving the information.

Please read through the instructions before you begin.

1. Hold up the grid, keeping it on the same plane as your eyes—remember Eleanor McCulley's device! If necessary, hold it at arm's length with both hands, to keep the grid on the picture plane—that is, in proper (perpendicular) relationship to your "line of sight." Move about your house or office or classroom with the grid until you find a view that you like, one that interests you.

2. Once you have selected the view you are going to draw, arrange yourself comfortably at the site with a table, board, or large book to hold the paper. Tape the paper down so that it doesn't shift about. Use a pencil, and keep an eraser handy.

3. Draw a format on your paper of any size you wish, but make sure to use the same proportions, width to length, as those of your plastic grid. (You can simply place the grid on your paper and draw around it, if that size suits you.) Lightly draw a matching grid on your paper. (This you can do most easily by placing your drawing paper over the grid, matching up the edges, then tracing the grid lines onto the paper, using a ruler if necessary.)

You may feel confident enough to omit gridding the paper. It is not really necessary, now that you understand the concept of the picture plane. But there is one important point (I warned you it was complicated!). On an ungridded sheet of paper, vertical and horizontal are represented by *the edges of the paper.* No matter what position your drawing paper happens to be in on the table, the two side edges represent vertical, and the top and bottom edges represent horizontal, as seen "out there." Hold in your mind the concept that the grid lines and the edges of the two formats (on the grid and on your paper) *all represent vertical and horizontal* "out there" in the real world, providing a glitch and the constants you must have in order to "really" see.

4. Now close one eye and fix the other on the small circle in the center of the grid. Then line up that fixed point with some chosen point on the scene in front of you, thus forming a three-point "fix" on a "point of view." This three-point lineup enables you to bring the grid back to the same position for each new sighting. Remember to close one eye for each sighting of the drawing and to keep the grid on the perpendicular picture plane.

5. Check the vertical line of the corner of the room against one of the vertical lines on the grid. (It too will be vertical: vertical edges of rooms, windows, doors, and other objects always remain vertical to the eye; it is the horizontal edges—ceilings and floors and table tops—that change to oblique angles.) Draw a vertical line to represent the corner of the room.

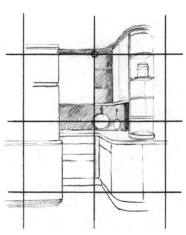

Fig. 17–11
Choose a "third point" on the scene in front of you to use for your three-point "line of sight": your viewing eye (the other eye closed), the small circle on the grid, and the chosen point "out there."

Fig. 17–12
A drawing of a room corner by student
Joe Jamilosa.

Fig. 17–13
What Joe Jamilosa saw through the grid.

6. Looking through the grid, now check the angle of the ceiling lines relative to a horizontal grid line. You may find that each angle is different. Even though you know the ceiling is *flat* and meets the walls at right angles, push away that knowledge and draw each angle just as you see it. Say to yourself, "Relative to the horizontal line on the grid, what is that angle?" Then draw the same angle on your paper *without thinking about it.* Don't make it hard; don't try to figure out why the angle is such and such. Your aim is only to see it *as it is* and to match that perception in your drawing. (Figure 17–12 shows an example of this sighting, but remember that the angles of *your* ceiling will be different if your "point of view" is different.)

7. As you progress, you will find gathered in the drawing more and more information about relationships. This progression provides redundant ways to check out any relationship; you can check the length of a line or the width of an angle against the grid, another line or another angle. This redundancy will give you confidence that your perceptions are right.

8. The lines you draw will define spaces and shapes, the drawing will go together like a jigsaw puzzle, and you may experience the feeling that the "puzzle" gets interesting as you go along. You may also experience the pleasure of realizing that you are gaining power, in a

192

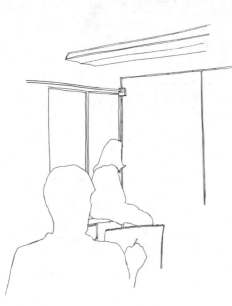

Fig. 17–14

Fig. 17–15
Student drawing: Room Corner.

sense, over space and the bafflement caused by three-dimensional images. L-mode, unable to prevail, will eventually quiet down, and at that point sighting becomes interesting—even fun.

Begin your drawing now. You can pause at any point to check back through the instructions for clarification if necessary. And when you have finished, I think you will be pleased with the discovery of just how accurately you have perceived—and drawn—that view. (Figures 17–14 to 17–16 show some student drawings of room corners.)

The Next Step: Just You, the Paper, and Your Pencil

Using your plastic grid with the necessary pauses to realign the grid and estimate the angles and proportions may have seemed somewhat cumbersome and slow. The grid, nevertheless, is a wonderful training device for the skill of sighting. You are ready now, however, to move on to a simpler, faster, and more elegant procedure in which the pencil you draw with becomes itself the only requisite aid to sighting.

Using this technique means that you need hardly pause at all to take sightings: the hand holding the pencil simply pauses for a moment, and you take the sighting by holding out the pencil at arm's length, as

Fig. 17–16
Writer and drawing student Peg Bracken chose to sight a corner that combined an antique sewing machine with a word processor sitting on top—a nice juxtaposition.

Fig. 17–17
Drawing by Alain,
©1955, 1983. The New Yorker
Magazine, Inc.

shown in the cartoon. Then the hand and pencil return to the paper and proceed with the drawing. At this point, sighting becomes quick and easy.

The point that needs to be made here is that the pencil functions as a sort of *movable grid line* (and a glitch), against which any angle can be sighted, any proportion determined, or any perception tested for validity. Thus, the pencil becomes a sort of shorthand version of the grid. Because of its elegance and simplicity, this is the method used by most artists. The only simpler method is "eyeballing"—sighting by eye— with no intervening device, which you may find yourself doing already, at least part of the time.

Let's try out sighting with only the pencil as an aid. *Please read through the directions before you begin.*

1. Persuade someone to pose for you, or, if you prefer, seat yourself in front of a mirror and be your own model. I will use French artist Edgar Degas's "Study for a Portrait of Diego Martelli" (Figure 17–18) as an instructional drawing. You will notice immediately that Degas, often called one of the greatest of all draftsmen, has gridded his drawing, as he frequently did.

Before you start your own "Study of a Model," I suggest the following quick exercise: use Degas's drawing to practice taking sightings. You can copy the drawing, if you wish, or only practice the sightings. You will then be ready to draw your model.

2. Prop the book up in front of you at eye level, if possible about

Fig. 17-18
Your "model," Diego Martelli, as seen through Degas's grid.
EDGAR DEGAS (1834–1917)
Study for a Portrait of Diego Martelli.
Courtesy of the Fogg Art Museum, Harvard. The Meta and Paul J. Sachs Collection.

three feet away. Sit in front of Degas's drawing. Draw a format edge on your drawing paper, the same proportional shape as the one in front of you. This boundary provides a more visible set of edges verticals and horizontals—than the paper edges alone. You may also want to draw Degas's grid within your format, to help assess angles and judge proportions.

3. Your hand, thumb, and pencil can function as a "viewfinder" to bound the object "out there" (Diego Martelli, in this case) by forming a right angle with your left hand (right hand for left-handers) and thumb. Then hold the pencil first in a vertical position to establish a third edge, then in a horizontal position to establish the fourth edge, as shown in Figure 17-19, forming with these movements a sort of "phantom" edge. You can move your hands closer to your eyes or farther away to "focus" the view you want to draw, fitting the model and the negative spaces comfortably within the boundary. (If you would prefer to make a "real" viewfinder, cut out a small rectangle in the center of a sheet of heavy paper, as shown in Figure 17-20. Using just the pencil and your hand-and-thumb as a viewfinder is quite easy, however, and allows you to draw without a mechanical aid.) In a second "Study of Diego Martelli," Degas changed the focus, bringing the figure closer to the viewer by drawing a larger figure relative to the format (Figure 17-21 on the next page).

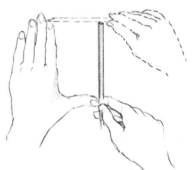

Fig. 17-19
A quick and easy "viewfinder."

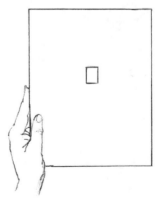

Fig. 17-20
Another kind of "viewfinder."

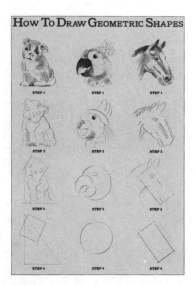

4. Returning to Degas's first "Study," take a mental note of the overall outside shape of the whole figure. This is a practice sometimes called "boxing up," that helps the artist keep in mind the general proportions and the general overall shape of the object. (Figure 17–22 amusingly reverses the procedure.)

5. To sight angles, close one eye and hold your pencil at arm's length on the imaginary picture plane (the pencil represents a "line" on the plastic grid in either a vertical or a horizontal position). Look at the angular shape between the pencil and Diego Martelli's left shoulder, shown in Figure 17–23. *Remember* that angular shape, and draw the edge of the shoulder at the same angle relative to the edge of your paper. Close one eye, check the next angle (perhaps the back of the head) with the pencil, and draw that edge. Continue to draw, moving from edge to adjacent edge, negative space to adjacent negative space. All angles can be determined by this means—a simple comparison with the constants, vertical and horizontal. And remember that you can cross-check any of these observations by shifting to the negative spaces.

6. To sight proportions, a different procedure is needed. The basic concept is that all parts of an object, a landscape, a person (a problem!) are locked into a proportional relationship which *you are not at liberty capriciously to change.* Your job is to see what that relationship is, and

to see it truly. Not what you think it *might* be, not what you think it *should* be, not what you think it *could* be, but *what it is*. We are talking about reality, what is really "out there," and of ways of seeing reality.

7. Holding your pencil at arm's length *horizontally*, place the top of the pencil at one side of the model's head, and mark the other edge with your thumbnail (Figure 17–24). Keeping your thumb in place, hold that measurement (called "one") and, keeping your elbow locked, turn the pencil vertically, and measure the length of his head (to the bottom of the beard). You will find that the relationship—the ratio—is about one to one and a half ($1:1\frac{1}{2}$) (Figures 17–25 and 17–26).

Keep that ratio in mind: $1:1\frac{1}{2}$. Now draw the head, making sure that it occupies the same proportion of the format (that is, that it is the correct size relative to the format). Degas's grid will help with that. Make sure also that the head is properly placed relative to the top edge of the format—Degas's grid will help with this also.

8. Next, ask yourself, "Relative to the length of the head, how far down is the edge of the waistcoat?" Again, take the sighting on the drawing ($1:1\frac{1}{3}$) and make a little mark to note the sighting. Use negative space to draw the arms, but be sure to sight the width across the upper arm. Go back to "one," the width of the head, and measure, "Relative to the width of the head, how wide is the upper arm?" You will find that

Fig. 17–23
Sighting an angle.

Fig. 17–24

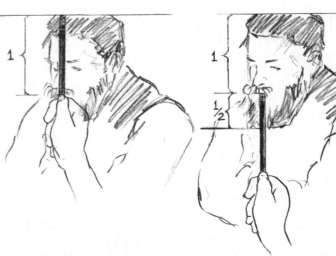

Fig. 17–25

Fig. 17–26. Sighting proportions.

Taking a Sight on Reason, Ratios, and Relationships

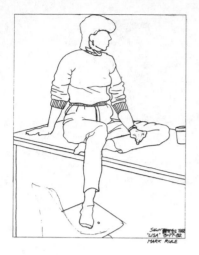

Fig. 17–27
An example of sighting in figure drawing by student Mark Rule.

Fig. 17–28
A plan and cross-section of Vincent van Gogh's room as he depicted it in his painting *Vincent's Room*, showing the artist sighting the scene by holding his paintbrush at arm's length. The diagrams are adapted from *Perspective and Other Drawing Systems* by Fred Dubery and John Willats, 1972.

the ratio is $1:{}^2/_3$. (The arm is two-thirds as wide as the head.)

9. Work your way right through the drawing, sighting any angles or proportions, always to determine *relationships*, and remember to use negative space as much as possible as a redundant check on your sightings.

After you have made the suggested practice sightings, take a new sheet of paper and start your "Study of a Model." Follow the same instructions: bound the form, using your hand-thumb-and-pencil as a viewfinder; draw a format; and begin to draw, taking any necessary sightings relative to vertical and horizontal, assessing proportional relationships, and cross-checking with the redundant negative-space information. (Figure 17–27 shows an example.)

When you have finished your drawing, I think you will find that everything "fits." And I imagine that you assessed many angles and proportions without even using the pencil-as-glitch—simply "eyeballing" the information by making quick assessments based on visual estimates; even, perhaps, easily bypassing the conceptual preprograms of the brain. R-mode is extremely fast and powerful in handling visual information (as is L-mode with verbal information). But for everyone who draws, knowing that an effective sighting procedure is always available to check "difficult" ambiguous or paradoxical views is very reassuring. Perhaps dictionaries and reference books perform the same function for writers, metronomes and tuning forks for musicians.

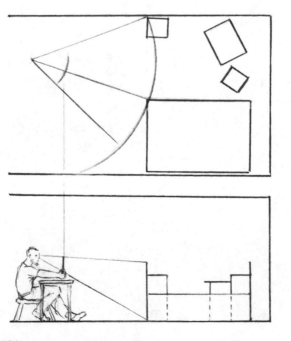

198

Drawing Away from Technical Explanations

Sighting, of course, is always approximate and subject to possible error. But the method, sometimes called "synthetic perspective," has been used by artists for centuries with satisfying results. Other systems of perspective are very useful to know, of course, and increase one's power over space. But for a beginner in drawing, sighting, when combined with the other component skills, is extremely effective. Vincent van Gogh, for example, who was largely self-taught, probably used the method in his painting *Vincent's Room* (Figures 17–28 and 17–29).

I certainly realize that all these explanations and exercises sound very technical and arithmetical and tedious. But keep in mind that at the same time you are learning the skill of sighting, you are also learning to integrate the first three component skills of drawing, the perception of edges, negative spaces, and proportional relationships. And while the complexity of drawing cannot be denied, once learned it becomes easy and almost automatic—like any other complicated, global skill.

Thinking in Proportion and in Perspective

To return now to our central concern, how do the skills of sighting relate to problem solving and the process of creative thinking? It is of obvious importance to see everything in our experience "in proportion" and "in perspective." Both proportion and perspective imply putting our perceptions in their proper relationships. They also imply their relative importance. How often have you heard these phrases: "He's blowing that completely out of proportion" or "She's completely lost perspective"?

Fig. 17–29
VINCENT VAN GOGH (1853–1890)
Vincent's Room, 1888.
Oil on canvas. Courtesy of the Art Institute of Chicago.

In either case, it would seem that a person who warrants such criticism has distorted a problem in some way—perhaps has overestimated or underestimated the importance of some part of the problem. Or perhaps the individual may be in an unrealistic *position* relative to the problem—perhaps too far away to "see" the fine details, or, conversely, too close to "see the whole picture." The visual skills of sighting, I believe, help train the mind to "measure" proportional differences and to put ourselves and our perceptions into the picture as it really exists.

Individual perceptions, of course, vary greatly. But in problem solving, constant factors are also important. Recall that constant factors by definition are things that can't be readily changed, against which other factors can be compared, measured, or contrasted. To ignore a constant, whatever the situation, to fantasize improbable changes leads to perceptual errors and ineffective solutions. Again, the visual skills of sighting help train the mind selectively to use constants against which a problem can be seen in proportion and in perspective.

Let's put this new skill of sighting to work in thinking.

Sighting Against Constants

Turn your mind to the problem at hand by taking out your Problem Analogs. *Read the following instructions before you begin.*

1. Looking at your analog drawing, ask yourself, "What are the constants of this situation—what is there as a *given* or a set of givens, facts of life that cannot be changed or manipulated which therefore help to 'set off' elements that may be changeable or impermanent?" One constant we all contend with, for example, is time. We are all allotted twenty-four hours a day, no more, no less.

2. Imagine the constants as a grid. Draw a grid on a piece of paper and label (in words) the vertical and horizontal lines. Each line may have a different label, or you may wish to work with two general labels, the equivalent of "vertical" and "horizontal."

3. Take a mental snapshot of the grid. Transform it in your imagination to a clear plastic grid. Now, in your mind, look at the problem through this grid of constants. (Or you may wish to lay the actual plastic grid used in sighting on top of your analog drawing, keeping in mind your labels for the grid lines.) Alternatively, you may wish to use a similar grid of only two crossed lines, as used by the advertising company, shown on pages 109 and 110.

4. Examine all parts of the problem in relation to the grid. What is revealed to you in terms of proportional size, placement above or below "eye level" (the midline of the grid), or to the left or right side? (Recall the importance of *placement within the format* of the Emotional State Analog Drawings.) What constant factors influence your perception of the problem as a whole? Is time a constant factor? Money? Family relation-

ships? A job? What happens to the problem if the grid lines —the constant factors—are removed? Is the problem still a problem? If not, are the constant factors the *source* of the problem? How could you come to grips with that possibility? Can the constant factors be influenced in any way? Can they be moved about, relative to the problem? For example, what happens if time is seen as *horizontal* (that is, ongoing and "tranquil"), rather than *vertical* (blocking and barrierlike)?

5. Put this new information into visual memory: the constant factors, tagged with words, and your new perception of the problem *in relation to* the constant factors.

Sighting to See Things in Proportion and in Perspective

1. Regard your Problem Analog Drawing again, or review in your mind the problem, the First Insight, and Saturation stages to date. Again using the plastic grid placed over the drawing, you will try next to see relationships between the parts of the problem.

2. Surveying the whole problem, choose one part or aspect to use as "one," against which something else (x) will be measured proportionally. Take a sighting on "one" and make the comparison: how big (important, urgent, significant) is (x) relative to "one"? Since these are nonobjective drawings (without recognizable objects), we need not use numerical ratios. Here are some important questions: What are the relative proportions of the parts of this problem? (You can assess relationships by checking them against the grid.) What "size" is your role in the problem, compared with the "size" of others? Does the problem have many small parts, or is it a large, single mass? Is the largest part high or low in the format—that is, above your "line of sight" or below? To the left of a centerline or to the right? Looking at the problem from this different, somewhat *calculating* point of view, what do you see that is new to you? Remember, sighting is a deliberate method, a *procedure*, for gaining access to visual reality. How does this new skill influence your perception of the problem?

3. Choose another aspect of the problem to use as "one," and "measure" (x) again.

4. Continue to check relational proportions until you have a good grasp of the parts that lie within the boundary of the problem. Again, take the important step of tagging your insights in writing, no matter how briefly, and then commit the new information—images and words—to memory.

Finding a Mental Glitch to Correct Misperceptions

You have just been using your plastic grid, which of course is a mechanical aid to perception, and a most effective glitch. But if you review in your mind other glitches, such as an upside-down orientation, the illusion drawings, or Daniel Dennett's "telling strategy" of dropping a bit of false information into the system to "catch a spy," you will be set to take this next step.

1. Review in your mind the principle behind using a glitch. The key point is that the brain tends to opt for the norm, what has always been tried and true, old concepts stuck in the memory, useful because they don't require fresh thinking or taking into account new information that doesn't fit the old.

2. Now, thinking again of your analog drawing and thinking of the problem it represents, search your mind for a glitch that might work with your project. Is there some bit of information that could be dropped into the system to see if it causes a new response to emerge, or if it *shows up*, so to speak, the falsity of an old response?

3. The glitch might be something as simple as a "What if . . .?" question or turning the problem upside down. Or it might be as elaborate as a hidden-image drawing, such as the "wife/mistress" or the "husband/lover." Might there be a "hidden image," equally valid, in your Problem Analog—something that looks like one thing, but turns out to be something else? For example, something that looks like "Anger" but, looked at another way, reveals itself as "Pleasure"? Something that you think is "X" but, paradoxically, can be seen with equal validity as "Y"? (Numerous scientific discoveries have appeared as "hidden images." An example is the discovery of penicillin: looked at one way, the key substance was a *mold*; looked at another way, it was a *cure for infectious diseases*.) And one further suggestion from the illusion drawings: if you gaze continuously at your drawing, might it turn itself inside out somehow, as did the Necker cubes, revealing a new perspective on the problem?

4. A famous glitch from the children's fairy tale "Snow White" was the mirror on the wall, which could only speak truly. Try holding your Problem Analog up to a mirror, thus reversing the image, and search for new perspectives on the problem.

5. If you are able to find a glitch, again "tag" your thoughts with words and commit your insights to visual memory.

Remember, sighting has to do with constants and with reason, ratios, and relationships. Having perceived the edges of the problem, having seen the negative spaces, you are now putting all that together into a relationship that is ordered and based on fresh perceptions of proportion and perspective.

Sighting as the Grammar of Drawing

Finally, imagine that you are seeing the Tweedledee and Tweedledum twins, verbal language and visual perception, side by side again. As components of each mode, I conjure in my mind that *words* in language and *edges* in perception are possible equivalents; that *context* (which helps establish meaning) in language is more or less equivalent to *negative space* in perception; and that *grammar* and *syntax* in language and *relationships* and *proportions* in perception are the third equivalent components.

If this is so—if grammar and sighting are equivalent—is it any wonder that the skill you have just learned is so often regarded as difficult and dull, just as grammar and syntax are often decried by students? And yet these skills are indispensable; language goes awry without grammar, just as drawing can founder without sighting. Learn them we must. And soon they both become automatic, integrated with the other skills, and indispensable in the accurate perception and interpretation of our experiences. In no other way can all the information, both visual and verbal, necessary to the Saturation stage of the creative process be fully assimilated.

"In the end, we will in all probability find that the way in which we think about human behavior and thought looks past—or through—such traditional divisions as artist and scientist, normal and brain-damaged, skilled or unskilled individuals.

"Yet in focusing on the arts, we may bring to light capacities and properties which have been hitherto neglected, and may discover as well that such aspects play a significant role outside the arts."

HOWARD GARDNER
"Challenges for Art," 1976.

18

Shadows that Light the Way

There is yet a fourth component skill of drawing necessary to accurate perceptions: the skill of seeing and drawing lights and shadows, a process that in art terminology is called "light logic," but that students often call "shading." What is its equivalent in language? I wonder. We speak of "highlights" in a story or novel, and of "shadowy" places. Perhaps light logic in perception is equivalent to the *setting* in language, which establishes mood, tone, and a sense of reality. So it is with light logic: "shading" establishes mood, tone, and makes things "look real," look as if they existed in space as three-dimensional objects. And unlike sighting, conceded by nearly everyone to be head-hurtingly difficult, the skill of seeing and drawing lights and shadows is truly joyful.

Learning light logic will be new learning for most readers, just as seeing complex edges, negative spaces, and relationships and proportions was perhaps also new. But this is the last of the visual skills that require teaching, since the fifth basic component, perception of the *Gestalt*—seeing the "thingness of the thing" or uniqueness of the thing perceived—emerges from the first four visual skills. The only instruction needed is to remind the reader to notice when perception of the *Gestalt* occurs, usually marked by a sudden appreciation of the uniqueness, complexity, beauty, and "rightness" of the thing being drawn.

The right hemisphere seems generally superior to the left in any task that involves complex visual recognition. These silhouette drawings, similar to those designed by Craig Mooney, test the ability to construct a whole, meaningful percept out of fragmentary information. Patients whose right hemispheres have been injured often have great difficulty in perceiving the faces in these drawings.
From COLIN BLAKEMORE
Mechanics of the Mind, 1977.

Leonardo's Device

Is there any adult, I wonder, who has not in some dreamy moment seen Viking ships and prancing horses in cloud formations, witches' heads and fire-breathing dragons in the floral wallpaper of a room? Many artists, including Leonardo da Vinci, have captured such imagined images in works of art, apparently by somehow "looking" at the imagined forms and drawing what is seen in the mind's eye.

For our purposes, we shall use this mental process that can make pictures out of coffee stains to help guide the drawing of lights and shadows. Moreover, in creative problem solving, we shall use the same mental process to help find patterns where information is incomplete or is somehow obscured.

Manipulating lights and shadows is one of the artist's most intriguing magic tricks. In this case, the trick is to supply enough information in the form of shadow shapes and light shapes to "set off" the imaging process in the minds of those who look at your drawing. Thus you, the artist, can make people see things in their imaginations that are not actually there in your drawing. In order to play this magic trick, the artist must provide just sufficient information to trigger and, in a sense, to control the viewers' imaging response.

The Magic Spell of Drawings

This is not to say that the artist is *only* laying cunning traps through the technique of imaging: it is so much more than that. The artist too is soon taken over by the image, which begins to work *its* magic spell on its maker. The image, in fact, soon begins to take on a life of its own, and imposes its will first on the artist and later on the viewers.

You will soon experience this strange crossing over of the controlling power of the image. But first, I will show you some eye-catching illustrations that illuminate the imaging response. You may have encountered these drawings before, but we'll be looking at them from a slightly different viewpoint.

Leonardo da Vinci's Device
Leonardo da Vinci wrote in his *Notebooks:*

"I cannot forbear to mention . . . a new device for study which, although it may seem trivial and almost ludicrous, is nevertheless extremely useful in arousing the mind to various inventions.

"And this is, when you look at a wall spotted with stains . . . you may discover a resemblance to various landscapes, beautified with mountains, rivers, rocks, trees.

"Or again, you may see battles and figures in action, or strange faces and costumes, and an endless variety of objects which you could reduce to complete and well-drawn forms."
Quoted in ROBERT McKIM
Experiences in Visual Thinking, 1972.

The English painter J. M. W. Turner was staying in the house of a friend who had three children. Turner had brought with him an unfinished watercolor landscape in which distant forms had been completed but the foreground was still unresolved.
Turner called the children to him and gave each a dish of water color, one red, one blue, and one yellow. He told the children to dabble color on the blank areas of the landscape. He watched intently as the children played together, then suddenly cried "Stop!"
He took the drawing, added a few details to complete the imaginary forms suggested by the children's marks, and thus the painting was finished.
From G. G. HAMERTON
The Life of J. M. W. Turner, 1879.

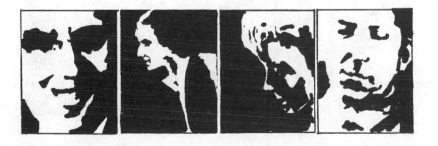

Shadows that Light the Way

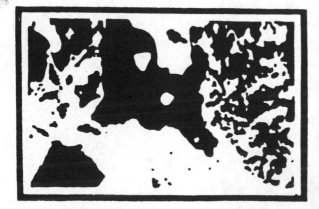

The strange-looking black shapes along the top of the page, when looked at differently, spell out the words "FLY" and "WIN." You can see the words, of course, by looking at the "negative" white spaces between the black shapes. Because one's immediate focus goes to the dark shapes, presented here as objects on a white ground, the spaces in between at first seem insignificant. Once the white spaces in between are seen as the "real" objects, however, the dark shapes recede in importance and the white letters somehow seem to acquire top and bottom edges, even though none are there. Also, once the letters are seen, you will find it quite difficult to see the black shapes once more as independent, separate objects.

Drawing on Patterned Lights and Darks

Next, look at the patterns of lights and darks in Figure 18–1. Try to watch your own brain at work as you scan the picture for meaning. The brain's drive to satisfy this quest for meaning is relentless, and to abandon the search is nearly impossible as long as the patterned lights and darks remain in view.

Once seen, however, the image seems inescapably obvious. (The picture is of a bearded man—Jesus, in some interpretations—wearing a white robe and standing against a background of foliage.)

"At some stage in the process of creation the creative product—whether painting, poem, or scientific theory—takes on a life of its own and transmits its own needs to its creator. It stands apart from him and summons material from his subconscious. The creator, then, must know when to cease directing his work and when to allow it to direct him. He must know, in short, when his work is likely to be wiser than he."
GEORGE KNELLER
The Art and Science of Creativity, 1965.

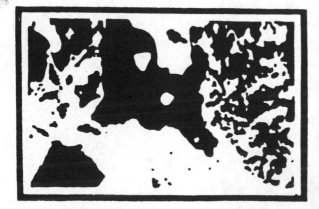

Fig. 18–1

Fig. 18–2

While we're going along in this brain-teasing direction, we may as well add the most baffling of these images, shown in Figure 18-2. Again, watch your own brain in its drive for closure. Watch as it seeks any recognizable clue, any hook to hang a meaning on. Watch also its persistence, and experience the sense of anxiety that gathers around this search for an answer.

Yes, it is a cow, standing with its head turned toward the viewer. A sketch (Figure 18-6) on the next page shows you the position, but try to see it on your own for a reasonable length of time. As with the bearded man, you cannot *not see* the image, once found, and it seems so obvious that you wonder why you were at first blind to it.

Drawing Out Images from Minimal Information

And last, an image of the most minimal information (Figure 18-3), a pattern of lights and darks that perhaps best illustrates the brain's ability to image a form complete in all its details from the barest scaffolding of suggested patterns of lights and shadows. If you can't make out the image at first, try holding the book at arm's length, squinting your eyes, and moving your head from side to side (or moving the book from side to side) while gazing at the pattern.

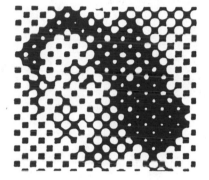

Fig. 18-3

The image will quickly emerge, and once it is perceived you will again find your brain hanging on to the "answer" as if for dear life, not allowing the image to dissolve again into a simple pattern of black and white squares and circles. Moreover, you will find yourself superimposing additional details on top of the minimal image—seeing things, in other words, that are not really there, things that help to "fill out" and complete the image. For example, you may see the young woman as smiling, looking directly at you; you may see shiny hair, high cheekbones, a sparkle in her eye, and so on.

Drawing on Shadows from the Down Side Up

Next, look at the upside-down image in Figure 18-4. You'll notice that it is somewhat difficult to decipher the image, though it can be vaguely seen as a man with his head thrown back. Notice specifically the oddly shaped black patches at the bottom edge of the image; they look quite meaningless upside down.

Fig. 18-4

Now turn the book the other way around and look at the image right-side up. Suddenly these same black patches take on form, seeming almost to disappear and to be replaced by a three-dimensional image. Can't you literally *see* the edge of the nose? There is nothing there— no edge at all. Your own brain is supplying that, superimposing an *imagined* edge onto blank paper.

Now turn the book upright once more to see again the apparently meaningless black shapes. Then look at the image right-side up again, to see one more time the imaging process at work as it changes random shapes to a solid three-dimensional form.

It's Only Light-Logical!

The drawing of Irish writer James Joyce by Augustus John (Figure 18–7) will illustrate a point that will seem quite obvious but must be stated nevertheless. It is this: when light falls on an uneven surface, the human face, for example, the shapes of the lighted areas and the shapes of the shadows are what they are because of the particular shape of the surface (the face). Given another face, lighted by exactly the same apparatus, the shapes of the lights and shadows would be different (see Figure 18–5).

From that statement, it follows logically that the reverse is true: given certain light/shadow shapes, a certain face will appear. Change those shapes and a different face will emerge. Thinking back to the hidden word images FLY and WIN, you can see the connection with the above statement: if the words were different, both the white shapes and the black shapes would be different.

Before you say, "Well, of course—that's obvious!" I must hasten to add that the most fascinating (but also the most demanding) thing about seeing and drawing lights and shadows is that each shape is unique. Nothing generalizes; no two shapes are alike. When Augustus John drew Joyce's portrait, for example, he had to see the shadow cast on Joyce's face by his eyeglasses as a *unique instance*. The shadow is the particular shape it is because of the shape of the eyeglasses *and* the shape of Joyce's face *and* the particular lighting arrangement that caused the shadow. Given another model, another pair of eyeglasses, or another kind of lighting, the shadow cast by eyeglasses would be different in each instance. Moreover, if Joyce had changed his position—say, a quarter-turn toward the artist—John would have seen an entirely *different* set of lights and shadows—although it was the same face—and each shape would have to be perceived anew and as it really was or there would be no resemblance.

This will not make your L-mode happy. As we have seen before, this kind of seeing goes directly counter to L-mode's need to find the general rule and stick to it. Furthermore, the shapes of lights and shadows as they occur on a human face, for example, have no relationship to the old symbolic forms developed during childhood and linked to words and categories (eyes, nose, mouth, ears, and so on). Yet paradoxically (to reassure L-mode), if the light/shadow shapes on the face are drawn exactly as you see them—that is, providing just enough clues about the shapes and no more—the imaging mind projects all the features onto the shadow shapes—eyes, nose, mouth, ears, and the rest! For example, if you look at Joyce's left eye, can't you see the eye, the iris, the lids, the

Fig. 18–5
Light logic. Light falls on objects and (logically) causes highlights, reflected lights, and "cast" shadows that *are what they are* because of the shape of the object the light is falling on.

Fig. 18–6

208

Fig. 18–7
AUGUSTUS JOHN (1878–1961)
Detail of *Portrait of James Joyce.*
National Gallery of Ireland.

Fig. 18–8
EDWARD STEICHEN
Self Portrait. Photograph.
Courtesy of the Art Institute of Chicago.

expression? Now turn the book upside down and look at the left eye. As you'll see, there's practically nothing there—no eye, no iris, no lids, no expression. It's just a smudge of shadow. Now, viewing the drawing right-side up again, can you see that *you* put those details into the drawing from your imagination? Best of all, your imaging mind *always gets the image right.* The artist doesn't have to draw in all the details; a couple of clues will do the job—and of course, Augustus John gave us just that and no more.

Drawing on Logical Inference

To try this out, you can draw a portrait of your own. Photographs will nicely substitute for life models, but if you can persuade someone to pose for you, that is even better. If you find no willing model, use the photograph of the American photographer Edward Steichen, Figure 18–8. Imagine that you are honored by the photographer's willingness to pose for you. Imagine further that you have arranged a spotlight so that

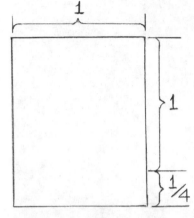

Fig. 18–9
Establish a format for your drawing. The proportional relationship, width to length, of the Steichen photograph in Figure 18–10 is about 1:1¹⁄₄.

Fig. 18–10
Prepare a smooth gray graphite ground.

it shines from above, highlighting only a few areas: the forehead; the nose; the white scarf; the hand, brush, and palette. Reflected light shines softly behind the figure, but the figure itself is mostly in shadow.

The instructions presented below relate to the Steichen photograph, but the same general instructions will apply if you are using another model.

Please read through all of the instructions before you begin your drawing.

1. Draw a format line on your drawing paper in approximately the same relationship width to length as the format of Figure 18–9.

2. Place your paper on a table, and using a hand-held pencil sharpener or a paring knife, scrape off some graphite from the pencil point, letting it fall at random on the paper. When you have scraped a sufficient amount to have a sprinkle of graphite over most of the surface, rub it into the paper with a paper-towel paid, using a circular motion. Continue rubbing, scraping on more graphite if necessary, until you have a smooth gray surface of a fairly dark tone, as in Figure 18–10.

3. Now regard the photograph of Steichen. Look at the shapes of the *lights*. Turn the book upside down if necessary to see these shapes clearly. While the book is upside down, notice that in the dark areas there is, again, very little to see—no clearly defined features at all. But when you turn the book upright, like magic, the features appear, with subtleties of expression that intrigue and mystify the viewer.

Your job in this drawing will be to duplicate this magic, providing a bare minimum of information so that the viewer (and you!) can see in the imagination features that you need not draw in. In fact, you will not even be using a pencil. Your drawing tool, to start with, will be an eraser. The eraser on an ordinary pencil is fine, or any other eraser you may have at hand.

4. You will be using all the four component skills of drawing: edges, negative spaces, relationships and proportions, and, now, lights and shadows.

Now look again at the light shapes of the photograph and take note of where they are located relative to the edges of the format. (You may lay the plastic grid from Chapter 17 over the photograph to help place the shapes and to size them correctly in relation to the whole format, or you may wish to simply "eyeball" the relationships. Remember that sighting relationships and proportions is involved in every drawing.)

5. The next step is important. Think of the light shapes of the photograph as the *letters* in the FLY and WIN patterns. In this drawing, you will erase out these "letter" shapes and leave the dark shapes, which function as negative spaces (remember the dark shapes between the letters). As a result, if you erase the light shapes of the photograph accurately, you

will have exactly described the particular three-dimensional surface of this particular face. Therefore, look very carefully at the first shape— for example, the light on the forehead; then work with the eraser until you have the shape right (Figure 18-11). Move to the next adjacent light shape—the light on the nose, perhaps—and erase that shape, placing it in proper size relationship to the first light shape (Figure 18-12). Then the light shape on the upper lip, then on the chin. And so on (Figure 18-13).

6. At each step, pull back a little from the drawing, squint your eyes a bit, or move your head back and forth, to see *if the image is beginning to emerge*, and if you are beginning to see things that aren't really there. When that happens, use the emerging image to reinforce, change, or correct your light shapes. You will find yourself shifting back and forth: drawing, imaging; drawing, imaging; drawing, imaging. At this point, you will be really seeing differently, experiencing the *Gestalt*, really drawing.

The experience is truly an amazing one. If you are drawing a person, rather than the photograph, you will surely see how beautiful that person is, seen through your eyes and mind in this different mode. If the person is well known to you, how astonished you will be that you never actually saw that person before, never noticed what beautiful eyes, what a wonderful nose, what a wonderful line of the chin! Even drawing the photograph, a sense of wonder will overwhelm you. How beautiful is this image in its mysterious lights and shadows! How beautiful is this person!

7. The image has come to life! When you have erased all the light shapes, you may wish to strengthen some of the dark areas by working over the gray ground with the pencil. Be sure to turn the photograph upside down to check on whether what you *think* you see is really there or not. Do not add unnecessary information, or you will spoil the "game."

Begin now. You will need at least an uninterrupted half-hour for the drawing.

In the Steichen photograph, a viewer *extrapolates* the features in the shadowed areas.

I have been intrigued to find that dictionary definitions of words often seem to present clues to R-mode imaging processes. The following definition closely parallels what happens in seeing into shadows:

extrapolate ek-strap'-o-late To infer values within an already observed interval; to project, extend, or expand known data or experience into an area not known or experienced so as to arrive at a conjectural knowledge of the unknown area by inferences based on an assumed continuity, correspondence, or other parallelism between it and what is known; to gain knowledge of an area not known or experienced. *Webster's Seventh New Collegiate Dictionary,* 1972.

Erasing out the shapes you *can* see (the lighted shapes) enables you to extrapolate (to "see into") the undifferentiated areas in shadow.

Fig. 18-11

Fig. 18-12

Fig. 18-13

Shadows that Light the Way

Fig. 18–14
Self-portrait by student David
Cardona.

Fig. 18–15
Self-portrait by student Carol Crofts.

Fig. 18–16
Self-portrait by student Ernie Antonelli.

Figures 18–14 to 18–16 show some examples of student drawings using the procedure described above.

Reversing the Process: Bringing Shadows to Light

Imagine that a young woman with the "head of an angel" has consented to sit for a portrait drawing (Figure 18–18). You have seated your model on a chair and you are seated on a drawing stool, thus looking down at the model who is seated slightly below your line of vision. You have arranged the lighting so that shadows play across her face (actually beautifully arranged for you by photographer Nancy Webber). Your model reminds you of Leonardo's "Angel" in his magnificent sixteenth-century painting, *Virgin of the Rocks*. (A detail of the painting showing the "Angel's" head is shown in Figure 18–17.) You have arranged your paper, pencil, and eraser on the table, and have taken a sight on the model, bounding the form and trying out various formats by using one hand as a right angle and holding the pencil to establish the third and fourth sides. Now you have decided on the format—the boundary shape that seems best for this pose—and you are ready to begin your portrait.

I will lead you through the drawing, but I suggest you read all of the following instructions before you begin.

1. Draw a format edge on a sheet of typing paper (or drawing paper, if available), duplicating the width/length relationship of the photograph.

2. Using the same process as in the Steichen drawing, shade the

212

DETAIL, HEAD OF ANGEL FROM VIRGIN OF THE ROCKS
BY LEONARDO DA VINCI

NANCY MAURER, ART STUDENT,
LOS ANGELES HARBOR COLLEGE

Fig. 18-17

Fig. 18-18. Photographic comparison by Nancy Webber.

paper with graphite, but to a fairly light tone.

3. With your pencil, lightly outline the *negative spaces* around the hair on the left side, the cheek, the chin, the neck and the shoulder. Then lightly draw in a line (called the "central axis") that passes through the bridge of the nose and center of the mouth. As you see in Figure 18-19, the central axis in this case is *slanted* (relative to the edge of your paper, which represents vertical). Next, lightly draw in a line to indicate the *eye level* (called the "eye-level line"). This line crosses the central axis. Make sure to note where these two important guidelines intersect the format edges.

4. *Do not draw in the eyes, nose, mouth, or ear.* These features will gradually emerge out of the lights and shadows.

5. Be very careful about placing the central axis/eye-level lines accurately, and be careful to note the relationship between the lower half of your model's head (eye level to chin) and the upper half (eye level to the top edge of the hair), particularly the eye-level line. The ratio, an impor-

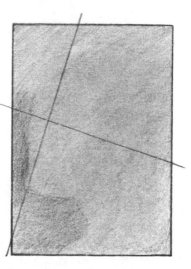

Fig. 18-19

Shadows that Light the Way

213

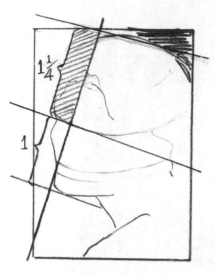

Fig. 18–20
Compare the size of the lower and upper halves of the head.

tant constant, is *1:1*. That is, for human heads the distance between the eye-level line, as measured along the central axis, and the bottom of the chin is exactly the same as the distance between the eye-level line and the top of the head. This constant applies to every adult human head with almost no variation. And since in this case you are looking down at the model from a slight angle, the ratio is $1:1\frac{1}{4}$ (Figure 18–20). Put another way, in this particular view, the features occupy *less than one-half* of the whole form of the head.

I must emphasize this last instruction, because the most frequent error made by students beginning to draw portraits is to enlarge the features by placing the eye level too high. This is a perceptual error, caused, I believe, by the brain's perceiving the features as all-important and therefore *seeing* the features as though larger than they actually are.

An example of enlarged facial features (probably deliberately done by the artist in order to emphasize the features) is shown in Figure 18–22. (The same enlargement also shows up in the student drawing (Figure 18–21) and in the face of the figure, said to be that of Jesus, on the Shroud of Turin, casting some doubt—in my mind, at least—on the divine origin attributed to the image (Figure 18–23).

6. By laying your pencil down on the photograph of your model, you can measure the relationship: in this view from slightly above the model, it is $1:1\frac{1}{4}$. You will notice that the bottom edge of the model's

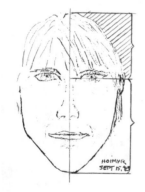

Fig. 18–21
A Pre-instruction drawing by student Haakon Hoimyr showing enlargement of the features, a typical distortion by students just beginning to learn to draw. While artists often use the distortion deliberately (as did artist Don Bachardy), beginning students are often unable to *avoid* the distortion.

Hoimyr's Post-instruction self-portrait, December 13, 1983.

214

Fig. 18–22
Compare the difference in the proportions of the model's head and the portrait head. The smile on artist Don Bachardy's face seems to invite the viewer to share the intent of the distortion. *Los Angeles Times* photograph.

Fig. 18–23
The "Shroud of Turin," a shadowed image of a figure on linen cloth, said to be the shroud or wrapping cloth of Jesus after the crucifixion. The image on the cloth is said to have been caused by contact with the head and body of Jesus. Photograph by Vernon D. Miller, 1978.

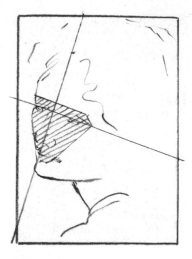

Fig. 18–24
Notice how small is the area occupied by the features.

Fig. 18–25
Erase the light shapes.

chin is slightly more than one-fourth up from the bottom of the format. Mark that point on your drawing, then mark the eye-level line, and then the top of the hair in the 1:1¼ ratio. Notice at this point what a small portion of the whole form of the head is occupied by the features (Figure 18–24).

7. Using the point of your pencil, begin to darken in the shadow shapes. Turn the photograph and your drawing upside down, if necessary, to help you see the shadows as shapes. As you work, notice that some shadow shapes are only slightly darker than the gray tone of the paper, but some are very dark—as dark as your pencil can achieve. Notice also the dark shadows in the hair. These too should be seen as shapes. At this stage of the drawing, avoid using lines if possible; try to regard even the "lines" marking the crease of the upper eyelids as *narrow shadows.* Continue to avoid drawing in the features, but begin imaging as you draw, trying to "see" the features, even though they are not yet there in your drawing. Be alert to any accidental mark that starts to "look right."

8. Next, you will use your eraser to erase out the light shapes, as in your previous drawing. Look at the photograph (and also the Leonardo painting) and ask yourself where the brightest light shape is located. You will see that it is on the eyelids, the bridge of the nose, and the cheeks. Since the lightest light you can achieve is the white of the paper, this is the area where you will erase out all of the tone you had applied. By turning the photograph upside down, you will see that this area has a definite shape, almost an oval (with some smaller lighted shapes remaining on the chin and shoulder.(Figure 18–25).

9. The darkest darks in your drawing (the dark shadow below the cheekbone, the dark negative space behind the head and so on), can be only as dark as your darkest pencil mark. In between the lightest lights (the paper) and the darkest darks is a whole range of tones, called "values." The relationships of these values are important.

Fortunately, beginning drawing students are quite good at estimating these relationships, once the two limits—the white of the paper and darkness of the darkest-possible pencil mark—have been pointed out to them. For example, the left side of your model's face is partly in shadow, the tone about halfway between the lightest light and the darkest dark of the negative spaces behind the head. Darker shadows appear, however, on the neck, under the tip of the nose, and under the lower lip; here the pencil presses harder. Notice that the lower edge of the jaw is defined by a slight edge of reflected light, but the tone here is not nearly as light as the lightest areas. Erase the tone much less vigorously here.

10. Now that you have drawn the large shape of the head, and most of the light shapes and the shadow shapes, imaging the features will come quite easily. Paradoxically, the features will look right only if the whole shape of the head is accurately drawn. Take a long look at the

photograph, and then, half-squinting your eyes, try to "see" the features in your drawing. Then make only enough marks to provide sufficient clues to trigger the imaging response. If you "lose" the likeness or the expression, don't panic. Rub the tone down again slightly, and again use your eraser and pencil to "draw out" the likeness. Have confidence that if you use the pencil to reinforce *your* imaging of the features, you will have a successful drawing.

At the same time, be careful not to overdo it! The viewer of your drawing wants to play the "game," and will "get the picture" with only a little help from you. Remember Augustus John's smudge!

11. As a final step, work over the drawing with your pencil and a small piece of eraser to bring the drawing to the desired degree of finish (Figure 18–26).

Begin your portrait now. Try to arrange for an hour of uninterrupted time. You will be absorbed by this drawing, once the struggle of integrating the complex component skills subsides and you are "just drawing." You will find yourself wanting to see ever deeper into the personality of your model with her dreamy, mysteriously *inward* expression. No doubt you will lose track of time, and somewhere in the midst of your drawing, your perception of the whole, the *Gestalt*, will occur. This experience is valuable; it will lead you to new insights into the drawing process.

When you have finished, again, bestow on your drawing a moment of esthetic appreciation. You have drawn a realistic and esthetically satisfying portrait, not as L-mode might have gone about the job, by saying, "That's an eye" and drawing a symbolic eye, but as R-mode does it, using its full range of perceptual skills—the basic skills, the basic components of drawing—and you have included as well the truly remarkable skill of imaging.

Fig. 18–26
"Draw out" the likeness from the shapes of lights and shadows.

PORTRAIT OF ANNA MEYER BY
HANS HOLBEIN

STUDY OF HOLBEIN'S PORTRAIT BY
V. VAN GOGH

ANDREA ANDERSON, CONCERT PIANIST

Fig. 18-27. Photographic comparison by Nancy Webber.

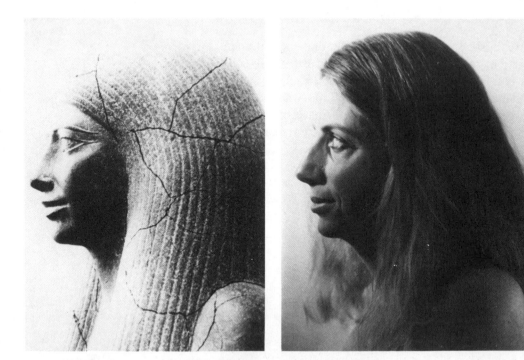

DETAIL OF SEATED STATUE OF SENNUWY FROM KERMA XII
DYNASTY, EGYPT

SUSANNA MEIERS, ARTIST

Fig. 18-28. Photographic comparison by Nancy Webber.

218

Figures 18–27 to 18–29 provide you with some additional "models" from Nancy Webber's imaginative and revealing "double images" (one, Figure 18–27, is a "triple image") to enable you to practice further the global skill of drawing. You will notice that each set of images emphasizes different components of drawing. The Holbein portrait (and Van Gogh's copy) emphasizes edges and negative spaces. It is instructive to note in Van Gogh's copy of the Holbein drawing the enlargement of the features and of the head itself in relation to the body. (You might try your hand at the Holbein in a little mild competition with the great Dutch artist.)

In contrast, the Egyptian sculpture and the uncannily look-alike model (Figure 18–28) both present light/shadow images, to be perceived and drawn by means of light and shadow shapes. Be sure to notice the 1:1 ratio of proportion of the heads, seen here in a straight-on line-of-sight view. This is a reminder that the component of relationships and proportions, of course, is embedded in all works of art, just as *grammar* is part of all writing.

And last, a more abstract image than those we have been observing (Figure 18–29). The Russian Expressionist Jawlensky has deliberately enlarged and simplified the features of the model, with great expressive effect. It would be instructive to try your hand first at a realistic rendition of photographer Nancy Webber's model (mainly a light/shadow image), then an abstraction of the features in the manner of Jawlensky. In this way, you can experience what goes on in the mind of a great artist when the goal in sight is to "abstract" the essence of the model.

Fig. 18–29
Photographic comparison by
Nancy Webber.

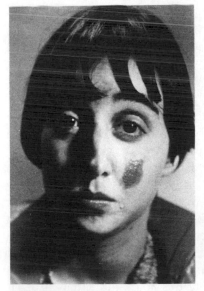

CAROL CLARK, PUBLIC RELATIONS

DREAMING HEAD BY ALEXEJ JAWLENSKY

Shadows that Light the Way

Drawing Problems out of the Shadows

The component of seeing lights and shadows rounds out your repertoire of newly acquired perceptual skills, and it also provides a new and particularly rich and profound way of thinking. The key points are that a little light thrown on any subject may be sufficient for you to extrapolate—to "see into"—the information still in shadow, and the shadows may enable you to see edges that may be "left out" at the moment.

This is accomplished by *imaging*, but note that I am not speaking of fantasy or pure imagination. Imaging that is useful in problem solving is derived from relationships of lights and shadows and is linked to reality, no matter how dimly lit. Recall Steichen's self-portrait: what is seen in the dark shadows depends on the exact nature—the reality—of the lighted shapes. Paradoxically, therefore, your ability to extrapolate into unknown areas depends on your ability to see known areas accurately—that is, without distortion.

Return now to your Problem Analog Drawings, and regard them from this new point of view. Even though you may not have included "shading" in your analog drawing, your imaging capability can come into play here. Can any of the shapes in your drawing be visualized as three-dimensional? If so, do they cast shadows on other parts of the problem? As you perceive the problem, what part is the light falling on? These are the parts that are clear to you, recognizable and unambiguous. Where are the soft shadows, shadows that do not entirely obscure the form (though the information is somewhat obscured)? Can you begin to "see into" those areas, to extrapolate from what is known in order to find out what is unknown? Where are the deepest shadows, so dark that no information is actually visible? With an effort of mind, can you find any clues whatsoever to begin to build a visualization of the configuration? What do the lighted shapes tell you about these dark areas? Is there any way to allow a little light from other areas to seep into these deep shadows?

Seeing the Problem as a *Gestalt*

As a final step, focus your mind on the problem itself as a whole, made up of many complex parts: words and concepts linked to perceptions and visualizations; edges, negative spaces, relationships and proportions, lights and shadows. You are seeing the "whole picture" as if you were going to draw it. Take a mental snapshot of it, trying to notice everything. Remember it. Allow the words you have used to "tag" your insights to flash through your mind, accompanied, if possible, by the drawings to which they were linked. Try to leave nothing out, but accept the fact that you may not see everything clearly. Try to hold all of that in mind, if only for a moment—not to attempt (premature) closure, not to find a solution right at this point, but simply to *see* it as a whole, as a *Gestalt*—the thing itself—almost in a Zen sense, without judgment. Store the image, the *Gestalt*, in your memory as a whole image.

Your mind is now saturated with this problem. You have conducted your research, gathering information up to the possible limits. You have arranged this knowledge in your mind in ways that link it to images and to visual strategies. The heuristics of perceptual thinking have provided new ways to look at the problem and new ways to submit L-mode sequenced, analytic, verbal concepts to R-mode simultaneous, analogic, perceptual synthesis. You have reached the end of the long Saturation stage; on this subject, your chosen area of research, you "know" and "see" all there is to know and see at this point.

It is time now to give your brain its instructions.

19 Drawing Close to the Magic Moment

Physicist Peter A. Carruthers, asked about his methods of research, said, "I have a very pictorial way of thinking." For Carruthers, the organizing patterns in a particular set of problems may take time to emerge, like an image on photographic film. "At some point," he says, "you suddenly see what's going on."
Carruthers' interviewer, *New York Times* science writer William J. Broad, said, "You get a feeling for the concreteness of it all in his notebooks, peppered with little line drawings and pictures."
From a series of articles on creative thought, 1981.

Poet T. S. Eliot took a somewhat different slant on Illumination:
"At these moments, which are characterised by the sudden lifting of the burden of anxiety and fear which presses upon our daily life so steadily that we are unaware of it, what happens is something *negative*: that is to say, not 'inspiration' as we commonly think of it, but the breaking down of strong habitual barriers—which tend to re-form very quickly. Some obstruction is momentarily whisked away. The accompanying feeling is less like what we know as positive pleasure, than a sudden relief from an intolerable burden."
The Use of Poetry and the Use of Criticism, 1933.

We are now approaching the crux of the matter. Your single-minded concentration on a problem or a set of problems—the long stage of Saturation—is over. The time spent on this stage is one of the requirements of creativity; First Insight, which comes into the mind with the glow of inspiration, must inescapably undergo the lengthy Saturation process.

Anxiety, another of the apparent contingencies of creativity, may have gradually descended on you during Saturation. Any possibility of solving the problem may have seemed to recede as rapidly as you gained new perceptions. Even now, having put in all that work, having looked at the problem from all aspects, having seen the subject in perspective and in proportion, having gathered the known information and composed it into a pattern of shapes and spaces, lights and shadows, you may find the sense of vagueness and anxiety increasing rather than diminishing.

The Pattern of the Process

This is all part of the process. According to the notes and journals of creative thinkers, the lengthy period of Saturation requires clear vision, patience, confidence, and courage. Interviewed in a recent article on creative thought, physicist Peter A. Carruthers said, "The *Eureka!* myth overlooks the long period of gestation for breakthroughs. Even in the vagueness and confusion, before the light comes, people know something is there, but they're not quite sure what it is yet." And as Rosamond Hardy in her book *An Anatomy of Inspiration* said of this stage, "Creation is not, in fact, always and at all times a pleasant process." Recall, for example, Charles Darwin's lengthy, exhausting search to gather information on the changes, over time, within species: years passed, and still the theory of evolution eluded Darwin. Then, at a certain moment, the key to the puzzle, the organizing principle, the *Illumination*, finally revealed itself to him.

Drawing the Threads Together

We are still some distance from that magic moment. Nevertheless, you have accomplished a great deal already. You have asked yourself the beautiful question. And in your search for the answer, you have opened your mind to see what could be seen. You have learned ways to "let in" perceptions previously overlooked. You have put a boundary around the problem, setting it off from the rest of the world. Using L-mode guided by R-mode heuristics, you have researched the problem up to the known limits at this time. You have looked at this information in new ways, searching for analogic insight. You have sought connections and patterns in the shapes and spaces that comprise the problem. You have envisioned parts of the problem that lay deep in shadow by extrapolating from parts that are sufficiently lighted to be seen. You have seen the problem as a whole. And yet . . .

The solution still eludes you. The pieces of the puzzle still do not seem to fit. Nevertheless, the mind longs for closure, while the answer stays just out of reach. And this, I believe, is the most critical moment in the creative process. You can succumb to the anxiety and give up, for fear that the problem may, after all, have no solution; or you can summon courage to accept the anxiety, keep the problem before your eyes and in your mind, and take the next uncertain step.

Incubation: The Short or Long of It

There seems to be little disagreement that the creative process *begins* with conscious efforts at creation or problem solving, but at some point in the process, often when fatigue or frustration sets in, the problem is "set aside" or "given over." The problem *shifts* to a different realm, so to speak, to develop or grow under conditions that are different from usual thinking. You are about to move to the next stage of the creative process.

The stage of Incubation—the time between the end of the search for information (Saturation) and the "Ah-Ha!" (Illumination)—can be long or short, a matter of weeks or months or years on the one hand, or an instant, on the other hand, as in musical improvisation. Writer Morton Hunt in *The Universe Within* pointed out in addition that Illumination can come as a slow-dawning awareness. For example, the seventeenth-century German astronomer Johannes Kepler experienced his discovery of the first two of the three laws expressing the movement of the planets as a slowly growing illumination. As Hunt quotes Kepler's words: "Eighteen months ago, the first dawn rose for me; three months ago, the bright day; and a few days ago, the full sun of a most wonderful vision; now nothing can keep me back. I let myself go in divine exaltation."

But much more usual is the Illumination that comes as a sudden,

Jacques Hadamard, the French mathematician, quoted the American psychologist Edward Titchener on his use of visual imagery in thinking: "Reading any work, I instinctively arrange the facts or arguments in some visual pattern and I am as likely to think in terms of this pattern as I am to think in words." Titchener continued that the better the work suits such a pattern, the better it is understood. Of his own thinking, Hadamard spoke clearly:

"(a) That the help of images is absolutely necessary for conducting my thought.

"(b) That I am never deceived and even never fear to be deceived by them."
From *The Psychology of Invention in the Mathematical Field*, 1945.

"We have learned that most of the work of the brain is done completely unconsciously, and we have come to have a healthy respect for the quality and the complexity of the computing/control functions that are carried out this way. Even in what we consider to be our conscious mental activity, we are actually aware of only a part of what is going on in the brain. There must be intricate switching and scanning processes under way that move related thoughts successively into our consciousness; we are aware of the thoughts, but not of how they get there.

"Such unconscious activity sometimes appears to extend to complicated logical thinking—how else can we account for the sudden insight or solution of a difficult problem that sometimes comes to us when least expected? Even when it seems to us that our conscious processes are completely responsible for our mental activities, we may be wrong; the real work of the brain may be that which is going on quietly behind the scenes."
DEAN E. WOOLDRIDGE
The Machinery of the Brain, 1963.

complete, and dazzling perception of the answer. The English poet A. E. Housman, speaking of his sudden intuitions, said that sometimes a whole poem came into his mind in finished form.

It Thinks

Whatever the length of the Incubation stage, it begins when it is time for your brain to "think aside," time for you to program your own brain to go to work on the problem and find a solution.

The formulation of this last sentence is deliberate, though it could also be said in the more usual way: it is time for *you* to "think aside" and for *you* to go to work on the problem. But I propose that the sentence as written is closer to the truth of the matter, that during Incubation the brain thinks on its own, in a way quite different from more ordinary kinds of cognition. The journal notes by and about creative individuals are clear on this point: Incubation proceeds while the *person* does something else.

Disagreements swirl furiously about the brain/mind dichotomy and whether it is the brain or the person that "thinks." But as anatomist J. Z. Young points out in the margin quotation, the arguments may be only semantic ones at this juncture of our knowledge of the brain. Therefore, following the lead of the creative thinkers mentioned by historian David Luft in the margin quotation, I have chosen to use the formulation "It thinks."

This formulation, "It thinks," has a somewhat different slant from the more usual idea that some unknown *something* going on in the subconscious mind eventually produces the desired illumination—the "Ah-Ha!" What I mean to imply is that the brain, focused on the problem and saturated with information linked to language but arranged in the form of visually patterned images (images such as the analog drawings), reaches a point at which the complexity and density of information is greater than can be handled in usual ways. You may have experienced some sense of this critical point in the creative process, and its accompanying anxiety, when, at the end of the last chapter, I suggested that you review the "whole problem."

This point, I believe, is somehow "recognized," and makes itself known at a conscious (L-mode) level. Beset with anxiety, the person casts about for some way out of the dilemma. "What shall I *do*? Give up? What—walk away from all that work? Something has to be done about this!" Finally, weary and perhaps even despairing, the conscious mode says, in effect, "All right. *You* find the answer." This deliberate "giving over" of the problem, I believe puts it out of conscious control, thus enabling (or perhaps *allowing* is a better word) R-mode, which is capable of dealing with enormous complexity, to "think aside." In its spatial manipulation of complicated structures, R-mode "looks at" the densely packed information simultaneously and globally, searching for "fit," seeking *meaning*, until the parts "fall into place" and the key to the *structural unity* of the data—the organizing principle—is "seen" at last.

Incubation, I therefore conjecture, is mainly R-mode manipulation of *visually structured* verbal and visual data, performed largely outside conscious awareness until that moment when the brain communicates the perceptual "Ah-Ha!" back to more conscious verbal processes. This communication translates the Illumination to a form accessible to L-mode: a *namable* image or dream, a verbal statement, a structured plot, a mathematical formula, an invention, a business strategy, or a musical theme ready for L-mode notation. In short, the solution to the problem.

The brain may even feel the solution "coming on." Some reported evidence indicates that the heart rate changes during different periods of problem solving, beating faster as the solution nears. Morris Stein, psychologist and professor at New York University, terms this "physiological awareness," and says that it occurs even when persons being studied do not yet know they have found a problem's solution.

Dropping a Letter into the Mailbox

If one can indeed initiate the mysterious Incubation stage by consciously giving the brain instructions to use the Saturation-stage information to find the solution, these instructions may vary from person to person, depending on the particular personality and, if I may say so, the relationship between the person and the person's brain.

The American poet Amy Lowell spoke of dropping a subject for a poem into her mind, "much as one drops a letter into a mailbox." From that point, she said, she simply waited for the answer to come "by return post." Sure enough, six months later she would find the words of the poem on the chosen subject coming into her head.

As another example, Norman Mailer, the American writer, in a recent interview used the term "unconscious," but his tone echoes Amy Lowell. Mailer linked his instructions to a subject he must by this time know rather well: marriage. "In writing," he said, "you have to be married to your unconscious. [If you've run across a problem in writing] you choose a time and say, 'I'll meet you there tomorrow,' and your unconscious prepares something for you."

And allow me to recount this small example of my own—actually one small part of the larger problem-solving experience of writing this book. I needed a name for the analog drawings introduced in Part II. From 1965 onward I had always called the drawings "Emotional State Drawings," for want of a better name. That unwieldy name never seemed to quite fit the concept I was trying to convey. When I started writing this book, I cast about for a more suitable name. No solution came to mind, and for lack of a name, I was forced to leave blank spaces in the

Jacques Hadamard stated that invention is *choice*—that is, choosing from available information—and that "this choice is imperatively governed by the sense of scientific beauty."
He then asked, "In what region of the mind does that sorting take place? Surely not in consciousness." Hadamard concurred with the great mathematician Henri Poincaré, who concluded that "to the unconscious belongs not only the complicated task of constructing the bulk of various combination of ideas, but also the most delicate and essential one of selecting those which satisfy our sense of beauty and, consequently, are likely to be useful."
HADAMARD
The Psychology of Invention in the Mathematical Field, 1945.

Writer Julian Duguid describes a procedure suggested to him by someone he met on board ship:
" 'You want to write stories?' he said. 'There is nothing easier. Your instinctive mind remembers every incident that has ever happened to you. . . . It will weave this experience into plots. You have only to rub the lamp.'
" 'And the technique of that?' I said.
" 'Our instinctive minds never sleep. It is the higher brain levels that are declutched each night when we go to bed. You can prove this very simply for yourself.'
" 'It sounds fascinating. What must I do?'
" 'It is fascinating. Just before you drop off, you must tell your subconscious what you want. Next morning a story will be ready for you. . . . By the way,' he said later. 'There is nothing to fear in this. . . . The slave of the lamp is your servant. . . . It is not a bad plan to call him by a name.'
"I decided that I should call the stranger within me the Helper."
DUGUID
I Am Persuaded, 1941.

And some further examples:
Julius King, a design executive for the General Motors Advanced Concepts Center in California, speaks of consulting with a "Companion" when working at creative problem solving.
King points out that Webster defines a *companion* as (1) a comrade, and (2) one employed to live with and serve another.
In conversation, Los Angeles, October 19, 1984.

Milton referred to his "Celestial Patroness, who . . . unimplor'd . . . dictates to me my unpremeditated Verse."
"The songs made me, not I them," said Goethe.
"It is not I who think," said Lamartine, "it is my ideas that think for me."
Excerpted from JAYNES
The Origin of Consciousness and the Breakdown of the Bicameral Mind, 1976.

Mathematician Jacques Hadamard quoted from a letter written to him by the linguist Roman Jakobson:
"Signs (images) are a necessary support to thought . . . the most usual system of signs is language properly called; but internal thought, especially when creative, willingly uses other systems of signs which are more flexible, less standardized than language and leave more liberty, more dynamism to creative thought."
Jakobson considered the most effective signs for creative work to be "personal signs which, in their turn, can be subdivided into constant signs, belonging to general habits, to the individual pattern of the person considered and into episodical signs, which are established ad hoc and only participate in a single creative act."
HADAMARD
The Psychology of Invention in the Mathemtical Field, 1945.

manuscript.

Several months went by. Finally, in frustration, I said aloud somewhat abruptly, "All right. *You* find it." By "you" I vaguely but quite consciously meant my own brain. I remember thinking that it felt rather good to say that—to give that instruction, to give the problem over, so to speak.

I put the difficulty aside and went to work on other aspects of the book—though still bothered, in some part of my mind, by the unsolved problem. Then one day, as I was driving to work on the freeway, thinking about something entirely different, there popped into my brain, actually breaking into my train of thought, the words "Analog Drawings." I said, "Thank you very much."

Step by Step to Incubation

To begin the Incubation process, then, you must first have reached a dead end in the Saturation stage, a point at which you can go no further in supplying information to your brain. You find yourself at the outer limit of available knowledge concerning the problem, yet no solution is in sight.

The following steps suggest ways to approach the Incubation stage, though there may be as many approaches as there are individual thinkers.

1. Assemble your entire set of drawings one last time, perhaps in a different order from that in which you drew them, so that the analog drawings—thought made visible by the pure language of line—are mixed in with the perceptual-skills drawings—realistic drawings of things seen "out there." You will see that the five perceptual techniques of drawing that you have just learned were already present in your analog drawings: edges, negative spaces, relationships and proportions, lights and shadows, the *Gestalt.* You used these techniques subconsciously and intuitively in these early drawings, knowing, at the time, more than you knew you knew. Conversely, you will also find the nonverbal language of line is present in your "realistic" drawings: placement within the format, heavy or light lines, jagged or curving shapes, expressive structural forms, again used at a subconscious, intuitive level. And you will find that your personal *style* of drawing—your unique mark—is present in all of your drawings.

Now review in your mind the visual information and the verbal interpretations your drawings have evoked.

2. At this point, take out your three Preinstruction Drawings and compare them with your later drawings. Like many of my students, you may feel almost shocked by them. Can you be the same person who drew these Preinstruction Drawings? Can you see what your "state of mind" was while you were doing the drawings (L-mode or R-mode)? See how

the visual information was translated into simplified, symbolic forms to fit with language concepts and programs in your brain? Consider for a moment how far you have come in your mastery of drawing techniques and in your ability to express yourself through drawing.

Now review in your mind the five components of drawing, and then transform them into heuristics for problem solving.

3. Then set everything aside, but focus your mind on the problem, *accepting* for the time being the inevitable anxiety that accompanies this transition stage from Saturation to Incubation. You want your brain to work on the problem; therefore, you must be willing at this point to face *not knowing* the solution. This requires a degree of fortitude, the degree depending, of course, on the problem's importance to you.

4. Now, having reviewed your knowledge of the subject up to its limits at this time, instruct your brain to find the solution you seek. The language you use for this instruction is entirely up to you. You might drop the letter into the mailbox; you might make an appointment with your brain for some date and hour in the future; or you might simply say, as I said, "All right. *You* find it."

5. You are now free to go on vacation, or to take up other work while your brain "thinks aside." The problem will stay somewhere in "the back of your mind," outside of your conscious awareness. Again, I think you can expect to experience a sense of uneasiness or anxiety, even acute anxiety if the problem is important to you. And the knowledge that this anxiety is part of the process won't help to alleviate the uneasiness. You must simply have courage enough to bear this.

Your brain will not fail you. One day, driving on the freeway or standing in the shower, the answer will come from out of the blue.

Illumination: The Exalted Moment

A curious facet of the fourth stage is that the person involved in the creative process immediately sees the Illumination as "right." Because it fits and reconciles all parts of the problem, the solution is joyfully embraced without intervening doubts or questions. In a sense, perhaps, the whole brain is satisfied with the answer. And while truly creative solutions in art, literature, and science often take additional time to realize, the idea, the strategy, the guiding principle does often arrive in a luminous moment.

Moreover, the creator often experiences a euphoric sense of esthetic pleasure at the beauty and elegance of the Illumination. Communicated back to the conscious mind, the solution's congruent wholeness, uniting the problem and its answer, seems like a work of art itself. During this magical moment, consciousness and unconsciousness for an instant become a creative unity, and Illumination lingers in memory with the rapture and delight of the moment.

Henri Poincaré, the great French mathematician, described the moment of sudden illumination that came to him as he stepped onto a tram:

"At the moment when I put my foot on the step, the idea came to me, without anything in my former thoughts seeming to have paved the way for it, that the transformations I had used to define the Fuchsian functions were identical with those of non-Euclidean geometry.

"I did not verify the idea.... I went on with a conversation already commenced, but I felt a perfect certainty. On my return to Caen, for conscience' sake, I verified the result at my leisure."

Quoted in HADAMARD
The Psychology of Invention in the Mathematical Field, 1945.

20 Drawing Power from Within

You are ready now to finish the work your imagination has begun. The creative process enters the final phase of Verification. The form of the final work depends on many factors, as varied as individuals are varied, and as diverse as fields of endeavor are diverse. I will therefore defer to the reader's expertise in his or her own field and will indicate only broad outlines of the Verification stage.

One of the functions of Verification is, as the term indicates, to check on the validity of the Illumination—to *prove* that it corresponds to reality. Given the detailed, careful preparation undertaken in the Saturation stage, the insight in most cases will prove correct and will uphold the feeling of absolute certainty that accompanied Illumination. The task of proof belongs to the conscious self, and throughout the last stage you will know, more or less, what you are doing.

The Long and Short of Verification

The time required to complete the work varies enormously. Verification can be as short as the time it takes to write down a poem or record a theorem's proof, or it can go on for years. In the case of Marie Curie, for example, verification of her brilliant prediction of a new element in pitchblende ore required years of intense labor to isolate one gram of radium salts from eight tons pitchblende. Fortunately, the euphoria and delight of Illumination linger in the memory and help the discoverer, as Madame Curie attested in her writing, to sustain energy through the last stage. Thus, the "Ah-Ha!" engenders confidence in the work, diminishes anxiety, enhances courage—and the will—to complete the project. The painting is painted, the song composed, the formula tested, the book, essay, or poem written, the experiment performed, the product manufactured, the business restructured, the advertising campaign charted; or, perhaps, a life's work begun.

During this last stage, isolation from others may not be the best circumstance unless the problem is a very personal one. If the goal of

"The creator is uniquely related to his creation; first, because he sees it as part of himself and as his personal gift to the world . . . a healthy ego requires its creations to be both communicated and accepted."
GEORGE F. KNELLER
The Art and Science of Creativity, 1965.

228

your creative project is to produce a useful new idea or product, it will at some point be put "out there" into the real world and you will hope for acceptance of your creation. The stage of Verification, therefore, can provide opportunity for testing out the product: the ideas can now be talked over with someone else, and you should invite criticism of the work. Again, courage—and faith in the work of your mind—are needed, perhaps even more at this stage than earlier. Remember, you are the care-taker of the insight given to you. If you shrink from this last stage out of fear that someone will disagree or disapprove, your creative endeavor may never take actual form.

Drawing Once More on Elements of Beauty

In Chapter Nineteen, I suggested that the logic and language skills of L-mode will come back into dominance in the last stage. For most projects, L-mode will largely control the mind-set for Verification. Never-theless, the whole aim of creativity is to produce something not only useful but also esthetically beautiful. Since Verification puts the insight into actual form, the esthetic sense of rightness and beauty will help ensure that the final product reflects the beauty revealed during the moment of Illumination. In truth, the esthetic sense seems to be deeply involved throughout the creative process, and Verification is not an exception.

I believe it is appropriate, therefore, to remind the reader once more of Aquinas' three requirements for beauty: *wholeness*, *harmony*, and *radiance*. These three can light the way for L-mode and help to amelio-rate its conscious task of Verification. Whatever product is entailed—whether writing a book, constructing a program, building a prototype machine, designing an investment strategy—truly creative work is never ugly, but is always beautiful, as Einstein clearly believed. Therefore, the heuristics of R-mode, now held in the back of the mind, are needed as guides for L-mode to *prevent the loss of beauty* while the conscious

An anecdote about Einstein:
"What I remember most clearly was that when I offered a suggestion that seemed to me cogent and reasonable, he did not in the least contest this, but he only said, 'Oh, how ugly.'
"As soon as an equation seemed to him to be ugly, he really rather lost interest in it and could not understand why somebody else was willing to spend much time on it.
"He was quite convinced that beauty was a guiding principle in the search for important results in theoretical physics."
HERMAN BONDI, quoted in G. J. Whitrow, *Einstein: The Man and His Achievement*, 1973.

The French poet and critic Paul Valéry said of Verification:
"The master has provided the spark, it is your job to make something of it."
Quoted by JACQUES HADAMARD, *The Psychology of Invention in the Mathe-matical Field*, 1945.

process moves forward step by step to a conclusion.

During the step-by-step process of Verification, then, hold somewhere in your mind Aquinas' three requirements:

First, as you validate your insight, continue to perceive the wholeness of the project, complete within its boundary line. This boundary
frames and separates the project from the immeasurable background of
space and time. Within the frame, the project is *one thing*, congruent and
unified, all parts consistent and appropriate. This is the *integritas* of
Aquinas, the unity of the whole.

Second, as you analyze and verify your project, passing from point to
point, try to perceive each part in relationship to each other part and to
the whole. Apprehend the proportion and rhythm of the structure, and
bring the parts into balance and accord. This is the *consonantia*, or
harmony, of Aquinas—the fitness, symmetry, and consonance of
the whole.

Third, use the Verification process to perceive your project as the
thing it is and no other: an original, unique product of your thinking that
did not exist before. As you give form to your idea, perceive that each
part fits together with the others as though inevitably—the only logical
and esthetically possible synthesis. This reveals the *quidditas* of
Aquinas, the radiant clarity, precision, and intelligibility of the whole.

When the last stage of Verification is completed, you—and now
others as well—will regard your creation and, seeing its wholeness,
harmony, and radiance, will experience the "luminous silent stasis of
esthetic pleasure."

Drawing to a Close

For most people, the question "How can I become more creative?" is a
deeply significant one. I believe the answer to that question lies within a
paradox: that one becomes more creative *not* by trying to be more
creative, but rather by further developing that part of the mind, the
visual, perceptual mode of the brain, which is so deeply involved in
creative thinking. I truly believe that learning to see in the artist's
mode of seeing is one of the roads that lead to the goal of greater creativity. There are doubtless other avenues, but the biographical notes of
creators are clear: visual, perceptual processes are central to creativity.

Unless one is an Einstein, gifted with visualizing powers, I believe
that any increase in perceptual skills will have a positive effect on creative
endeavors. It seems only logical that adding visual skills to already existing language capabilities stands a very good chance of increasing the
overall power of the brain.

Drawing as Empowerment

Moreover, learning to draw is truly a wonderful experience, very difficult to put into words. Drawing gives one a feeling of power—not power *over* things or people, but some strange power of understanding or knowing or insight. Or perhaps it is just the power of connection itself: through drawing, one becomes more connected to things and people outside oneself, and perhaps it is this strengthened connection which seems to signify personal empowerment.

In drawing, there is always the sense that if you can just look closely enough, see deeply enough, some secret is going to be revealed to you, some insight into the nature of things in the world. Learning through drawing, therefore, can fill a lifetime, since such secrets lie at the bottom of a bottomless well, and the searcher never wishes the search to end.

As the reader has already experienced, drawing and creativity are both replete with paradox. That the never-ending search is tantalizing yet deeply satisfying is one of the striking paradoxes of drawing. One always feels that the *next* drawing will reveal what one searches for, and the next, and the next. Another paradox is that by looking outward and seeing the world around you in the artist's mode of seeing, you gain insight into yourself. Conversely, by looking inward to find the artist within, you gain insight into the world outside yourself. These paradoxical insights, I believe, form a basis for wonder and lead one toward further creative endeavors.

Once you have embarked on the path of drawing, it becomes the most natural thing to shift frequently to the artist's mode of seeing. Your responses to people, things, and events then change in some subtle way, because you see things differently. Since whatever you draw reveals its often unexpected complexity and beauty, you become more curious and more observant, and images remain in the memory with a vividness and clarity not obtained through ordinary ways of seeing. In time, the mind becomes rich with images, a storehouse on which to draw when thinking is in progress.

But most important, perhaps, drawing can release the artist within, that part of the personality too often locked away from consciousness. The joy of releasing your true potential for creating beauty is right there, right within your grasp, if the mind wills it.

"I think this heightened sense of observation of Nature is one of the chief delights that have come to me through trying to paint. . . . The whole world is open with all its treasures. The simplest objects have their beauty. . . . Obviously, then, one cannot be bored. . . . Good gracious! What there is to admire and how little time there is to see it in!"
WINSTON CHURCHILL
Painting as a Pastime, 1950.

BIBLIOGRAPHY

Adams, James L. *Conceptual Blockbusting*. New York: W. W. Norton, 1979.

Agor, Weston. *Intuitive Management*. Englewood Cliffs, N.J.: Prentice-Hall, 1984.

Alberti, Leone Battista. *Kleinere Kunsttheoretische Schriften*, H. Janitscheck, ed., in *Quellenschriften für Kunstgeschichte*. Vienna: 1877.

Arnheim, Rudolf. *Entropy and Art*. Berkeley: University of California Press, 1971.

_____. "A Plea for Visual Thinking," in *The Language of Images*, W. J. T. Mitchell, ed. Chicago: University of Chicago Press, 1980.

_____. *Visual Thinking*. Berkeley: University of California Press, 1969.

Austin, James H. *Chase, Chance, and Creativity*. New York: Columbia University Press, 1978.

Barrett, F. D. "How to Be a Subjective Manager," *Business Quarterly*, April 22, 1976, p. 85.

Bill, Max. "The Mathematical Approach to Art," in Tomas Maldonado, *Max Bill*. Buenos Aires, 1955.

Blakemore, Colin. *Mechanics of the Mind*. Cambridge: Cambridge University Press, 1977.

Bloomer, Carolyn M. *Principles of Visual Perception*. New York: Van Nostrand Reinhold, 1976.

Bondi, Herman, in G. J. Whitrow, *Einstein: The Man and His Achievement*. Cambridge, Mass.: Harvard University Press, 1973.

Boorstein, Daniel. "Creativity in the United States." Carnegie Symposium on Creativity, Inaugural Meeting of the Library of Congress Council of Scholars, Washington, D.C., Nov. 19–20, 1980.

Bouma, Erin. *World Student Times*, March 11, 1982, p. 11.

Breton, André. *Le Manifeste du Surréalisme*, 1924, in Patrick Waldberg, *Surrealism*. New York: McGraw-Hill, 1966.

Broad, William J. Interview with Peter A. Carruthers, "Creativity," *New York Times*, 1981.

Bruner, Jerome. "The Conditions of Creativity," in *Consciousness: Brain, States of Awareness, and Mysticism*. New York: Scientific American, Harper & Row, 1979.

_____. *On Knowing: Essays for the Left Hand*. New York: Atheneum, 1965.

Champlin, Charles. *Los Angeles Times*, June 30, 1984, Part V, p. 2.

Churchill, Winston. *Painting as a Pastime*. New York: McGraw-Hill, 1950.

Cochin, Charles N. "Essai sur la vie de Chardin" (1780), published in Précis analytique des travaux de l'Académie des Sciences, Belles-Lettres et Arts de Rouen, *Beaurepaire*, Vol. LXXVIII, 1875–76, pp. 417–41.

Connolly, Cyril. *Previous Convictions*. New York: Harper & Row, 1963.

_____. *The Unquiet Grave*. New York: Harper & Brothers, 1945.

Darwin, Charles. *The Life and Letters of Charles Darwin*, Francis Darwin, ed. 1887.

Dubery, John and John Willats. *Perspective and Other Drawing Systems*. New York: Van Nostrand Reinhold, 1972.

Duguid, J. *I Am Persuaded*. London: Jonathan Cape, 1941.

Edwards, B. *Drawing on the Right Side of the Brain*. Los Angeles: J. P. Tarcher, 1979.

Einstein A., and L. Infeld. *The Evolution of Physics*. New York: Simon and Schuster, 1938.

Einstein, Hans Albert, in G. J. Whitrow, *Einstein: The Man and His Achievement*. Quoted in *Einstein: A Centenary Volume*, A. P. French, ed. Cambridge, Mass.: Harvard University Press, 1979.

Eliot, T. S. *The Use of Poetry and the Use of Criticism*. London: Faber & Faber, 1933.

Emerson, Ralph Waldo. "Self-Reliance." 1844.

Field, Joanna. *A Life of One's Own*. London: Chatto and Windus, 1936; Los Angeles: J. P. Tarcher, 1981.

Franck, Frederick. *The Zen of Seeing*. New York: Random House, 1973.

French, A. P., ed. *Einstein: A Centenary Volume*. Cambridge, Mass.: Harvard University Press, 1979.

Gardner, Howard. "Challenges for Art," *Scientific Aesthetics*, Plenum Press, June, 1976, Vol. 1, No. 1, p. 31.

_____. *The Shattered Mind*. New York: Alfred A. Knopf, 1975.

Geshwind, Norman. "Specializations in the Human Brain," in *The Brain*. San Francisco: Scientific American, W. H. Freeman & Co., 1979.

Getzels, J. W. "The Psychology of Creativity." Carnegie Symposium on Creativity, Inaugural Meeting of the Library of Congress Council of Scholars, Nov. 19–20, 1980.

Ghiselin, Brewster, ed. *The Creative Process*. Berkeley: University of California Press, 1952.

Gilchrist, A. *Life of William Blake*, 2 vols. London: Macmillan & Co., Ltd., 1880.

Goldstein, Nathan. *The Art of Responsive Drawing*. Englewood Cliffs, N. J.: Prentice-Hall, 1973.

Gollwitzer, Gerhard. *The Joy of Drawing*. New York: Sterling Publishing Co., 1963.

Gregory, R. L. "The Grammar of Vision," *The Listener*, 83:242, 1981.

_____. *Mind in Science*. Cambridge: Cambridge University Press, 1981.

Guilford, J. P. "The Psychology of Creativity," *Creative Crafts* (no date), 6015 Santa Monica Blvd., Los Angeles, Calif. 90038.

Gunderson, Keith. "Asymmetries and Mind–Body Perplexities," in D. N. Rosenthal, ed., *Materialism and the Mind–Body Problem*. Englewood Cliffs, N.J.: Prentice-Hall, 1971.

Guptill, Arthur L. *Freehand Drawing Self-Taught*. New York: Harper & Brothers, 1933. Reissued, New York: Watson-Guptill, 1980.

Hadamard, Jacques. *The Psychology of Invention in the Mathematical Field*. New York: Dover, 1945.

Hall, Edward T. *The Dance of Life*. New York: Doubleday, 1983.

Hamerton, G. G. *The Life of J. M. W. Turner, R.A.* London: Seeley, Jackson & Halliday, 1879.

Hanks, K. and J. Parry. *Wake Up Your Creative Genius*. Los Altos, Calif.: William Kaufmann, 1983.

Hanson, N. R. *Patterns of Discovery*. Cambridge: Cambridge University Press, 1958.

Harding, Rosamond. *An Anatomy of Inspiration*. Cambridge: Heffer & Sons, Ltd., 1948.

Harrison, Andrew. *Making and Thinking*. Indianapolis: Hackett Publishing Co., 1978.

Hill, Edward. *The Language of Drawing*. Englewood Cliffs, N.J.: Prentice-Hall, 1966.

Holbein and the Court of Henry VIII. Catalog for the Exhibition, The Queen's Gallery, Buckingham Palace. London: Lund Humphries, 1978–79.

Holton, Gerard. "On Tracing the Nascent Moment." Carnegie Symposium on Creativity, Inaugural Meeting of the Library of Congress Council of Scholars, Washington, D.C., Nov. 19–20, 1980.

Hunt, Morton. *The Universe Within*. New York: Simon and Schuster, 1982.

Hutton, E. H. *Einstein: The Man and His Achievement*. Quoted in *Einstein: A Centenary Volume*, A. P. French, ed. Cambridge, Mass.: Harvard University Press, 1979.

Huxley, Aldous. *The Doors of Perception*. New York: Harper & Row, 1954.

Ivens, William J., Jr. *Art and Geometry: A Study in Space Intuitions*. New York: Dover Publications, 1946.

Jaynes, Julian. *The Origin of Consciousness in the Breakdown of the Bicameral Mind*. Boston: Houghton Mifflin, 1976.

Kandinsky, Wassily. *Concerning the Spiritual in Art*. New York: Wittenborn, 1947.

_____. *Point and Line to Plane*. New York: Solomon Guggenheim Foundation, 1947.

Kenyon, F. G. *Life and Letters of Robert Browning*. London: Smith, Elder and Co., 1908.

Kierkegaard, Søren. *Philosophical Fragments* (1844), David F. Swenson, trans. Princeton, N.J.: Princeton University Press, 1962.

Kimmelman, Michael. Interview with John Elderfield, *Art News*, May, 1984, p. 73.

Klee, Paul. *Altes Fräulein*, 1931. Paris: Spadem, 1976.

Kneller, George. *The Art and Science of Creativity*. New York: Holt, Rinehart and Winston, 1965.

Koestler, Arthur. "The Act of Creation," 1964. Quoted in K. Hanks and J. Parry, *Wake Up Your Creative Genius*. Los Altos, Calif.: William Kauffmann, Inc., 1983.

Krishnamurti, J. *You Are the World*. New York: Harper & Row, 1972.

Kronsky, Betty J. "Freeing the Creative Process: The Relevance of Gestalt," *Arts Psychotherapy*, Pergamon Press, Ltd., Vol. 6, 1979, pp. 233–40.

Kubie, L. S. *Neurotic Distortion of the Creative Process*. New York: Farrar, Straus & Giroux, 1961.

Langer, Suzanne K. *Philosophy in a New Key*. Cambridge, Mass.: Harvard University Press, 1942.

Leibowitz, Herschel W. *Visual Perception*. New York: Macmillan, 1965.

Leonardo da Vinci. *Leonardo da Vinci's Advice to Artists.* Emery Kelen, ed. Nashville, Tenn.: Thomas H. Nelson, 1974.

_____. *The Notebooks of Leonardo da Vinci*, Pamela Taylor, ed. New York: Mentor Books, New American Library, 1960. Quoted in Robert McKim, *Experiences in Visual Thinking*, p. 59. Monterey, Calif.: Brooks/Cole, 1972.

Levy, Jerre. "Children Think with Whole Brains: The Myth and Reality of Hemispheric Differences and Interhemispheric Integration." Paper presented at New Orleans Conference on Student Learning Styles and Brain Behavior, National Association of Secondary School Principals, November, 1981.

_____. "Possible Basis for the Evolution of Lateral Specialization of the Human Brain," *Nature* 224 (1969): 614–15.

L'Hermitte, Françoise. "Thinking Without Language," *Réalitiés*, April, 1979, p. 60.

Lowenfeld, Victor, "Basic Aspects of Creative Thinking," in *Creativity and Psychological Health*, M. F. Andrews, ed. Syracuse, N.Y.: Syracuse University Press, 1961.

Luft, David S. *Robert Musil and the Crisis in European Culture, 1880–1942.* Berkeley: University of California Press, 1980.

Maslow, Abraham. *The Farther Reaches of Human Nature.* New York: Penguin, 1976.

McKim, Robert. *Experiences in Visual Thinking.* Monterey, Calif.: Brooks/Cole, 1972.

Miller, Jonathan. *States of Mind.* New York: Pantheon Books, 1983.

Moholy-Nagy, Laszlo. *The New Vision.* New York: Wittenborn, 1947.

Murphy, Thomas P. "Eureka! Venture Capital," *Forbes*, May 7, 1984, p. 218.

Musil, Robert. "Ansätze zu neuer Aesthetik: Bemerkungen über eine Dramaturgie des Filmes," *Der neue Merkur*, March, 1925, pp. 672–74.

_____. *Tagebücher, Aphorismen, Essays und Reden*, Adolf Frise, ed. Hamburg: 1955. Quoted in David S. Luft, *Robert Musil and the Crisis in European Culture, 1880–1942.* Berkeley: University of California Press, 1980.

Nemerov, Howard. "On Poetry, Painting, and Music," in *The Language of Vision*, W. J. T. Mitchell, ed. Chicago: University of Chicago Press, 1980.

Nicolaides, Kimon. *The Natural Way to Draw.* Boston: Houghton Mifflin, 1941.

Nierenberg, Gerard I. *The Art of Creative Thinking.* New York: Cornerstone Library, Simon & Schuster, 1982.

Nietzsche, Friedrich. *On the Genealogy of Morals*, 1887; New York: Vintage Books, Random House, 1968.

Orwell, George. "New Words" (1940), in *The Collected Essays, Journalism, and Letters of George Orwell*, Vol. 2, *My Country, Right or Left*, Sonia Orwell and Ian Angus, eds. New York: Harcourt, Brace & World, 1968.

Osborn, A. F. *Applied Imagination: Principles and Procedures of Creative Problem-Solving.* New York: Scribner, 1957.

Ovary, Paul. *Kandinsky: The Language of the Eye.* London: Elek Books, 1969.

Pagels, Hans. *The Cosmic Code.* New York: Simon and Schuster, 1982.

Pascale, Richard Tanner. "Zen and the Art of Management," *Harvard Business Review*, March–April, 1978, p. 155.

Perkins, D. N. *The Mind's Best Work.* Cambridge, Mass.: Harvard University Press, 1981.

Rauzino, Vincent. "Conversations with an Intelligent Chaos," *Datamation*, May, 1982, pp. 122–36.

Rawson, Philip. *The Art of Drawing.* Englewood Cliffs, N.J.: Prentice-Hall, 1984.

Rogers, Carl. "Towards a Theory of Creativity," in *Creativity and Its Cultivation*, H. H. Anderson, ed. New York: Harper & Row, 1959.

Ryf, Robert S. *A New Approach to Joyce.* Berkeley: Perspectives in Criticism Series, University of California Press, 1962.

Sargent, Walter, and Elizabeth Miller. *How Children Learn to Draw.* Boston: The Atheneum Press, Ginn and Company, 1916.

Sperry, Roger W. "Bridging Science and Values: A Unifying View of Mind and Science," *American Psychologist*, April, 1977, p. 237.

_____. "Hemisphere Disconnection and Unity in Conscious Awareness," *American Psychologist* 23, 1968, pp. 723–33.

_____. *Science and Moral Priority.* New York: Columbia University Press, 1982.

Springer, Sally P., and Georg Deutsch. *Left Brain, Right Brain.* New York: W. H. Freeman & Co., 1981.

Strunk T. and E. B. White. *The Elements of Style.* New York: Macmillan Publishing Co., 1972.

Suojanen, Waino W. "Management and the Human Mind: On the Three Kinds of Contingencies," in R. Carleton Bessinger and Waino Suojanen, eds. *Management and the Brain: An Integrative Approach to Organization Behavior.* Atlanta: Georgia State University Business Publishing Division, 1983.

Taylor, Gordon Rattray. *The Natural History of the Mind.* New York: E. P. Dutton, 1979.

Thomas, Lewis. *The Lives of a Cell.* New York: Bantam Books, 1975.

Tolstoy, Leo. *War and Peace.* New York: Heritage Press, 1938.

Uris, Auren, and Jane Bensahel. "On the Job: Quick Solutions to Job Problems," *Los Angeles Times,* July 20, 1981, Part IV, p. 2.

Von Oech, Roger, *A Whack on the Side of the Head.* Menlo Park, Calif.: William Kaufmann, Inc., 1983.

Warshaw, Howard. *Drawings on Drawing.* Santa Barbara, Calif.: Ross Erikson Press, 1981.

Webber, Nancy. *Women in Art.* 1217 Silvius Avenue, San Pedro, Calif. 90731.

Webster's Seventh New Collegiate Dictionary. Chicago: Rand McNally, 1972.

Wertheimer, M. *Productive Thinking.* New York: Harper & Row, 1945.

Wooldridge, Dean E. *The Machinery of the Brain.* New York: McGraw-Hill, 1963.

Wylie, Laurence. *Beaux Gestes.* Cambridge, Mass.: The Undergraduate Press, E. P. Dutton, 1977.

Young, J. Z. *Programs of the Brain.* London: Oxford University Press, 1978.

Zaidel, Eran. "The Elusive Right Hemisphere of the Brain," in *Engineering and Science,* California Institute of Technology, Sept.–Oct., 1978.

INDEX

238